"There is such vibrancy, adventure, mystery, and lucidity in this book. The country and its history will look different to anyone who reads it, if they can escape the categories that tell us this is merely a tale of music, popular culture, or the like. Using the oldest materials, *Backbeat* tells a new story."

—Greil Marcus

"Earl Palmer . . . is, in fact, inarguably one of the most important figures in the development of popular music in the second half of the 20th century. . . . He is one of the gods of our music who still walks among us. . . . His biography is filled with the unmistakable sound of his voice and the stories only he can tell, and it belongs in the library of every music-loving American."

— *Gambit Weekly*

"The meticulous biographer has freed Palmer's voice. By editing his story down from 125 hours of tape-recorded conversations with Palmer, then backing Palmer's memory with primary research, Scherman has made a valuable historical contribution. In so doing, he has brought rock's original backbeat to the front, where it belongs."

—*Cleveland Plain Dealer*

"It isn't until nearly the end of the book that Earl Palmer makes passing reference to the Rock and Roll Hall of Fame. Yet by that point in Tony Scherman's "Backbeat: Earl Palmer's Story," the reader has long since been convinced that the exclusion of rock and roll's pioneering percussionist renders inclusion an empty honor—that his impact, influence, and accomplishment are far greater than those of the vast majority enshrined."

—*Austin American-Statesman*

"A fascinating American life. . . . [T]he concluding appendix of 'Selected Singles, Albums, and Film and Television Soundtracks Featuring Earl Palmer' is a treasure trove, the real monument to his musical stature."

—*New Orleans Times-Picayune*

BACKBEAT

Earl Palmer in the studio, Los Angeles, ca. 1961.

BACKBEAT

EARL PALMER'S STORY

TONY SCHERMAN

DA CAPO PRESS

Scherman, Tony.
    Backbeat: Earl Palmer's story / by Tony Scherman.— 1st Da Capo Press ed.
        p.   cm.
    Reprint. Originally published: Washington : Smithsonian Institution Press, 1999.
    Includes bibliographical references and index.
    ISBN 0-306-80980-X (pbk.)
    1. Palmer, Earl. 2. Rock musicians—United States—Biography. I. Title.
ML419.P38 S34 2000
786.9'164'092—dc21
[B]   00-031689

First Da Capo Press Edition 2000

Published by Da Capo Press
A Member of the Perseus Books Group
http://www.dacapopress.com

1 2 3 4 5 6 7 8 9 10——04 03 02 01 00

FOR THELMA, NITA, AND COLLEEN

CONTENTS

FOREWORD

New Orleans musicians love to talk. They're great storytellers, too. My growing up was filled with tales of great musicians like Lester Young, Coltrane, Dizzy, Bird, Miles. What they did—what they said—how they felt—what they knew. Tales of legendary New Orleans musicians—Fats Domino, Professor Longhair. "This is how Fess played it. Son, check this out." If you were late, don't ask my daddy for a ride!

The passing of some empty lot or dilapidated weed-grown buildings would inspire time-sweetened memories of local hot spots like the defunct Dew Drop Inn. "That's where the Dew Drop was, man. Too bad you missed the Drop, baby. Sheeet! We used to play all night, wooo! —damn! Too bad you missed your appointment." Yes. They love to talk about New Orleans musicians who became famous but still liked pork meat in they red beans, and tail, too. In more sober moments they would discuss musicians who left because there was no work, too much prejudice, too much ignorance, or just because. Then the name of Earl Palmer would come up. "Earl didn't take no shit. That's why he had to get away from this backwards ass town."

The musicians I knew were all strugglin'. A lot. But they loved to play! And did. Some succumbed to dope and died like Nat Perillat. Others got a day job and raised a family, like Warren Bell. Still other diehards, like my daddy, kept playing those nonpaying local gigs in the one or two jazz clubs that were open. But no matter the circumstance, the feeling of New Orleans and of jazz defines these men. It's in the way they greet each other with an embrace. It's in their stride, in the rhythm of their voices, and in the way they listen. Impossible to describe but unmistakable.

To some people, I guess, these musicians must seem crazy, living in a dreamworld of cats, gigs, bread, axes, and so on. But when you get to know them, you come to feel that maybe theirs is the only real world. Their understanding of "what is" without illusion, without judgment, comes from knowing jazz music. That's why Earl Palmer, inventor of the "straight-up backbeat" that changed the world of rock and roll and thus the entire world of music, wants you to know: he is a jazz musician.

From his childhood years as a vaudeville tap dancer to his ascendance as the rock drummer of choice and a first-call Los Angeles studio musician, Earl feels and understands life in the ironic, syncopated way of jazz. But for all of his hard-earned individualism, he exemplifies the jazz musician's ultimate credo, "live and let live." Jazz musicians—that's a mysterious world with its own language, humor, morality, and code of conduct. Show people, night people, dope addicts, pimps, con men, shit talkers, and hustlers are surrounded by day people seeking a taste of the night. Day and night people swung together in a desperate dance, all night long.

If you wasn't there, you missed it. New Orleans in the 30s, 40s, 50s, gumbo, Claiborne Avenue, Mardi Gras, the Big Easy, the ceremonies, the celebrations! s e g r e g a t i o n   There wasn't too much talk about that after it was all over. Not much at all, considering how important segregation was to the swing. It gave the music of Earl's generation an acerbic sweetness. Made nightlife more absurd. "You niggers sho' play good, make me and my old lady hot as can be, but stay away from those white gals, ya heah." Jazz and men and women and white folks and black folks and drinkin and dope and dancin and laughin, cryin, and the wang dang doodle dandy. Oh! And the good ole stars and bars. The livin, the lovin, the lyin. And the listening. That's what makes these musicians different. Earl and them know how to listen.

Earl voices what they all know. Life is an octopus. Stay above or go down tangled. He's seen it many times. But beneath the surface, etched into the lines on the faces of jazz men and women, embedded in the eyes just past the humorous twinkle or melancholic gaze, a little deeper than the staccato *"motherfucker"* that juts out of almost every sentence, is the key. They speak from above in the language of the low. "The world is full of bullshit and bullshitting. But even though it choose you, you don't have to choose it." And that's not a matter of race, politics, or sex. That's Earl, brother.

Wynton Marsalis

ACKNOWLEDGMENTS

Many people helped this book take shape. Several were extraordinarily helpful. Jim Keltner first made me aware of Earl Palmer. Peter Guralnick, with whom I've shared many a rambling conversation since 1990, pushed me past my early wafflings. Rip Lhamon, who became my E-mail pal late in the game, doesn't know how much encouragement he provided; Tad Jones was an unselfish and incisive guide to New Orleans music, history, and music history. Mark Hirsch of the Smithsonian Institution Press opened the door, and thanks to the National Endowment for the Humanities, what was starting to feel like a fool's errand ended as it had begun: a labor of love.

Each of the following deserves thanks, too: Alex Albright, Jennifer Allen, Dave Bartholomew, Bill Bentley, Shirley Bird, Peter Brosius and Rosanna Staffa, Bart Bull and Michelle Shocked, Armand Charbonnet, Pamela Doqui, Colin Escott, Paul Feldman and Iris Schneider, Fred Goodman, Bill Hewes, Bob and Helen Hughes, Carol Kaye, Cynthia Keltner, the Louisiana Endowment for the Humanities, Carol and Allison Monahan, Albert Murray, Earl Palmer Jr., Donald, Pat, Penny, Ronald, and Shelly Palmer, Walter Pichon Jr., Andy Rabinbach, Bruce Raeburn and Alma Williams at the William R. Hogan Jazz Archive, Suze Rotolo, Ben Sandmel, Richard Snow, the late Leroy Sonier, Ross Spears, Genevieve Stewart, Jack Stewart, Dan Thress, and the late Red Tyler. I've tried to recall everyone; I'm sure I haven't.

INTRODUCTION

[I]n spite of what is left out of our recorded history, our unwritten history looms as its obscure alter ego, and although repressed from our general knowledge of ourselves, it is always active in the shaping of events. It is always with us, questioning even when not accusing its acclaimed double, and with the two locked in mute argument. —Ralph Ellison, "Going to the Territory"

Earl Palmer, a great musician, has lived his life below the threshold of fame. The historian ignores this stratum at his peril, for it is where much of a nation's culture is created. The conspicuous figures aren't necessarily the crucial ones; history works its wiles behind the backs of headline writers. Only with hindsight, after the parade goes by, can the cultural investigator get to work.

This is the story, in his own words, of one man's passage through the twentieth century. Earl Palmer's life is a many-chambered vessel. When we first spoke, doors opened unexpectedly onto vital and underexamined corners of our nation's recent past: New Orleans's protean musical culture from the 1930s through the 1950s (after jazz's first wave, that is), the daily lives of black New Orleanians during the same years, the world of Negro vaudeville in its twilight, the experiences of black soldiers in World War II, and the working and personal lives of the musicians who steered rock and roll from the margins to the mainstream. As I've listened to Earl remember, I've been struck again and again at how remarkable it is that somebody who is very much alive has lived through so many now-vanished eras. Without his witness, these chapters would be even more firmly shut.

Earl was no mere onlooker, to put it mildly indeed. He is among the most important popular musicians of this century's second half, a shaper of millions of Americans' musical tastes. No sixties rock fan had the slightest idea who Tommy Tedesco was, or Ernie Freeman, Carol Kaye, Hal Blaine, or Red Callender, but in those days you could hardly listen to your radio for twenty minutes without hearing them play: the recording-studio elite of Los Angeles, essential names (though you'll rarely find them) in any cultural history of the sixties. As often as not, it was their skill and inspiration that turned flimsy material memorable. None was a more consistent alchemist than Earl Palmer.

A drummer of tremendous power and subtlety, he arrived in Los Angeles in 1957. For the next decade he practically lived in the studio, cocreator of hundreds of hits (though he never shared royalties or credits). He played on Sam Cooke's "Shake," Ritchie Valens's "La Bamba," Eddie Cochran's "Summertime Blues," Johnny Otis's "Willie and the Hand Jive," Larry Williams's "Slow Down," the Righteous Brothers' "You've Lost That Lovin' Feelin'," Ike and Tina Turner's "River Deep Mountain High," and literally thousands of songs by the Beach Boys, the Supremes, Marvin Gaye, the Ronettes, Bobby Darin, Tim Hardin, Glen Campbell, the Mamas and the Papas, and others (I'm omitting his substantial later credits). He played jazz and big band pop with Frank Sinatra, Count Basie, Dizzy Gillespie, Ray Charles, Nat "King" Cole, and Sarah Vaughan, and was one of Hollywood's most sought-after film and television soundtrack musicians. To succeeding generations of studio musicians, Earl Palmer is a legend.

Yet if he had never played a note in California, Palmer's place in music history would be secure. In fact, his pre-California contribution is what he will (or should be) remembered for most. In his native New Orleans in the early to mid-fifties, he laid the rhythmic foundations of rock and roll. "If any single musician can be credited with defining rock & roll as a rhythmic idiom distinct from the jump, R and B, and all else that preceded it," wrote critic and music historian Robert Palmer in 1990, "that musician is surely Earl Palmer." It was Earl Palmer who transformed rhythm and blues's lope into the full-tilt thrust of rock and roll, bowling listeners over with a power previously unheard in popular music.

He was the force behind New Orleans's "Studio Band," rock's first great recording-session band (the prototype for such later house bands as Motown's). Between 1949 and 1957 he propelled almost all of Little Richard's hits ("Tutti Frutti," "Long Tall Sally," "Slippin' and Slidin'," "Rip It Up," "Lucille," "Good Golly Miss Molly") and many of Fats Domino's: "The Fat Man," "My Blue Heaven," "I'm in Love Again," and "I'm Walkin'" (Earl's favorite drum part from his New Orleans years, with its buoyant parade-band beat). He played on records by Lloyd Price ("Lawdy Miss Clawdy"), Shirley and Lee ("Let the Good Times Roll," which he also arranged), Roy Brown ("Let the Four Winds Blow"), and dozens of artists less well known at the time: Professor Longhair, Smiley Lewis, the Spiders, etc. Before America's cultural and moral arbiters had even begun to condemn rock and roll as aesthetically barren, Palmer's sophisticated licks had already proven them wrong (not that anyone heard that sophistication until years later).

Ironically, given his specific achievement (and the rock drummers who idolize him, from the Rolling Stones' Charlie Watts to Bruce Springsteen's Max Weinberg), Palmer doesn't consider himself a rock drummer and has little use for rock and roll. It was his day job. His passion was jazz. "Bebop and modern jazz never took hold here," writes jazz historian Frank Driggs about New Orleans, "the 'traditional style' was too entrenched." While not exactly wrong, Driggs, like most researchers, is unaware of a lively bebop subculture that sprang up in the Crescent City in the forties. The names—Warren Bell, Son Johnson, Weedy Morris, Jack Lamont—roll off Earl's tongue, but no jazz fan knows them. Although it produced jazzmen of major impact (Ornette Coleman's great drummer Edward Blackwell, for instance, or Ellis Marsalis, patriarch of America's current leading jazz family), New Orleans bebop remains a secret episode. Rock and rollers for whom Earl's significance begins and ends with Little Richard and Phil Spector would do well to probe Palmer's jazz roots, the source of his rock and roll's special suppleness.

Earl didn't become a musician until he was twenty-two, one of almost a million black veterans of America's last segregated army. His war remembrances are a sardonic counterpoint to our official national memory of "the good war." After years of neglect, there has lately been a surge of interest in World War II's black soldiers. Yet this interest tends to focus on the few who managed to fulfill the army's, and mainstream America's, notions of conduct—heroes, in other words. Earl's army career wasn't exactly distinguished. He went AWOL, issued ammo to his noncombatant mates (so they could shoot back at trigger-happy whites), was busted from sergeant to private, and wound up on a two-week joyride through France, gaily taking advantage of a bureaucratic foul-up. Yet rather than consider his behavior reprehensible, it makes sense to see it as an understandable, even rational, response to an especially galling form of hypocrisy: Jim Crow disguised as Uncle Sam. On the face of it, Earl's army performance is the exception to a life of achievement. Look a little deeper and you'll see that it's fully congruous with the rest of that life: a black man's life, in all its counterstating richness, in white America.

Earl's rhythmic sophistication is rooted not only in jazz but in an area of Afro-American rhythmic invention whose day has come and gone (though it keeps making semi-comebacks): tap dancing. By virtue of a very early start— he was on the road at six—he gives us a first-person window onto black vaudeville, a world already in eclipse when, "pretty as a little pimp," Earl starred in the great blues singer Ida Cox's *Darktown Scandals* traveling revue. A blues-singing headliner supported by comedians, tap dancers, scantily clad chorines, and any number of novelty acts strikes us today as an almost surreally eclectic bill. Within the vaudeville format a blues singer, a jazz soloist, and a trick cyclist were equally entertainers, at the service of the community; any claim by the former two to be artists, freed by their muses from the imperative of pleasing five audiences a day, would have been ridiculed. When a troupe's orchestra, often composed of first-class jazzmen (as we'll see, a young Clark Terry spent time with the *Darktown Scandals*), took the spotlight, its members added all sorts of low-comic effects: anything for a laugh. The very thought of a jazz modernist, a John Coltrane or a Max Roach, augmenting his impact with a little mugging, a comedy bit or two, is preposterous. Sixty years ago it was de rigueur. Vaudeville, in other words, was a unity, deeply embedded in people's lives, that has long since splintered.

Good liberals today, of whatever color, are revolted by the burnt-cork makeup and craps-shooting jokes that were black vaudeville's stock-in-trade. But the stereotypes merely disguised the winks and nods, the Aesopian humor, with which black show folk communicated with their audiences. Instead of reflexively condemning what was in fact a series of masks, we should be investigating the skill with which these masks were donned and doffed—the ways, in other words, in which black vaudeville was a survival guide for dangerous times.

In the last fifty years it has become an American piety to look at black urban life solely in terms of poverty, crime, and social disintegration. Regardless of who holds it, this viewpoint amounts to an espousal of middle-class standards. It is blind to the life that flows between and behind the statistics. Earl's memories of his New Orleans childhood challenge any such assumptions about what it means to grow up in a so-called slum. His New Orleans stamping ground, the Tremé district, has a longer and richer history than most American communities of any ethnic makeup. As poor as it already was in Earl's day, it had a proud lineage of craftsmen, writers, businessmen, and political leaders; its family life was supportive, not dysfunctional; its residents weren't browbeaten, they were cocky, with an enviable capacity to savor life. It's easy to see how the Tremé produced an individual as intelligent, ambitious, tough, and

creative as Earl Palmer. There is no substitute for mother wit, of course; if re-
liable intelligence tests had been given in the thirties, I believe Earl would
have scored over the moon. But this is not simply a self-made man. Earl is
Tremé-made.

I met Earl Palmer in the spring of 1991 at the New Orleans Jazz and Heritage Festival. I came into our relationship aware of his musical achievement;
it was something else that made me decide almost immediately to undertake
this project. Earl spoke pure vernacular poetry. "I've got a touch of emphy-
sema," he said delicately, bumming a cigarette. Partly a matter of the verbal
flair of the native New Orleanian, black or white, Earl's expressiveness is at
bottom his alone. It isn't an exaggeration to speak of Earl's verbal artistry, the
unstoppable creativity with which he spins phrases (and the pleasure he de-
rives from his knack). Wayne Newton was a "long-legged short-torso kid,"
Strom Thurmond "that old live-too-long motherfucker"; a plain woman Earl
once knew was "not shapely, not pretty, just female." A homicidal arsonist
"soused the place with gasoline," which evokes the action a lot better than the
proper word.

"If you can use rationale with somebody," he told me, "fine. But sometimes
you turn the other cheek, he'll break that one too." Again: "Confidence and
ego are somewhat the same but a lot different: you're up shit creek if you don't
have one, you're an asshole if you got too much of the other." And in a bleak
mood Earl allowed that "the American and the African got together and made
a new race—the nigger."

Most of these came from later in our relationship, but it was obvious at once
that Palmer could make language come alive. In the preface to his pioneering
oral history *Mister Jelly Roll*, Alan Lomax writes of his travels as a folklorist, his
efforts to "tap into the wild currents of word slinging that Americans are so
good at. The people I met spoke sentences that wound across the page like
rivers or mountain ranges. Jelly Roll spoke like that." So does Earl. As important as its subject matter is, this book stands or falls on whether I have caught
the cadences of Earl's speech.

We conducted a few interviews in summer 1991, but life intervened; it wasn't
until late 1993 that we reconnected. Between January 1994 and September
1995, I flew to Los Angeles for two two-week sessions and one four-day session.
Earl came to New York for two weekend sessions. At each of these we worked
daily for 7 or 8 hours. We began a session with questions I'd previously drawn
up, road maps from which we freely strayed. We also spent countless hours on
the phone, with tape rolling. The result was more than 125 hours of raw material. I transcribed the tapes myself, winding up with well over a thousand single-

spaced pages. Editing the transcript took three-plus years of part-time work. In December 1996 I received a National Endowment for the Humanities fellowship, which let me work full-time on the book for a year: finishing the editing, conducting secondary interviews, fact checking, and writing the supplementary material. I finished work in January 1998.

I mention fact checking because too many oral historians receive their subjects' words as a kind of demotic holy writ. The result, while stamped with a flavor missing from more formal approaches, is often studded with inaccuracies (for some reason jazz oral historians are especially ill-disposed toward fact checking). Although Earl Palmer has a remarkable memory, neither of us assumed it was error-proof. I spent many hours and lots of NEH money poring over primary materials and grilling elderly New Orleanians, corroborating (and occasionally and regretfully jettisoning parts of) Earl's story. Memory plays tricks, especially at a fifty and sixty years' remove. I can't claim that the result is error free; I can claim to have worked hard to make it so.

A penultimate note, on the endnotes. They range from brief references and asides to short essays that were too detailed to be included in the chapter introductions and interludes. Instead of flipping back and forth, you may want to read the narrative straight through before turning to the endnotes. This is a story first, a study second.

This book represents what is hopefully the start of a larger attempt to correct the distortions in our picture of rock and roll's early days. The efforts of historians like Lawrence Levine in *Black Culture and Black Consciousness* to focus more on the American past's supporting players than its luminaries have hardly been extended to this most democratically inclined of all American art forms. Very little in the way of *any* serious historical research has been devoted to rock. A sort of macrohistory has been sketched, with an overemphasis on stars and their impact. If there is a movement afoot to study the context and the process of pop-music creation, not just its most conspicuous products (whether song or singer)—to assess, that is, the role and importance of session musicians, songwriters, soundtrack composers, arrangers, recording engineers, producers, contractors, and all the others involved in the process of contemporary song making—let this be one of its early stirrings.

Note to the paperback edition: Earl Palmer was inducted into the Rock and Roll Hall of Fame in March, 2000, one of the first inductees in a new category, Sidemen.

1

THE TREMÉ JUMPED
NEW ORLEANS CHILDHOOD, 1924–1942

Human beings may give high-octane performances on low-octane fuel.
. . . After all, a human being can always wish and dream, and he can
never be reduced to zero. —Albert Murray, "The Storyteller as Blues Singer"

This is the Tremé, the Sixth Ward. This particular corner, Dumaine and
Claiborne, is one of the most famous corners in New Orleans. Dumaine
and Claiborne, Dumaine and Robertson: these were swinging corners.
You can see that lady over there swinging today, and this is some fifty
years after it all happened. She's still swinging. She got the vibrations
and she feels the spirit. —Danny Barker, New Orleans musician, 1978

Earl Palmer, 7 years old, should be a "whip" when he grows into a
youth. Already he has 12 different dance steps in his routine . . . and an
eye for the ladies. —*Louisiana Weekly*, March 12, 1932

Most musical histories of New Orleans still ride heavily on the
distinction between "uptown" and "downtown," the former the
home of dark-skinned, blues-playing American blacks, the latter of
French-speaking black Creoles and their politer music. As useful as
this time-honored schema has been, it doesn't do justice to the city's
motley nature. For New Orleans is a city of neighborhoods, each
with its own character and history. Tighten your focus, and the old
Creole downtown resolves into several very different communities,
the largest of which are the Seventh Ward and the Tremé.

In the years of Earl Palmer's childhood, the Seventh Ward was the stronghold of the descendants of the old *gens de couleur libre*, antebellum New Orleans's French-speaking, Catholic Creoles of color. The Seventh was staid and genteel, its residents fighting a rearguard battle for their ebbing prestige. "In the Seventh Ward," says restaurateur Leah Chase, who grew up there, "everyone thought they were the Pope."

The Tremé was older—in fact, it is North America's oldest black urban neighborhood—but livelier. Whereas the Seventh Ward is tucked away downriver, the Tremé is near the heart of the city, wedged between Canal and Esplanade Streets, just behind the French Quarter. This is where Earl Palmer was born, on October 25, 1924, and raised. It was a neighborhood at once insular and cosmopolitan, with a big-city bustle and a Southern country town's tangled bloodlines and down-home conviviality. As Earl says, "The Tremé was the party action."

Nightspots abounded here, from the 2,000-seat Coliseum on Derbigny and Conti to smaller halls like the San Jacinto, where top local bands held cutting contests and the Sunday matinee was nine hours long; from well-appointed nightclubs like the Gypsy Tea Room to corner dives where rough barrelhouse pianists rambled till the butcher cut them down. "'Little Willie,' a well-known piano plunker, died last Sunday from a heart attack after playing his instrument around St. Philip and Dumaine Streets all day," the *Louisiana Weekly* reported on February 6, 1937. "[T]hey picked up money to bury him."

Neighborhood sports loitered on the corner of Claiborne and Dumaine, the Tremé's hub, laying bets and ogling girls and talking trash. Claiborne Avenue was black New Orleans's main artery and among the busiest black thoroughfares in the South. Its wide, grassy median—"neutral ground" in New Orleans parlance—graced by azaleas and a double row of live oaks, was the Tremé's backyard, a haven for kids, ballplayers, trysting couples. At Mardi Gras the city's black community massed at Claiborne and Dumaine to view the parade. "Everybody came in under the oaks," says longtime resident Norman Smith, "and we'd all picnic and watch the activities. If you saw the Zulus [the black Mardi Gras krewe, whose outrageous costumes and pageantry lampooned white Mardi Gras], you were fortunate."

New Orleans's two oldest cemeteries, St. Louis I and II, bordered the Tremé. At least once or twice a month funeral bands came marching down Claiborne, somber before the burial, raucous after. "I grew up on the fringes of the Tremé, real near the cemetery," Earl Palmer's lifelong friend, the late Red Tyler, recalled. "You'd hear somebody shout, 'Second line at the cemetery!' and you ran to see the band and join the second line": the impromptu procession that invariably accompanies a New Orleans marching band. "We had more second lines in the Tremé," says Norman Smith, "than any place on earth."

Nor was a parade necessary to get people dancing in the street. "Musicians would form a band and go from joint to joint on a horse and wagon," says Earl's contemporary Walter Pichon Jr. "Put a drummer on there, put a trombone on there, and the people come out and danced in the mud—none of them streets were paved. After the musicians got a drink, they moved two blocks down to another bar, and a new bunch came out and danced." Music undergirded everything here; even the draymen's cries were soulful: "Hey water-mel*uhhn. . . .*"

Tremé people were nourished by a deep fund of lore (it wasn't seen as lore, of course; it was the social air you breathed). There were neighborhood heroes like the pimp Louis Henry, real as day but touched by myth. Money wasn't really a token of status; nobody had any. What mattered were flair, good looks, athletic and musical prowess—*style*, not in the sense of veneer or superfice but the ability to spin the raw, often mean stuff of daily life into something pleasing and memorable.

"You came up hard in the Tremé," says Earl. Yet as a source of expressive culture, of style, this place held riches. "The housing in the Tremé was not the best in the world," says Norman Smith, "but these were very proud people; they were very, very enlightened into the cultural aesthetics of living." When Walter Pichon Jr. recalls some of the men of his childhood, you get a sense of the elegance with which these members of a "deprived" community carried themselves. "Ratty Cady, Jim Conan, Leon DeLisle, Paul Gross— these were all good-looking men. They were better looking than their women! Paul Gross—one of the best-looking men you'd ever want to see! They were dressers, you know. They wore three-piece suits and suspenders with gold chains. You don't see people walking

around the Tremé like that today—oh, no indeed!" Pichon himself
is in this number, one of the last, debonair at seventy-five in wind-
breaker and fedora, a career maître d' in some of the city's best
restaurants and nightclubs.

Twenty years ago a West Coast friend of Earl's took a trip down
South. She found herself driving through the Tremé. Shocked by its
blight, she realized, she says, how far Earl had come from such
humble beginnings, against such odds. Admittedly, the place this
woman saw had deteriorated from the Tremé of Earl's childhood.
But she probably would have been almost as appalled by the old
Tremé; she probably would have seen only the poverty. She did not
understand that this neighborhood hadn't handicapped Earl—it
had given him a head start. On these blocks the boy grew into a
man of humor, curiosity, and resilience: very, very enlightened indeed in the aesthetics of living.

You know one of the reasons New Orleans got the nickname "Big Easy"?
Why, because you could feed a family of seven on twenty-five cents!
In my neighborhood, the Tremé, you'd go to a store and buy what they
called half portions. That's a nickel a portion. You'd get a half of red beans,
half rice, half loaf of bread, and a hunk of smoke sausage, big as that. Our lux-
ury was pickle meat. A bottle of jumbo sarsaparilla soda for a nickel and you
got you a meal; feed a family of seven, man, off a quarter.

It's not that my mother didn't make no money—she sent money home. But
you see, we were such that a whole unit within our family might not be working. If my Uncle Freddy was out of work, his family moved in and we all
bunked together. One time there must have been five different branches of the
family staying together: my aunts and uncles and their children and my grandparents and my mama and me. My mama raised three children that wasn't even
related to us! We always took people in, man, it didn't matter, it was so cheap
to live. You got used to living cheap like that, where you always wanted something. It was a part of life.

That's pretty poor when you're getting half rice, half bread, and half beans,
but I was never hungry. In New Orleans your mama could always go to a family down the street and say, "Listen, we ain't got nothing now, take care of my
baby, feed my baby." You'd go over there and eat and didn't feel anything
wrong with it. Their child might do the same next week. They themselves
might do the same next week!

I never knew my father, never saw a photograph of him, don't know what he looked like, his age, nothing. This is all I was told: he was a cook on a whaling vessel and he sailed out of Newfoundland and had an accident and got killed on the ship.

My mother met him when she went to New York to get some singing jobs. As far as my Aunt Josephine, who was kind of the family historian, said, Edward Palmer's family came from Virginia. He had a brother and a nephew in White Plains, New York. Aside from that I don't know a thing about his family. As for the name of Walter Fats Pichon and whether anybody by that name had anything to do with me being born, I guess I'll never know the answer. But we'll get to that.

My mother's father, George Theophile Sr., was a porter for the L & N Railroad, that's Louisville and Nashville. Exactly how my mother got interested in show business is something only my Aunt Nita would have known, and Nita passed last year. I'm the oldest in the family now.

My grandfather looked to be a tall white Greek man. I have a picture of the family, my mother, my aunts, my grandmother, everybody: all different colors. My Uncle Freddy looked like a perfect little Greek, blue eyes and curly, curly black hair, white as white. You see, as far as I could understand from my Aunt Josephine, my grandfather was mixed with Greek and French. His name was pronounced the French way, "tay-o-feel." His sister Ernestine, we called her Aunt Teen, lived in St. Louis and was very, very white and a redhead. My grandfather could easily have been considered white. But he stayed with us, he stayed among black people. He didn't have some black woman he was having children by and then he went home to St. Charles Avenue. He didn't have any family but us.

The races here were so mixed up! My own theory why there wasn't a hell of a lot of lynching round New Orleans is that a sumbitch would never really know who he was lynching. Could be his own cousin!

"Hey, who's that hanging from the tree? Aw, it's Cousin Louis! Why y'all did that?"

"Man, we didn't know it was a relative! He was black, wasn't he?"

There was white families in our neighborhood that got along fine with us. I'd fall asleep at their house listening to *Amos 'n' Andy* or *Inner Sanctum*, get up in the morning, get a big old hunk of bread with red gravy and go to the black school; they'd get up and go to the white school. If they fell asleep at our house they'd get a hunk of bread loaded with condensed milk, just as sweet and as filling and as fattening.

And there was people like the Spadonis—that family was white, man, they

"I have a picture of the family, my mother, my aunts, my grandmother, everybody: all different colors." Earl's grandmother Octavia Theophile and her children. *Above left to right:* Freddy, Thelma, George Jr., Josephine, Nita; *below left to right:* Leonora, Octavia, Leonard.

were white *people,* but they were born and raised right there on St. Ann between Galvez and Johnson and they were part of our neighborhood. They was a little mixed but they were mostly white. Everybody knew it, nobody cared. Because they didn't act white, they didn't want to be white, they were uncomfortable in the white culture. Johnny Spadoni would work a white job to take care of his family, but he'd never go to Bourbon Street and drink. He drank at the bar across the street. The Spadonis didn't even go to a white school; they put down on the paper that they were black and went to black schools like Joseph A. Craig and Albert Wicker. In those days in New Orleans, if you were white and decided to be black, they let you.

Of course, they also had a lot of light-complected blacks that didn't want to be around blacker blacks; call you nigger fast as any white man. There was a

little animosity there all the time. You didn't find it so much in my neighborhood, because we had a mixture of the *passe a blancs*, the real light-complected
blacks you saw in the Seventh Ward, and the darker ones you saw uptown.
The Tremé was a mixture.

My grandfather was a quiet strong man who used to pick me up on his lap
and kiss me. He died of cancer of the throat when I was five years old. I ran
three blocks to call Miss Marie Andrews, the family's midwife. "Miss Marie,
my grandpa dying, my grandpa dying!"

I was my grandparents' boy, spoiled rotten. When my grandpa came in from
work, I took all his tips out of his coat and put them on the table. Twenty-four
cents—fourteen cents for carfare, ten cents for two cups of coffee—that's all I
let him keep. I brought the rest straight to my grandma, never kept any for myself. I considered this my responsibility and a very big one, man—as far as I
knew, this was the money we was living on!

My grandma took me everywhere. "Cissy's boy." Seems I don't remember
going anywhere in that part of my life with any other woman but my grandma.
Sometimes we walked all the way down Canal Street to bring my grandfather
his lunch. The L & N station was by the river, right next to where the aquar-
ium is today: big old-fashioned railroad station with a glass ceiling. The engineers were old white men. They let me up into the cab, and the nicest one let
me blow the whistle. He never called me Earl, always "boy," but I felt a kind-
ness in him.

The French Market was further down the waterfront. My Uncle Rene
worked there, at J. Tedesco's Fruit and Vegetable, hauling fruit, stacking veg-
etables, loading trucks. Uncle Rene was much more important than a steve-
dore. He didn't make as much, but because there was so many stevedores
scrambling for jobs, we considered them lesser than somebody with a special
job in the Market. *My* uncle worked at the Market!

We lived on Bienville Street when I was born, that's two blocks north of
Canal. What we really call the Tremé, the Tremé proper, starts three blocks
north of Bienville, at Lafitte, and runs over to Esplanade. The Tremé is in the
Sixth Ward. If you came from the Sixth Ward and went down to the Ninth,
you could easily have trouble. They'd stop you on the street. "Where you
from? Man, you Sixth Ward niggers . . ." Happened to me plenty.

The further you got into the Ninth Ward the more rural it was. Just below
the Ninth is an area they call Chalmette. Until I began to look into the history
of New Orleans, I didn't know there's a whole big battlefield in Chalmette. In
the War of 1812 the American forces, which were the Cajuns and the Creoles

"In those days Claiborne Avenue had a great big what we called a neutral ground, big wide grassy area where we played football and baseball and the Mardi Gras clubs paraded." The Tremé's main thoroughfare, Claiborne Avenue, as it was in 1955, before the trees were pulled out and an expressway built overhead. (Historic New Orleans Collection)

and them, picked that site. The British thought, "Oh, okay, this'd be good. We'll back them sumbitches right into the river. Drown em." But they did not contend on Jean Lafitte the pirate coming in from the river, and we kicked the British's ass right there in the Battle of New Orleans.

We lived in a block of little row houses and knew everybody on the whole block. To one side of us was the Taylors: Miss Gussie and her sons Gabe and Alvin and her daughter Rosemary, my first girlfriend, and Rosemary's sisters Gloria and Dunnie. A few years later Andrew Young, who became the mayor of Atlanta, lived around the corner on Prieur Street in what we called the big house because it was nicer than the rest.

They had an old policeman in the neighborhood, Big Aleck, a walking beat policeman. Big Aleck was the first cop I remember, because he had been on that beat for years and years and years. He was a big red-faced dude and a drunk, and in that heat, with them regulation-issue hot black shoes—man, Aleck had bad feet all the time. Couldn't catch us when we ran.

"Aaahh Big Aleck you big red *neck!*"

My family moved around a lot, but always in that same neighborhood—I never lived outside the Tremé until I left New Orleans for good. From Bienville we moved to 823 Claiborne, between Dumaine and St. Ann, then Dumaine between Claiborne and Derbigny and then St. Philip between Claiborne and Robertson. After that came St. Philip and Robertson, on the corner; then 1526 St. Philip, between Robertson and Villere, and the last place we lived before I went into the service was 918 Claiborne, between Dumaine and St. Philip. We didn't own any of those houses, landlords did. Joubert was the name of the big real estate people we paid rent to; I don't know if we ever even knew who owned the damn houses. They were all pretty much tenements, one was never any nicer than the other. Bigger, maybe.

Not all the streets in the Tremé were paved, by any means. North Claiborne was — it was the main drag. St. Philip was, but Robertson was dirt, Villere was dirt, Marais was dirt. In those days Claiborne Avenue had a great big what we called a neutral ground, big wide grassy area where we played football and baseball and the Mardi Gras clubs paraded.

The main congregating point was the corner of Claiborne and Dumaine, where the Chattard brothers, Robert, Noel, Lowell, and Shack, had their barbershop. A half-Chinese, half-black guy, Wong, worked for them, who later opened his own place between St. Philip and Ursulines. Out front of the barbershop was Big Al Dennis's shoeshine stand. Al Dennis sent his kids through Grambling off that stand.

Big Lo, Lowell Chattard, was kind of a fight manager, so the barbershop is where everyone gathered on Sundays to talk boxing. Big Lo had one of these big loud mouths and knew more than anyone about boxing. According to him, anyway.

Around the corner on Dumaine was Joe Sheep's sandwich place, no bigger than somebody's little kitchen. Joe Sheep had the best hot sausage sandwiches in town for a dime, but he was the meanest old sumbitch you ever met. You'd come up there to get a sandwich.

"What you want, little nigger?"

"I wanna hot sausage sandwich."

You going through your pockets, pulling pennies out.

"Hurry up, you little motherfucker you." Oh, he was a terrible old man, but them sandwiches was delicious!

Across Dumaine was a bar they used to call the Keno, had a racehorse book gave you the results from the fairgrounds. I'd go in and get buckets of beer for my uncles, Coca-Cola for my grandmother. Behind the bar was a gambling joint where my Uncle Son dealt monte, cotch, and twenty-one. Vernel Fournier's daddy George was one of the dealers in there for years.

Joseph A. Craig Elementary, where I went to school, was on St. Philip between Villere and Marais. Still is. Benny Powell grew up across the street on Marais and he'd play hooky, hang out his window making faces at us in the geography room.

"Miz Gair, Miz Gair, Benny's not sick, look at him!"

Teacher turned around and Benny ducked. Soon as she faced us again he'd pop up, stick his tongue out.

I enjoyed masking at Mardi Gras with the other kids, putting on a costume and dancing up and down the street, following the bands, doing the second line. Everybody's door was wide open; you could walk right in, have some red beans and gumbo, and go right back out again, masking and dancing. Mardi Gras afforded you to do things you couldn't any other time. I'd go in houses I wasn't supposed to; go in Miss Olga Manuel's looking to see the prostitutes, though they was all out masking.

The Baby Dolls were women that masqueraded as little baby girls. It just started as a comedic gesture, these great big fat women in baby doll outfits, bonnets tied under their chins, and little socks, and sometimes they wear a diaper. Thighs this big sticking out of their tiny bloomers. Some of them got a little nasty sometimes. But we're talking about the days when they wasn't allowed to do anything real nasty, as opposed to now when they show their pussies on Bourbon Street. The Baby Dolls wouldn't dare do that!

When you're little, some of the maskers' costumes are really scary. The scariest were the skeletons, where these guys took a pair of long johns, dyed them black, and painted skeletons on. They made big papier-mâché heads that looked like a skull and carried bones from a slaughterhouse and rattled the bones as they walked and went "*Grrrgggghhhh!*" and I mean this scared you to death, scared us kids to death, right out there in the bright sunlight.

When I got big enough to know these weren't real skeletons, I got interested in the Indians. The main tribes were about four: the Golden Eagles and the others from uptown, and the one tribe that was indigenous to the Seventh Ward, the Yellow Pocahontas. The police didn't let the Indians in the Quarter; mostly they went up and down Claiborne. They're still not allowed down Canal. They were known as belligerent and violent maskers, get drunk and loaded off weed and cut each other up. Many times people got killed.

But oh, you'd be waiting for them! If they'd vowed they was going to fight, that's what they did. Right in front of the crowd—hell yeah! These were bloodbaths, man. They actually thought they was Indians. One tribe run into another one they considered not friendly, or the tribes was jealous, or one tribe's costumes were prettier—any kind of stupid, illiterate idea.

The groups that have the funeral parades—"plantings," that's my joking terminology for them—is the social and pleasure clubs. Social is from your dues, you do some good, donate money to the poor, make up Christmas baskets; pleasure is having parades and throwing affairs for your members' fun. Going to the cemetery, you went slow and the band played the normal sad songs— "Nearer My God to Thee," "A Closer Walk with Thee"—and they'd cut the coffin loose. As soon as they got out of the cemetery, the band starts to play snappier music. The band played a tune, then the snare drum played for a block or two, then they all struck up another tune and the second line started dancing behind the band and that's when they'd really get to second-lining and shaking it down all the way back to the neighborhood. Every bar in the Tremé filled up. "To Louie!" "That little motherfucker!" Lot of crying going on.

I was in the second line a lot. We lived right between two of the main funeral parlors, that's Llopis on Dumaine and Labat on St. Philip, so I was right there when the parades formed.

Being born into a vaudeville family, I was a dancer by the time I was five. In fact, my first memories are learning to dance at home with my mama and my Aunt Nita. I remember being pulled onstage at the Lyric Theater when I was four or five, maybe less. Didn't take a lot of coaxing either, I just went out there and tap-danced along like I was part of the show. Even earlier, I've been told, my mother would come off, nurse me between numbers, and run back on. I was in a milk crate instead of a cradle. We were poor people, and cradles wasn't important long as you had somewhere to lay.

When my mama and Aunt Nita left town there was a little tap dancer friend of the family that taught me, Joe Toy. I learned from other dancers as I came along, like my Uncle Benny Williams, Benny Rubberlegs Williams we called him, because he did a real limber-leg dance like somebody that's got rubber legs. Benny did what we called eccentric dancing, which is when you do a routine that's not just straight-out tap dancing, you're combining contortionist movements and backflips and all kind of stuff.

Everybody around New Orleans knew my mama and my Aunt Nita. They did regular vaudeville shows in town and then they went on the road, back and forth. My mama did pretty much whatever she wanted to, because she ran the show a lot at the Lyric; she made extra money doing that, she and a guy named Eddie Lemons, who had a heck of a reputation for having been big.

My mama was a wonderful woman at organizing things. Once when she was home for a while, she stuck together a troupe of kids and called us the Rinky Dink Revue. We had a girl named Doris Francis who was a good little singer, and Doris's cousin Erna Ferrand—Erna was a chick who could dance, man—and another little girl, Irene Andrews. Ernest Phillips was the only other boy, Love, we called him. We also called him Tee-Bat. My mama worked out routines for us and put us onstage at the Lincoln, the Palace, and the Harlequin.

By the time I was a growing young man, it had become pretty much knowledge to me that my mother'd had some gay relationships with people. I'm telling you, a lot of these so-called aunts of mine! My Aunt Nita, my real aunt, that is, never married, because she was also involved with a few relationships. I had a lot of aunts, man. I was probably the only feminine thing my mother ever did!

My mother was very argumentative around the house. She had a hell of a mouth on her, too. I'll tell you the kind of thing she said. When I went to Los Angeles in 1950 with Dave Bartholomew's band, my Uncle George, who lived there, had just had a prostate operation. I got home and my mama said, "How's your bighead *parran?*" — your godfather.

"Well, he just had an operation on his *gogo,*" his ass.

"Nigger had to go all the way to California to get a new asshole?"

She loved to play the dozens with Big Ike, who lived next door. She'd be sitting at the table playing pitty-pat and say, "Ike—"

"Don't start with me now, Thelma."

"I just wanted to say I don't see how Ophelia"—that was Ike's wife—"how Ophelia can stand your big funky ass laying all over her."

"Her big ass is as big and funky as mine!"

"Lord have mercy!" my mama would say.

She'd get on my Uncle Rene about his mother, Grandma Sally: "Rene, I just saw your mama down on the longshoremen's line!"

Uncle Rene was always kind of sheepish and guilty because he was fooling around with a woman on Burgundy and Orleans. One night the family was playing pitty-pat and Rene comes in drunk, wants to hug on my Aunt Leonora, his wife, and kiss her.

"Oh, Leonora, my little—"

"Get away you pain in the ass, I'm trying to watch my cards!"

All of a sudden Rene goes on a crying jag. Reaches in his pocket for a handkerchief and pulls out a pair of women's drawers! Blows his nose, dabs his eyes, and don't even notice what he's using. We all do a double take and *crack* up laughing.

"You son of a bitch!" yells Aunt Leonora. "What are these?"

"Why, it's just my handkerchief, Leonora!" He finally looks at what's in his hand. He left the room and I didn't see him for another couple of days. To tell you the truth, I always knew about Uncle Rene and his girlfriend. My buddy Jimmy Narcisse lived next door to her, and Jimmy and I saw Rene over there plenty times. We always hit him for money—we knew he was thinking, "or else. . . ." We set poor Rene up, man. He always was kind of weak-willed, but he was good to me. When all the kids in the neighborhood were getting bikes, my mother was off on the road and hadn't sent no money, and this man bought me a beautiful gray-and-red Western Flyer bicycle.

Grandma Sally lived down in Oakville toward the Gulf, and Rene took us kids there by the weekend. The main thing we went for was the food. Grandma Sally had chickens in the yard and pigs and pecan trees with big, *big* pecans, and Grandma Sal could cook. The one thing we didn't like was that old Baptist church with those big sweaty ladies and you're scared one of them's going to fall on you, jumping around the way they did. We didn't jump like that at St. Peter Claver. We stood quietly and made the sign of the cross and nobody sang but the priest because he was the only one knew the words. Down here everybody sang and tried to show off how much they could faint.

My best little neighborhood friend was Butsy. We didn't become buddies until we had to fight. He was a bully, bullied me and everybody else too, until one day I beat him and then we was friends. Butsy had a sister Marguerite, and many people didn't know if she was a guy or a chick, because Marguerite always had chicks, man. She was a pimp around there. Then there was Andrew Martin, we called him Porkchops, and Alton Harris, whose nickname was Tee-not, but there was another nickname for him called Uncle Ford. New Orleans is funny for nicknames. My cousin Arthur Landry is Bo Weevil, damned if I know why they call him that. My mother's nickname was Sal, and I never knew why they called her that either. Sal? Sal? What does that have to do with Thelma? I know why my nickname was Slack—I always had loose pants in the back, never had no big old ass like some dudes. Used to have a flat butt, man, all the time. My friend Steve Angrum called me Slack until the day he died. Red Tyler almost never called me Earl. He exclusively called me Gus. I called him Gus. I don't know why we picked Gus. We didn't think anything of it, we done it so long. Steve got to calling us Gus, too, he got in on it. But we never called him Gus.

Everyone had a lot of sayings, too. People think "Where yat?" is new, but I said it as a kid. If you asked somebody, "Where yat?" and they didn't feel good? "I'm fucked." Another was "How you percolating?" That's real old, grownups said it when I was a kid. "Is you sticking?" meant "Got any money?" A guy talking about his chick called her his quiff. If you wanted a girl's pussy, you'd say, "I want some of that trim," but a woman's private parts was also her coosy. If you were going to work, you said, "I'm going on my slave." You also called it your yoke. When someone got in a fight, that was a humbug. Doorpopping was eavesdropping. My ex-mother-in-law was a doorpopper: "There's Odile—

do'popping again!" Marijuana was muggles and we also called it mootah. A boy and a girl messing round were doing nasty. Thelma Milton's stepfather caught Thelma and me doing nasty. Neither of us knew what it was, we just doing it because it was nasty. I heard her stepdaddy coming down in the basement and I got up and ran out the back, down the alley and up the street and I was gone! But he must have seen my shirttail flapping because when I got home my mother kicked my butt, spanked me, and called me a couple nasty little names.

When we lived on Dumaine, there was a dog on the next block that came charging all the way from the back of the yard every time someone passed by. His owners put up a picket fence, but you could see him coming. Mean. He had a little extra animosity toward me — I'll admit I teased the hell out of him. I'd stop and yell at him, spit at him. He'd go *rrrgggghhh*. . . . One day I came passing by and he cleared the fence. I caught him, and even though he scratched me all over, I never turned him loose. I choked him to death. And I might have done the same if it had been Butsy back before I knew him, or anybody coming at me.

Round there it was protect yourself. You came up hard. The Tremé is the ghetto; the gangbangers and the drug dealers will rob you there. It's not a safe place to be! Back then it wasn't like it is now, but it was always tough. They had this chick named Ruth, she was known to be a tough chick around there. Stand straight up like a man and fight you with her fists. On Robertson between St. Philip and Ursulines, Ruth and another woman fought with knives to the death. Women were crying. I was crying, because I knew Ruth. People begged them, "Please stop, y'all, please don't, y'all gonna kill each other. Somebody please stop them!" Al Dennis tried to break it up, and Big Red, big light-complected guy. These were guys you'd expect could just walk in there and stop it — couldn't get close. I saw the other woman fall down for good, and Ruth kept on stabbing her. She was dead by the time the ambulance came. Ruth was on her knees, groggy, looked like she didn't have the strength to fall over. Blood running everywhere in the dirt. We later heard Ruth died in the hospital; she may have died on the way there. The ambulance driver probably took his time, didn't give a shit how long it took two niggers to kill each other.

Nobody gave too much of a damn what blacks did as long as they didn't hurt no white people. If blacks killed other blacks, nobody cared. Hell, no. Shit, no. My mother could get anybody out of jail if they hadn't hurt no white man, stole nothing from no white man. Eddie Grochell that owned the Dog House where my mama worked, he had an in with the police. Any blacks got in trouble, they came right to my mother.

The first trouble I had with a white man was getting my ass kicked, literally, in the Donze brothers' store on Dumaine and Robertson. Ol' Donze was loaded and didn't give me my right change.

"Mr. Don, you didn't gimme all my money."

"You little black motherfucker you, get the—" and he kicked me right in my ass. Not to excuse him, but this was the day he and his brother found out their sister Rosie was taking their money and their drugs—they sold drugs, too—*and* was fucking Burnell Santiago, a black piano player.

When I was little, Louis Henry was about my biggest hero. Louis Henry was a top pimp and he looked the part. He wore silk pongee shirts with a garter on the sleeve, tailor-made slacks with suspenders, diamonds everywhere, gold all across his mouth. The first time I was ever on top of a woman it was Louis's main woman Effie. I was five or six and she was laying up in bed and Louis said, "Go ahead on, get some of that!" and he puts me on her and starts pushing me up and down.

Being a pimp was lucrative and acceptable. A top pimp wasn't an outcast, he was a big *shot*. People loved you. The pimps were the Robin Hoods of the community. "Coach," Miss Olga Manuel, sweetest woman in the world, man—ran prostitutes. That's the way New Orleans was. Here's a woman ran a house of prostitution, but everybody loved her. However she made that money, she was always giving it to someone. I'll tell you someone that had aspirations to be a pimp, because he hung with Louis Henry sometimes, and that's Louis Armstrong. He had a lot of women, man, he loved women and they loved him. He wanted to be a pimp.

Every big shot pimp had what we called mascots and I was Louis Henry's. The mascot dressed exactly like the pimp. Louis had my little outfit made up by Harry Hyman, a Rampart Street tailor known for fine custom clothes. Nobody bought clothes ready-made; a number of tailors along Rampart Street did custom tailoring, and some of them did it very cheap. You'd pay down on a pair of tailored pants or a suit, five dollars a week, until you'd paid your twenty-five dollars and got your suit.

They had another pimp by the name of Pete Robertson, who quit pimping and became a master baker. Many times Louie and Pete took me to Heinemann Park to see Satchel Paige. They had the Negro leagues then and got eleven thousand people in Heinemann. They had the white Southern League, too: the New Orleans Pelicans, the Atlanta Crackers, the Birmingham Barons. But none of them drew any bigger than the black teams: the Homestead Grays, the Pittsburgh Crawfords, the Black Yankees.

Satch would come over to Lou's box, and Lou would say, "How many you going to strike out today?"

"All them motherfuckers. I'm going to strike them all out." Then Satch would turn to Pete, because Pete had played ball, and say, "Come on behind the stands, I'll strike out your big black ass too!"

I met Paige on the road later on, and more than once, because places they didn't have no colored hotels, white people often put up black ballplayers and entertainers. I met Josh Gibson, too, out at Heinemann. Paige was far more extroverted; Josh Gibson was a reserved type of man. But I'll say one thing: I have never, except for maybe a couple of people, seen anybody hit a baseball as hard as Josh Gibson. He had something about a fluidity in his swing and he could slam that ball on a drive, man—I'm telling you!

I wasn't Louis Henry's mascot long: a year, maybe two. When I started dancing in the Quarter for tips, my heroes became the tap dancers who were better than me. Hats and Coats, for example. John McElroy was originally called Hats and Coats all by himself, I have no idea why. When he combined to work with John Green, he became Hats and John was Coats. When I joined I was Buttons. Hats was a terrific tap dancer, Green was even better. They were both heroin addicts. Me being little, I'm sure they thought, "Little kid like this, we can steal his money." Cousin Joe, who became the famous blues singer and guitarist, joined the group later on because he wanted to learn to tap-dance. Joe sang and played ukulele, so he was our band. He was Pants. When he joined, my mother was very happy because she trusted him to keep an eye on Green and McElroy.

So Cousin Joe played and we got out there and danced, on the streets and in the clubs, black and white clubs both. Actually we did very little dancing on the street. We did if things were slow or if there was a lot of tourists around. But we were street dancers, know what I mean? We danced for tips. We had no steady job, we weren't hired anywhere. We went in clubs up and down Bourbon Street, one to the next, and did our little show.

In the white clubs, which was mostly tourists even back then, the emcee would say: "And now for a special treat we're going to bring on some little nigger boys to dance for you all!" First we'd do a chorus together, more than likely what they called the old B.S. Chorus, that's the Bullshit Chorus. The B.S. Chorus was pretty much the standard routine for dancers, the first group of steps you learn. Time step, cross step, kick step, and pulling the trenches. Sometimes it variated from that, but it was usually them four steps. The time step sets the tenor, the time. You do it for the first eight bars and then you do a stop-time break called the separator. Then you did the cross step: *taka taka taka* and you cross-your-leg, *taka taka taka* and you cross-your-leg. The Shim Sham Shimmy was a whole dance they had that derived mostly from the cross step. Next was the bridge, which would probably be some sort of kick step. Then came your big, your closing, step. It might be pulling the trenches, where both arms are swinging and your legs are sliding behind you one at a time — some guys could make it look like they were really skating on ice. But the trenches wasn't the only closing step. I liked to do what I called the stomper, which you do with the back of your foot.

After the B.S. Chorus we danced individually, then we'd close out all together. How long we danced, that depended on how long they threw money. Some nights people be stuffing it in my coat pocket, just shoving dollars in and I hardly knew it. Nights like that we might make a hundred, hundred fifty dollars, not counting what Hats and Coats stole. That was a lot of money in those days, a lot of money. Then some nights we'd make twenty-five.

We might make extra at a place like Beverly Gardens out on River Road. We made good tips there, and we'd get an extra five, ten dollars for one little bit I did. Louis Prima was just beginning to get popular and that's where he played. Prima, remember, was a very comedic-type man. He'd be making an announcement and I'd go out onstage, a little guy five, six years old, and keep pulling his coat.

"Go away boy, you're bothering me. I'm trying to talk."

I kept pulling his pants until finally he hollered, "What do you want?"

"Daddy, Mama wants you on the telephone!"

Of course, the crowd roared. Prima says out the side of his mouth, "Here, kid, take this and beat it." Slips me five or ten, like he doesn't want the people to know. Then he introduced us: "Ladies and gentlemen, here's Hats, Coats, and Pants, and this is my son Buttons!" and we did our routine and got more tips. That was a good little job for us, especially on a Saturday night. They threw a lot of money on that floor.

I had one little rival, Porkchops, but I was pretty much the top kid around there. When the *Our Gang* kids came through on a personal appearance, Buckwheat, the little black kid, took sick. I went up for an audition, but they said I was too light! They wanted to put burnt cork on my face. My grandma said, "Bull*shit* you're putting cork on his face. He's black enough as it is, too black already." And she turned the audition down.

I was cocky. You know what I had a big head about, more than anything else? The fact that I was all of these things: a dancer, a good athlete, not bad looking — hell, I thought I was as pretty as a little pimp! Even when you ain't acting cocky, they had grownups who felt that because you had this talent, you were a cocky little asshole. "Well, well, well. You think you cute." Apt to want to take you down a peg. Octave Crosby was a piano player who was crazy about

"I was pretty much the top kid [dancer] around there. . . . I was cocky." "Baby" Earl Palmer in a New Orleans photographer's studio.

Olivette West, a pretty dancer friend of my mother's who quit Octave because he was an obnoxious, rude son of a bitch. He wanted my mother to put in a good word for him but my mama said, "I ain't got nothing to do with that."

He cussed my mother out and Aunt Nita, too.

"You bitches won't say nothing to her for me."

I was standing there and went, "Teeheehee"—you know how a kid can laugh at somebody that's been embarrassed. Well, Octave came for me later and slapped me. When my mama found out, she had a big humbug. She went right after his ass. So did Hats, who was known to be a tush hog.

"I ever hear about you laying a hand on this kid, I'll break your neck."

"I didn't touch him, Hats!"

"If you even say that again, I'll break your neck!" Hats was bad, Hats was a hog.

Guys like Hats and Coats protected me since I didn't have a father. They were picking my pocket, but that's for drugs—they'd steal for that from anybody, that had nothing to do with their relationship with me. But it wasn't often they did that. They were very shy about stealing from me. They weren't going to lose the goose that's laying the golden egg, the little kid dancer.

Before long, I joined my mama and Nita, the Theophile Sisters. We danced at the Dog House on Rampart and Bienville; at the Silver Slipper on Bourbon; at the Entertainers on Franklin near Customhouse; at the Plantation Club, run by Pete Herman, the famous ex-bantamweight champion from years ago; and at the Big 25, an entertainers' and pimps' hangout on Franklin. The Pentagon Ballroom was downtown on Galvez and St. Bernard, across the street from another little bar called Little Ferd's.

There was the Budweiser on Iberville and the Kingfish, which they also called the Pig Pen, on Decatur and Ursulines. And there was the Gypsy Tea Room on St. Ann and Villere, Ethel Grant was a waitress there because what I recall, my Uncle Benny was going with her. God, she was pretty. God*damn*, she was pretty. Buddy Tureaud was the emcee and spoke the worst English in the world. "Y'all get ready, we going bring y'all so-and-so, boy shit can she sing!" A couple that played the Gypsy Tea Room used to fight all the time, Billie and De De, you pronounced it dee *dee*. Big Billie was the woman, De De was a trumpet player. I mean really fight. She'd be punching him like she was another man. They were good musicians, good entertainers. Everybody that played trumpet did a Louis Armstrong imitation, and De De was kind of known for that—he had one of these gravel voices anyhow. Billie sang all kind of risqué songs and played the piano. If she played the wrong note, De De said, "You ain't playing the right goddamn notes!"

"Fuck you, play your damn horn, don't tell me how to play!" Fistfight right there.

We played the Palace Theater, too, on Iberville and Dauphin. The Lyric was before the Palace. It used to be on the very next corner, at 201 Burgundy Street—Burgundy and Iberville, downtown back-of-town side. The Lyric closed when I was practically a baby; there's been a parking lot there for years.

Because of dancing I learned the structure of songs, which was a boon to me as a drummer. I learned how to improvise. That's all tap dancing is, improvising. They have set steps, but you make up plenty of your own. Any time dancers find themselves together, it becomes a jam session. "See this? Can you do this one?"

You need stamina as a dancer, and that's what drove me to play an instrument that takes stamina. I always liked the drums, even as a little kid. First drums I owned I was four years old, a cheap little toy-type set my grandfather bought at Morris Music Store on Claiborne Avenue. I played snare drum in the Craig School marching band, had a hole knocked right through the drumhead when we went marching down St. Philip Street and somebody threw money. I was furious! I never played in a funeral band. I always wanted to, but that was relegated to the old dudes, it was the highest of prestige.

I wanted to play tenor sax at one time and took clarinet lessons from Professor Tureaud, who was eighty-something years old and the only teacher my mother would let me go to. But he wouldn't take me on tenor, not until I learned clarinet, and my cousin stole my clarinet.

The first music I knew was the songs I danced by, like "Rose Room," or the songs my mother sang, like "Am I Blue?" "My Buddy" is another song I remember from early. ". . . the nights are long since you went away/I dream about you all through the day, my buddy. . . ." Kids didn't have no money to buy records, black kids anyhow, and there weren't any black radio shows or black disc jockeys. We listened to what the white stations played: *Amos 'n' Andy, Inner Sanctum*. You don't know how many years it took black people to realize it wasn't black guys doing *Amos 'n' Andy!* The sound of their voices was so typically black. Those guys did a hell of a job. They must have lived in black culture and really observed.

One year of high school is as far as I went. How could I learn about tap dancing in school? I'd known all my life what I wanted to be: something in show business. I went to Joseph A. Craig Elementary, Albert Wicker Junior High, and St. Peter Claver's Catholic school. I wasn't valedictorian or none of that shit, but if I didn't do well I wouldn't get to be in concerts or on the basketball team. So I did pretty well, except in subjects pertaining to numbers.

By the time I was seventeen I had been intimate with maybe fifteen, twenty girls, not counting casual acquaintances I met in other parts of town. Altogether I'd say I had maybe thirty, forty girls. That ain't a lot, not when you living where pussy's as free as the wind.

Blanche Thomas was the first chick I had anything to do with. I was about twelve, she was three or four years older and lived on Dumaine Street, between Claiborne and Robertson. It was the kind of thing where the grownups are gone and you're in the house. Blanche was a very forward girl. She dared me.

"You don't know how to do nothing."

Being a young, feisty dude, I said, "Yes I do!" You know, that kind of brag-gadocio attitude.

"I bet you never had no girl."

"Sure I did!"

"Aw, you don't know what to do."

"Yes I do, I'll show you!" I had sensed this was going to be the time. But I still wouldn't have been surprised if she'd slapped me and said, "Get the hell away from here!" I was kissing on her and feeling on her and I told her I was going to put it in her.

"Yeah, you keep saying that."

Next thing you know, that's just what I did. I remember thinking, "Jesus, I really don't know how to do this!" All I could think afterwards was, "I should have done this earlier!"

That's when I started looking for girls; before, I'd always let them take the initiative. You never took your clothes off, you had to be ready to run out the back door—we were kids, man! Those houses all had back doors and little alleyways and you'd go running out the alley.

It wasn't long after, I had a little finagling with a cousin of Blanche's, Angelina Ferrand, a pretty, pretty girl whose nickname was Sailor Mouth. Motherfuck this, motherfuck that. And pretty as a little speckled pup! It went on between me and Angelina for years, man. With a certain few people, you'd do it almost any time. Me and Angelina were friends, but we were fucking friends.

Actually, it wasn't that unusual for a girl in my neighborhood to maintain her virginity. The large percentage, you see, were Catholics and was afraid of the priests and the sisters—and them priests found out every time. I'm Catholic born and raised, I was even an altar boy at St. Peter Claver. I think they were short of them. That's where I learned to drink. The father turned me on to wine, man, the wine they made the blessed sacrament with. He drunk it like a fish when he wasn't drinking Irish whiskey. Do you realize there was a time they didn't allow no blacks in Immaculate Conception? A Catholic church! I was put out of Our Lady of Guadeloupe on St. Louis and Rampart when I was eleven or twelve. I went in there for Ash Wednesday, and the priest said, "You can't come in, go to St. Peter Claver." I was shocked! After a while I wasn't shocked anymore, and that's the reason I never had much faith in the Catholic Church.

THE DARKTOWN SCANDALS ACROSS THE USA, 1930–1942

Miss Cox, an ebony edition of Sophie Tucker . . . whams with "My Handy Man," topped by a shiver dance that rocks the house. . . . In Ida Cox the unit has a star. — *Variety* review of Ida Cox's *Darktown Scandals,* Roxy Theater, Salt Lake City, Utah, November 28, 1937

Word comes from Chicago that "Baby" Earl Palmer "broke up" the Sunset Club Saturday when he was sent for from Bloomington, Ill. . . . Earl, Thelma and Nita Theophile . . . were playing the Majestic Theatre in Bloomington. — *Louisiana Weekly,* April 25, 1936

Moore's Golden Lily Show wishes to contact chorus girls, musicians and performers who can produce a real show; no boozers or agitators wanted. —Chicago *Defender,* April 18, 1936

In the early thirties Earl joined his mother and aunt on the black vaudeville circuit, where he spent a good part of the decade. Of the several shows he joined, he spent the most time with Ida Cox's *Darktown Scandals Revue.*

"The Uncrowned Queen of the Blues," Cox had ridden the crest of the twenties blues craze, selling hundreds of thousands if not millions of records. By the thirties, big bands reigned; blues singers were passé. Miss Ida had played the Apollo in 1929 and a week at Chicago's great Regal in 1930. Within two or three years she was plying the back roads, bringing country people what they considered a touch of big-city class.

Early twentieth-century popular entertainment was an undifferentiated mass, yet to divide itself into genres, formats, and markets. A grab bag of music, comedy, dance, and anything else capable of holding an audience, vaudeville was the ideal genre for these prespecialized times, America's most popular form of entertainment from 1895 to 1930, among blacks as well as whites. In the mid-twenties some three hundred theaters specialized in so-called black cast vaudeville. It's a misconception that these shows' audiences were also all-black. Earl estimates that in half the theaters he played, the audience was either all-white or mixed.

"It was the most marvelous life a kid could ask for," says Earl of his show days. He thrived in a dying genre. Crippled by radio and talking pictures, vaudeville was finished off by the Depression. Black vaudeville suffered even more than its white counterpart; the audience had fewer discretionary dollars. "Admitting their white brothers have been caught in the year of theatrical depression and nationwide unemployment," said *Variety* on December 31, 1930, "Negro show producers, theatre operators and players have apparently been caught deeper. Colored show biz just creeps along— going and getting nowhere." In 1930 the Chicago *Defender*'s weekly list of show routes still teemed with names—the *Black Bottom Revue*, the Brownskin Models, Butterbeans and Susie, *Tan Town Revels*, *Pickings from Dixie*, Ida Cox's *Raisin' Cain* (the predecessor to the *Darktown Scandals*), the Whitman Sisters, the Black Peppers, the *Chocolate Snaps of 1930*, and many others—but by the mid-thirties the *Defender* no longer ran the weekly itineraries. In his weekly *Defender* column, retired vaudevillian "Uncle Bob" Hayes reported the illnesses and deaths of his old pals with relentless, and finally lugubrious, regularity. Only a few troupes and shows carried on: the Brownskin Models, *Silas Green from New Orleans*, the Whitman Sisters, the *Darktown Scandals*, and various organizations calling themselves the Georgia Minstrels. They were lucky if they broke even. On May 9, 1937, the *Louisiana Weekly* reported that after a week at New Orleans's Palace Theater, Ida Cox "made no money here. Which isn't bad for a road show these days." A vaudevillian named June Brown "is hiding here till the winter blows over," said

the *Louisiana Weekly* on February 6, 1937. "He made it here from
Kansas City and Memphis and says it's tough up the line."

Black vaudeville was its own insular world, held together by word
of mouth and black newspapers' entertainment pages (the Chicago
Defender especially was a lifeline for twenties and thirties show people,
its "amusements" page a combined mailbox/opinions and
forum/bulletin board). This world had a rough romance but no lux-
ury; performers scraped hard against life's unbuffered edge. Pay was
minimal, especially as the Depression deepened. In 1937 the orchestra at New Orleans's Palace Theater struck for a fifty-cent raise; the
players earned $7.50 for three shows a week. A chorus girl earned
perhaps $15.00 a week and did not travel in style. The great jazz
trumpeter Clark Terry, a member of the *Darktown Scandals* orchestra as a boy, remembers the show's bus: "That little rusty-ass bus, it's
a wonder we didn't all catch pneumonia. We wrapped croker sacks
around our feet and plugged the windows with paper." On a hill
outside Huntington, West Virginia, the bus shuddered to a halt.
"Ida said, 'All right, everybody get out and push,' and everybody got
out and pushed, except a little midget named Prince. Ida goes, 'I
said everybody out!' Prince says, 'But Miss Ida, I'm so small.' 'Get
your ass out there,' says Ida, 'we got a little bitty place just for you.'
That bus was always pumping and humping and barely making it
over the terrain. We came in town once and the engine burst into
flame; someone in the press said, 'Ida Cox's red-hot show rolled into
town on fire.'"

Below the Mason-Dixon line, the everyday could instantly turn
nightmarish. Traveling with the venerable Reuben & Cherry carnival just before joining the *Scandals*, Clark Terry was almost lynched
twice. He and a band mate were in a dime store in Jacksonville,
Florida, when Terry's companion accidentally stumbled against an
elderly white woman. "She started yelling," says Terry, "and we were
suddenly running from a mob." They hid under a rubbish heap.
"We're lucky they didn't have dogs." In Meridian, Mississippi, Terry
made the mistake of answering a white railroad man's question
without adding "sir." "He beat the hell out of me with a blackjack
and left me lying in a puddle, screaming and moaning. The train
crew found me and carried me back to the show car. They told me
later that this man came back with fifteen Caucasians with picks

and axes and shovels and chains and bricks and bats, and they said,
'Where's that nigger?' They were going to finish me off."

The *Defender* was full of such stories. January 31, 1931: "The trials
of a small road show playing below the line [are] shown in a letter . . .
received this week, asking assistance in locating one 'Jolly Snow.'
The letter reads: 'Doc Livingstone's show was playing at Little
River, Fla., when the Klan rode up with whips in their hands. Pig
Jones and several others beat it for the woods, pursued by the Klux-
ers. All have been found except Jolly Snow.' "

Sometimes the bookings ran out, sometimes the owner. Getting
stranded was a routine hazard. " 'Shufflin' Sam' Left Stranded in
Knoxville," ran a *Defender* headline of December 13, 1930. The
company manager had shuffled off, "leaving the entire troupe of 21
holding the proverbial sack on three weeks salary and a sheriff's at-
tachment staring them in the face." From the October 4, 1930, *Defender:* "Sweetie Walker wires us of the sad closing of 'High Brown
Follies,' leaving a cast of 65 on the rocks at Natchez, Miss. SOS calls
are being made to friends and relatives of members of the cast."

However grim the circumstances, the performers were often first-
rate. Aurora Greeley, object of Earl's peeping Tom exertions, was
briefly the toast of Harlem, headlining at the Ubangi Club in 1936.
Comedian Jazzlips Richardson, who traveled with Earl in 1936, had
starred on Broadway in 1929 and crossed the ocean to appear before
England's King George. Drummer Kidd Lipps Hackett of the
Brownskin Minstrels stopped shows by diving fifteen feet from the
box seats to the stage (while executing a perfect flip), landing at his
drum kit to hit the song's last beat: an impressive way to end a tune.
Although *The New Grove Dictionary of Jazz* (indeed, every standard
jazz history) ignores him, Hackett also excelled at straight-ahead
swing, starring in Buck Clayton's orchestra in the mid-thirties.

Earl's vaudeville years were vitally important to his later musical
success. It isn't merely that tap dancing, as is often pointed out, is
drumming with your feet, that tap gave Earl (and Buddy Rich,
Louis Bellson, Philly Joe Jones, Steve Gadd, Hal Blaine, and others) a rhythmic facility he drew on as a drummer. Years spent sweat-
ing to make an audience applaud gave Earl an intuitive knowledge
of how to achieve emotional effects, how to build tension to the
point of climax and catharsis—how to sell a song, as the old-timers

say. You can hear it in his drum fills on a big band album like Mel Tormé's *Sunday in New York and Other Songs about New York* or a rock tune like Sam Cooke's "Shake," in the understated but extraordinarily expressive licks with which he graced thousands of recordings. As Earl's old friend the recording engineer Cosimo Matassa says, "Some people didn't do it, they were it. It was in their bones. Earl is one of those people. Earl is an entertainer." In Earl Palmer, ex-vaudevillian, sixties rock and roll benefited from a showbiz tradition that had vanished years before.

I loved Miss Ida and she called me her baby. "Earl! Come here, baby!" She'd grab me and hug me and put me on her lap. Many times I fell asleep on them boobs of hers, man. Like pillows! Actually, Miss Ida wore a corset most times; if she hadn't, she'd have looked like a bale of cotton with the middle band busted. Miss Ida was a hell of a woman. She carried people when they needed to be carried, gave them plenty of opportunities when they messed up.

I traveled in vaudeville off and on for eleven years and a fair chunk of that was with Ida Cox's *Darktown Scandals*. My mother took care of a lot of business for Miss Ida because Miss Ida *drank* a lot in those days. She always thought she was as good a blues singer as any and hadn't been recognized. I remember a tune she did, something about he stokes her furnace, lights her fire, does everything that fulfills her desire, because lawdy lawdy lawdy he's her handyman. That was my favorite.

I sat on Bessie Smith's lap, too, in Montgomery or Mobile. She and Miss Ida and my mother were talking in Miss Ida's dressing room and Miss Bessie picked me up and hugged me. I smelled booze all over her but I was used to it. Bessie looked like she might've been a nice rounded fairly cute Betty Boop–type woman once, but you could see the dissipation coming into her. I stayed and listened to her and Miss Ida, just two drunken women talking, a mutual admiration society and neither of them meant it worth a shit.

Now, when I was twelve was the last time I danced in the Quarter for tips. Being out on the road, I'd become a consummate professional. Street dancing was below me now, it wasn't anything you'd do after you realized you was a little more of an artist.

Aside from Miss Ida's I was with a show called the Georgia Minstrels for eight, nine months in 1936. They had a famous comedian named Jazzlips Richardson who had big, big lips and made them flutter. Black comics in

"Miss Ida was a hell of a woman. She carried people when they needed to be carried, gave them plenty of opportunities when they messed up." Ida Cox in the mid-forties. Note the cast of the advertised film—apparently Miss Ida forgave the wayward Birdina Hackett. (Frank Driggs Archive)

those days did lots of stuff like that. Jazzlips did a backflip, the first I ever saw. He wore shoes that were big and long and wide and he slapped them down like boards.

They had another show I was on, too, the Rabbit's Foot Minstrels. My mother and them joined it for a good while but I was on it no more than a month. It was a tent show and traveled just like a carnival: the equipment on trucks, the people in buses and cars. It was a very famous show but the one thing I can't remember is who was in it.

Minstrel shows started way back before vaudeville. In a minstrel show everyone sat out on the stage and the interlocutor, who was the master of ceremonies, began a conversation with each performer. That's what led up to your act. You sang, danced, told jokes, same as in vaudeville; it was just a different

"I was gorgeous as a little pimp!" Dime store photo of Earl, mid-
thirties.

form of presentation. Minstrel shows was known to be a very circus-type of at-
mosphere. They'd parade through town when they got in; we never did that.

A vaudeville show opened with the chorus: usually an eye-catching spicy
number where the chorus girls did lots of kick steps and showed a lot of leg.
Then came the acts, starting with the comedians. In those days teams was considered necessary for comedy. Single comedians like they have today, stand-
ups, didn't come along until later. One guy was the straight man, the foil, the
other was the dummy, and it was always a job for the straight man not to crack
up. Blackface was standard for comedians. It was what audiences were used to
seeing, including black audiences—they laughed as hard as whites. It was just
something that was considered comedic and I didn't think twice about it.

After the comedians came the girl singer, then another number by the cho-

"They [the Georgia Minstrels] had a famous comedian
named Jazzlips Richardson." Jazzlips Richardson in a snap-
shot from Nita Theophile's photo album, mid-thirties.

rus, featuring the soubrette—that was the lead chorus girl, which in Miss Ida's
show was my mother. Next a tap dance team, then maybe your male vocalist.
The star closed the show, singing however many numbers he pleased. Miss
Ida sang five or six. The chorus did one last number and then came the finale,
usually something lively and up-tempo where everybody came out, took a
bow, sang one chorus, and ran off. The last to take a bow was the star.

We did three and four shows a day, at least. On Saturdays, depending on the
laws, we did what you called the Midnight Ramble, where kids wasn't allowed.
The jokes had double meanings and the chorus did a little more shaking and
shimmying. It was risqué, but nowhere near as risqué as today. Nobody took
their clothes off—no, indeed, that was against the law then!

My mother and my Aunt Nita had a featured spot. It was a good act. They

"A vaudeville show opened with the chorus: usually an eye-catching spicy number where the chorus girls did lots of kick steps and showed a lot of leg." The Georgia Minstrels chorus line, 1936. Nita Theophile is at far left; Juanita Gonzales is second from right; Thelma Theophile is at far right.

were good dancers, good singers—they were good entertainers. What made their spot special was they did it as a boy-girl act. My mother played the male counterpart. She wore pants and a cap. She never had a lot of bosom; it didn't jump up and down, anyhow. Nita was what they called the baby girl, in a little frilly tutu.

My mama handled that male part well. She'd sing, "Ain't she sweet/When she's walking down the street" and point to Nita, who did some little cute dance. Nita toe-danced and did Russian-type dancing—she was very, very good at that. Then they'd do some tap steps together, depending on what was in vogue, and my mama took her cap off and her long hair fell down and the audience gasped. Don't forget, we were playing a lot of little towns where they was easy to fool.

My mama and Nita worked out new stuff all the time, between shows, on the bus, in the dressing room. We had time. I'd suggest things, or my Aunt

Mattie Jackson would suggest things. She was Nita's girlfriend and Benny Williams's stepsister.

Before I got my own spot I was in my mama's. I came in and did my little dance, to "Rose Room" or something like that. I had four, five minutes, then they'd announce me as her son and I'd run off. Other than that I did anything they could use a kid for: conduct the orchestra, play the drums, fake playing the piano. Sometimes I did a chorus or two with Benny, who often joined the show.

We had another male dancer, Reggie Grant, a strict, straight-out tap dancer and a very good one. He was also the emcee, usually. A lot of guys hit on my mother and never got anywhere, but the one man I think may have was Reggie Grant. Reggie gave me my first conk. I was smitten with it—oh, it looked beautiful! I said, "Damn, all of a sudden I got good hair!" My head burned like a sumbitch—not as bad as I expected, but I yelled anyway. For some reason Reggie always called me Mustard. I can hear him, clear as a bell: "Hey *Mustard!*"

After I got my spot I did maybe six minutes. Reggie announced me—"Earl Palmer the Kid Wonder!" or "The Tap Dancing Sensation" or "The New Orleans Flash!"—whatever nonsense came in his head. I'd come out, bow, and open with something eye-catching, maybe "I Got Rhythm." Then I'd level off and do a chorus or two where the audience could hear me tapping, not just watch. Something that showed my prowess. "Rose Room" was especially good for that. It had built-in stop time—you didn't have to cut out any of the melody, it had plenty sections where the music stopped cold. "Tea for Two" is more continuous, it stops only once. Then came your big, your closing, chorus, where I'd do something like "Liza," using what we called flash steps, fast and flashy.

I wore a white tux onstage. Not just a plain tuxedo: tails. Tails was more or less de rigueur for entertainers in those days. I wore white tails, black tails, sometimes fancy red-and-blue tails.

There were about thirty of us in Miss Ida's: eight or ten girls in the line, eight to twelve pieces in the band, and maybe another ten in the featured acts. We used one bus with a big sign on the side, "Ida Cox's Darktown Scandals Revue." Miss Ida took a double seat all to herself, right behind the driver. She put her feet up, leaned a big pillow against the window, and slept. Snored like crazy. Otherwise she'd be talking and drinking with the rest. Miss Ida wasn't drunk all the time, just frequently.

When Mr. Jesse Crump was on the show, he took a double seat, too, because he was a big fat man. Mr. Jesse played piano, ran the band, and was Miss Ida's accompanist. He was from Paris, Texas. He was Miss Ida's old man at the time, though I don't know if they were married; I always thought they were.

They'd sit up front and have normal husband-wife conversations or talk about the music. Get in arguments all the time. Ida was a volatile woman and Jesse Crump was no pussy of a man. He might say, "Ida, why you got to drink?"

"Don't tell me what the fuck to do."

"Goddamn right I'll tell you what the fuck to do." Miss Ida was a strong woman but Jesse was her man.

There wasn't a lot of money in circulation then, so prices were pretty reasonable. Shoes were two dollars, two-fifty; a good meal was thirty-five, forty-five cents. We couldn't afford nothing very expensive anyway, not that they had expensive places for blacks, not down South. I once heard Sammy Davis Jr. say he never ran into prejudice until he was in the service. That's bullshit, because I ate with Sammy Davis in a restaurant kitchen. That's where you ate in white restaurants down South. They cleaned off the dirty-dish counter and put a tablecloth on it.

Buses didn't have no toilets then; when you had to pee, we stopped by the side of the road. That bus broke down all the time, too. If it was something Dallas the driver couldn't fix, we'd have to get a mechanic from town and everybody would get out and stand around. Dallas looked exactly like Lew Chudd, a record producer I later worked for. The strange thing about Dallas was, here was this Southern white man who not only hung around black people but took such abuse from them! The way Miss Ida talked to that man!

"Goddamn it! Don't you know where you going?"

"Well, Miss Ida, we have to go this way."

"Shit! Look like it taking a goddamn long time." And he just loved her! Everyone on the bus is whispering, "Why is she fucking with that man, he ain't done nothing to her!"

She was a mean drunk. When she had nothing to bitch about, she brought up stuff that was already resolved. If somebody made an entrance at the wrong time, about a week later Miss Ida would say to herself out of the blue clear sky, "I wonder how long the bitch has to be a dancer before she realizes when she supposed to come on the goddamn stage."

Just sitting up there by herself, loaded. Everybody whisper, "Uh-oh. She's reached that point again."

I never saw her hit anyone. I saw her threaten people. She threw her hairbrush at me once when I wouldn't get out of her dressing room. A girl got a little too friendly with a local guy and Miss Ida assumed she was turning a trick. Maybe she was and maybe she really had eyes for the guy, but Miss Ida threatened her and fired her. Turning tricks was a no-no; show people were very protective of what reputation they had left. My mother slapped a chick named

Lorraine for turning a trick. My mama had spoken up about it and Lorraine said it was none of her business.

"I knew that when I opened my mouth," my mama said, "but I'm making it my business."

"You ought to keep your mouth shut," Lorraine said. My mama slapped her. She started to fall and my mama pushed her on her back.

"Get up and I'll kick you in the face." Lorraine just lay there glaring.

I saw a lot of things I wasn't supposed to. A little boy is a hell of a peeping Tom and I made it a point to peep at Aurora Greeley. I had a huge schoolboy crush on her. She was in a team called Broomfield and Greeley, one of the most class acts the show ever had, Leroy Broomfield and Aurora Greeley. They did a lot of ballroom routines, had a thing where the guy's a gigolo and he beats up the girl and she spins across the floor and comes back to him, still loves him, and he knocks her across the floor again and she turns a flip. Boy, was that woman beautiful! Had a body on her I can never forget. Aurora was always very aloof from everybody on the show. I never did catch her completely undressed, but what I saw was enough.

Some of the rank-and-file names on the show was Juanita Gonzales, Sweetie and Stella Walker, Jennie Smith, and Rookie Davis. There was Rae Carter, a trumpeter who'd been with the International Sweethearts of Rhythm, and Birdina Hackett, a chorus girl, a laughing, outgoing, bubbly type. Jenny Smith was a comedienne who doubled as a chorus girl—these girls, you see, doubled a lot. Rookie Davis read books that were over our head. Sweetie Walker was a comedian, Stella was his foil. We had an old comedian named Leroy White; when I was a kid, man, Leroy White looked to be seventy-five. Big, tall, very funny man, did a lot of things off the top of his head and if it was funny he kept it. He did a routine where a guy's trying to get out of paying alimony for seven children. Finally some straight man, which was anybody from the band gone and put on a police jacket, nails him. "We finally got you!" As it turns out, none of the kids is his.

We had a saxophone player named Eddie Johnson who drank a lot, had one of those heavy burned-out whiskey voices. He did me something, I don't remember what, scared me, cussed me, threatened me. I said, "I'll fix him." I just thought I'd give him a little problem and loosen a key on his saxophone, but the screw came off and rolled away. I couldn't find it. The moment he picked up his horn, the key fell right off. Everyone was backstage—it was during the afternoon movie—and Eddie Johnson was *ohhhh!* He raised hell. He had a big solo, too, and couldn't play it. I was afraid he'd find out and kill me, but he didn't even suspect. Probably because he thought I'd never dare do

Georgia Minstrels chorus members on the road, 1936. *Far left,* Juanita Gonzales; *far right,* Nita Theophile.

something like that—he'd kill me, *kill* me. Chase me right through the movie screen into the crowd, like in the cartoons. In those days, you see, it wasn't only your mother could whip your butt. Anybody that caught you doing wrong could spank your ass. *And* tell your parents about it, so you got another spanking.

Van Epps was a gay dancer I called my Uncle Van, and Clifton Phelps—another good, hell of a good, tap dancer—was what you might call Van's old lady. When I was coming up I didn't know nothing about no closet gays. I didn't consider someone was gay until I saw him bend his wrist and I saw a lot of that. Juanita Gonzales was gay, Rae Carter was gay. Clifton Phelps reached out to grab me once and my mother went after him, called him every kind of sumbitch in the world. Van had already taken care of him. Clifton was crying and apologizing. If it hadn't been for him and Van having a pretty good act, I think my mama would have gotten Miss Ida to let him go.

We didn't have anyone running from the law but I'd hear about that, people who'd changed their names and gone out on the road because they'd done something bad. I remember seeing the police come for musicians from other shows. That never happened to us except once, when they came for Johnston.

The whole thing started when Miss Ida found out that Mr. Jesse was carrying on with Birdina Hackett. Did they have a screaming match! Miss Ida was raising hell about how Mr. Jess considered her a damn fool and that's the end of him having to do with that bitch Birdina, she was going—both of them was going.

Now, Birdina was also seeing a saxophone player named Johnston, a good-looking West Indian man. Johnston was his first name, I don't remember his last. When he found out about Birdina and Mr. Jesse, he cut Birdina. Put a gash down the side of her face all the way under her chin. He almost slit her throat. He was known to carry a knife, he was known for that, man. You could hear Birdina scream. I saw her right after he did it and I yelled like I was the one been cut. He did it backstage. They rushed her to the hospital holding a towel to her neck but the blood soaked right through it, blood all over.

Johnston didn't even run. He went and sat in the seats, put his head in his hands, and waited for the police. Birdina stayed in the hospital when the show left town. Mr. Crump left the show, too, and I never saw any of them again.

Miss Ida was pretty broken up. I can't honestly say I studied it—at my age I wasn't studying grownups' emotions. She must have had an idea this was going on. Everybody knew it. Mr. Jesse was a philanderer, he sneaked around. But Ida cared enough for him that she ignored it until she couldn't anymore.

The stabbing was in some small town in the Northwest, some town we seldom played, like Sioux Falls, South Dakota. Wherever it was, it was extremely fucking cold. I remember the blood coagulating when it dripped on Birdina's clothes and on the floor.

We played a lot of towns like that. Mr. Schenck was a wizard at booking us places, man, where you'd never think they'd hire a black show. Jack Schenck. He was a wizard at that. His son Lawrence came on the road too; Lawrence ran the business of the show while Mr. Schenck was out what they called front-manning, booking ahead, because he was a bitch at booking. He was a road manager par excellence. He could sell you something, boy. Anytime you got a black singer like Ida Cox playing Newton, Iowa, not a single black in the audience and the theater is packed, someone is selling that package. Either that or there was a lot of white people loved the blues.

After Jesse Crump left, Mr. Schenck took that other front seat. Before long he started going with Miss Ida. It was supposed to be a secret but everybody knew. That was about the only black-white relationship I was aware of then, except Birdina. She fucked Jack Schenck too. Birdina was a social climber, man. When Lawrence came on the show, she tried to fuck *him*. Lawrence mingled a lot, sat in the back of the bus, anywhere in the bus, playing cards and talking basketball.

When Leroy White or Reggie Grant was on, I'd watch the show from the wings. Otherwise I might be in the dressing room playing solitaire. If I was finished I might be gone, gone out in the streets. See, I was little enough to sleep in the overhead luggage rack on the bus. The grownups sat up all night; when we got to a town in the morning, they wanted to stretch out. Rather than rent hotel rooms everybody lay down in the theater lobby on those nice thick carpets and slept until the theater opened for the movie; then they went backstage and slept a couple hours more. Me, I'd have slept all night so I was out meeting the townskids.

"You with the show come in?"

"Yeah."

"Well, what do you do?"

And you'd make friends. In towns where there was damn few black kids, they knew you was there for some special reason. So I'd meet the white kids. I always wanted to be accepted by the kids I met. Keep a little change in my pocket for ice cream or milk shakes—right away I was popular. They figured I was a star anyhow; I was with the show, right? I was hardly making a quarter, but I always kept a couple dollars in my pocket.

In Lead, South Dakota, they had a big hill behind the theater. The local kids climbed it all day long.

"Want to come up the hill with us?"

"Sure."

But you couldn't get down like you went up. The coming down was steep! I hadn't realized that; I wasn't no hill climber like these kids. I got stranded up there, man, scared to come down. I tried to scrape down on my behind and tore the back of my pants. The fire department had to get me. My mother kicked my butt, my butt that was already sore. I don't know if I even went on that day, my ass burned so.

Those kids in Lead had become my friends and I just wanted to stay and have more fun, so I let all the air out of the bus's tires. Nobody ever found out it was me, they thought it was kids in town. Or anybody, some bigot, maybe, because things used to happen all the time, us being an all-black troupe. There were towns we passed through, they'd throw rotten eggs. Tomatoes. In Dothan, Alabama, someone threw something that cracked the window. When something like that happens today, you stop, get out, and kick some ass. Back then if you stopped, you *got* kicked. So you just kept going. Didn't shake your fist, didn't stick your head out the window, hell, no. You did nothing. You got on away from there as fast as you could and called yourself lucky. They could catch your ass, put you in jail, beat you up, lynch you. An incident could explode into anything. It only depended on you, on how you reacted, and the best reaction was to get the hell away.

There was little towns you came through and a sign said, "Nigger Don't Let the Sun Going Down Catch You in This Town." You was careful not to upset anybody and I don't care how mad they made you. Forget about being your-self. Yourself was not the kind of sumbitch you could be, not when you're wor-rying if someone's going to get pissed off and beat your ass up. Forget com-fortable. It was not comfortable. Your comfort was not what they had in mind.

Prejudice wasn't even something you could easily admit you disliked. It was going to be that way everywhere. To be daring you might step out of line, do something you knew you shouldn't: walk where you knew you shouldn't be walking, drink from a fountain you knew you shouldn't use. But the sign said you couldn't do it and the law said the same. And if you got caught, whatever punishment you suffered, you felt was justified.

When you're a kid dancer, everywhere you go somebody's always bringing in the local favorite, the new fast gun. "Aw, we got a local kid better than that." They don't realize that what they saw you do onstage isn't all you do. They don't know that as a professional you can turn it on, pull out the hard stuff, and cut his head. We called it bucking each other.

This was mostly with black kids; I only remember one white kid coming backstage, in Boulder, Colorado. I wiped him out, outdanced him so bad he went home crying. That happened a number of times until in Kansas City I ran into these two kids who took me down a peg. Two brothers, bitching dancers. Kicked my ass. They both kicked my ass, boy. Taught me some hu-mility, which I needed; I was beginning to feel I was badder than bad. They was tap dancing asses, boy. Here I was, thought I was big, and these local townskids, kids that wasn't doing nothing, whipped my ass. One was named Connie. That little mother, man, I remember just burning with shame. "He cut my head!"

The show was laid off for a while and I got to be friends with those two. Af-ter they kicked my ass, I wanted to impress them. At the playground on Paseo Parkway I tried to show them how fast I could swim, got a cramp and almost drowned. Both those brothers jumped in and got me out of there.

Of the few professional kid dancers I met out on the road, the best was Sammy Davis, a motherfucker, a dancing sumbitch. I ran into him a number of places. They'd be somewhere the week before us, leaving as we came in: the Will Mastin Trio. Sammy and I danced a little once, near the Frolic The-atre in Birmingham, fooling around. To me he was just another kid dancer; I didn't come to see how good he was until later, when I mastered certain things and realized, "Goddamn, he was doing this back then?"

But I was good. Had I kept going I'd have been very high echelon. Known. It has nothing to do with ego. It's a matter of fact.

"I was beginning to feel I was badder than bad." Earl in the mid-thirties.

Sometimes I was on the posters. My mother and aunt often were. "Ida Cox's 'Darktown Scandals,' Featuring the Theophile Sisters." Sometimes we hired a big act. You may remember the Step Brothers, who joined us briefly. Oh, could they dance! Maceo Anderson and Al Williams and Prince Spencer. Whenever they were on, I watched. They did things like jump over each other from a push-up position. They'd crisscross, the guy on the left leapfrogging over the guy in the middle, the guy on the right leapfrogging over him, all the while parallel to the floor. Then they'd get up and tap-dance their butts off.

They showed me things too—toe stands, where you dance a couple of beats on your toes, and the wings they did were different from any I knew, more difficult. Prince Spencer was the best dancer I'd seen up to then. Who I recognize now as great, that I only saw once, much later on, was a drug addict named Baby Laurence. Ohhh! You know how scat singers put lyrics to famous jazz solos? Well, Baby Laurence tap-danced to solos. He hummed the melody once while he tapped it, just so he knew what song it was. Then he tapped the solos. Try to imagine somebody tap-dancing to Bird's solo on "Donna Lee"! I saw Baby Laurence in a club in Chicago not long before he died. He was the best I ever saw.

Sometimes we carried a peg leg dancing act—a good peg leg dancer, that was a hell of a draw. We had two at different times. Peg Leg Parker, little short guy with a long head, and Peg Leg Jefferson, heavyset, looked like a football player. I was pretty blasé about stuff like that, one-legged dancers. If I was curious it wasn't for long; my main interest was in seeing how good they were. Once I found out, they were just dancers with one leg.

If we were doing very well, Rookie Davis was my tutor, man, because she'd been an accredited teacher. Depended where we were. Down South they didn't give a damn if a black dude was in school. Up North the truant officer came around a few times. They had to make some kind of showing.

"Ain't that boy in school? What do you do for schooling, don't you know it's school time?"

And there was places they assumed I was a midget. When people think you're the midget, you can go in a lot of places kids can't go. In Kansas City we played Scott's Theater restaurant and stayed at the Hotel Booker T., which you'd find in damn near every big city in the country at that time: the Booker T. Washington Hotel. They had a fish joint near the corner of Vine and Eighteenth. For years I didn't know what that fish was. Delicious! It's called buffalo. Across Vine was a joint I went in with Reggie and a couple of guys; the piano player looked to be thirty-five, forty, kind of fat, and I hadn't heard anybody play the piano that fast since Burnell Santiago, the little junkie in New Orleans. I also knew one thing: Burnell was very crude compared to this man. That's how I came to see Art Tatum.

I did more traveling with Miss Ida, in the USA, than I've done since. Out of forty-eight states I'd say we played thirty, working the big circuits and the small. The real big circuits, the Loew's-Warner, the Keith-Orpheum, were mostly up North; down South they had combines like the Barrasso Brothers that specialized in black theaters. They'd book you in all their theaters and you went from one to the next.

"We played middle-sized and small towns mostly: Carlsbad, Albuquerque, Santa Fe, Las Cruces, Galveston, Shreveport, Des Moines, Omaha, Racine." *Darktown Scandals* chorus member Rookie Davis in front of a poster for the show.

We played middle-sized and small towns mostly: Carlsbad, Albuquerque, Santa Fe, Las Cruces, Galveston, Shreveport, Des Moines, Omaha, Racine. Huntington, West Virginia. Lincoln, Nebraska, where they had the first soap-box derby; I wanted to get in that so bad I cried and cried. Flint, Michigan, the coldest place I ever was in my life. Across the border to Windsor, Ontario. Weed, California, where they had a little small theater and we played for lumber workers and I saw Mount Shasta, the tallest mountain in California. I used to love to go flying, and you could pay to go up in a biplane. Nita loved it too, and the first time I went a white guy took both of us, some guy that was interested in the girls on the show and figured this was a good way to introduce himself. You didn't go too high, you weren't up in the stratosphere in no Fairchild biplane. I went up all over the country, man, every chance I got.

Miss Ida played cities, too: Houston, Denver, St. Louis, Kansas City, wherever there was a big black population. Memphis, Birmingham, Atlanta, these were all good towns for black vaudeville. It was a week in the cities, one-night stands in the small burgs. Sometimes we did fifteen, sixteen one-nighters in a row. In towns like Fresno where we played for migrant workers, we always had a packed house — we were the only entertainment those people got. The point was to get the hell out of a place like that before the work season broke down, or there was a good chance you'd strand. You could see a strand coming: a week of one-nighters dwindled to three gigs a week, then two, and finally the show just went on the blink. Miss Ida went home to Knoxville and we caught work where we could.

We stranded once in Flagstaff but it wasn't on account of not having no work. Those iron weights they had in old theaters, curtain raisers, one of them tore loose and hit my mother on the head. Cracked her skull. I didn't see it but I heard it. *Rap.* Just like a rock hitting a piece of wood. My mama's blood flowed all over. They carried her unconscious to the hospital and put six clamps in her skull. The doctor said, "She's lucky it didn't hit her square on the head, but she'll have to be here six to eight weeks at least."

The closest place for work was El Paso, so Nita and Mattie and I went there and found a cheap hotel. An old couple ran it that was raising their grandsons, Miguel and Pablo. I got to hanging with these kids and ate frijoles and beans and learned to speak Spanish damn near fluently. Their mother had been busted weed-smuggling and couldn't come across the border, so they went to Juárez nearly every day and I went along. This was the 1930s and Juárez was wild, Juárez was a town you didn't want to go to jail in. They didn't have no roof on the jail in Juárez. The further into that town you got the more it deteriorated into a real slum, into nothing, into shit.

We found work with a nine-piece band led by a light-complected wavy-haired Mexican-looking guy named Bat Brown. He treated us like stars. I was featured doing my little tap dance and conducting the band — Bat Brown made a thing out of turning the band over to "our little mascot."

He played all across that territory: El Paso, Abilene, Midland, Odessa, Lubbock, Sweetwater, Amarillo, and up into New Mexico. Outside Carlsbad, New Mexico, we met a guy took us rattlesnake hunting, a dude who knew Mex, Bat's bus driver. The snakes were short and thick, man, this big around. They sold them to the hotels. I understand the meat is delicious. They made steaks from these thick, thick rattlesnakes and considered it a delicacy.

Mex's friend told me, "Don't go off by yourself," but I strayed out turquoise hunting, out in the middle of all this mesquite and rocks. Suddenly all I could hear was rattles going off, rattles all around. I screamed. "Don't move!" I heard somebody yell. That's the last thing they should have said, because I took off in every direction at once. I don't even know when I stopped. If my mama'd been there she'd have beat my butt.

"It was the most marvelous life a kid could ask for." Earl (rear center) with members of the Bat Brown Orchestra, somewhere in the Southwest, mid-thirties. Mex the bus driver is at lower left.

We were with Bat Brown three months and I cried many times; I missed my mother terribly. There were times, man, we thought we'd lose her. Nita and Mattie would tell me, "She's not doing too well." We were afraid they'd tell her she was healed just to get her out of the hospital. I talked to her once or twice and started crying. "Mama, when you coming by us?"

And then she came back. Mex carried Nita to Flagstaff to get her. She recovered a while and then we rode a bus as far as we could, to Beaumont, East Texas. Someone showed Mattie how to hop a freight train, so the four of us went down to the rail yards early one morning. You had to wait until the train started moving, then you ran alongside and grabbed them iron handles and jumped on. I remember getting lifted into the car from behind. Nita jumped on after me, then my mama, then Mattie. The train was only going maybe five miles an hour. Not even dangerous, just enough to be a little fun. I slept a long, long time and when I woke we were on the outskirts of New Orleans, out where all the marshes are. That was the first time I saw men in waders, out there marsh fishing. The train stopped in a rail yard way outside of town. Come to think of it, my Uncle Papa was there to meet us in his Buick.

We stranded a few years later in Pennsylvania. My mother and Nita found work in Philly and we lived there a while, on Sixteenth between Fitzwater and Bainbridge. I had to stay in during the day because of the truancy officers, so I'd sneak out to buy lunch at the Father Divine restaurant on South Street where they served good meals cheap. I played basketball every night at the Elks lodge and this guy Shine, who ran the gym, he tried to get me to stay in Philly and go to Overbrook High—like most kids from New Orleans that played sports, I was a little hotshot.

I could look out our back window onto Sims' Paradise, a big-name club on Broad and South. If they wasn't out of line with the club's transom, I could see Erskine Hawkins, Tiny Bradshaw, Lucky Millinder, the Savoy Sultans. I could see Pha Terrell, who sang with Andy Kirk, or Avery Parrish, Erskine Hawkins's piano player. Then again, right on our corner was the Two Bit Club, where Anita O'Day and Roy Eldridge played. I went by that neighborhood thirty years later and couldn't recognize anything until I saw the window where I'd looked down on Sims'.

I met a white girl in Philadelphia, Peggy Gould, who lived in Camden but came across the river every Saturday for piano lessons. We sat and held hands in the Earle Theatre and watched the cartoons and fantasized about the things kids dream about: getting married, having babies, the future. That was the second time I experienced what felt like love, not just lust. The first was a year or so earlier in Seattle, when another white girl came to watch the show every day for a week. I went and sat next to her, the next day we held hands, and pretty soon I fell in love. Her name was Susan Young, a little fragile-type blond girl, hair like corn silk. I thought about her often, and we even kept in touch a little while. Five or six years later I was at a Tulane-LSU football game and I swore I saw her on the field, a cheerleader for LSU. I looked in the program— there was her name. I said it out loud. I told them I was carrying a message for somebody so they'd let me pass into the white section to have a better look at the field. It was definitely her. And I remembered that she'd always said, "I'm going to go to college in Louisiana, where you live." Maybe it had stayed in her mind, even if she forgot me by the time she got there. I didn't look her up—this was Louisiana, not Seattle. I would have been afraid someone would find out which nigger was trying to contact this young white lady and why. You never knew; she might say, "This nigger's bothering me, some nigger I met a long time ago." It wasn't worth it and I let it go.

Puppy love! I knew that seeing these girls was nothing I'd do in Louisiana, but I knew something else—I wasn't in Louisiana. It may not have been exactly acceptable in Philly or Seattle, but it wasn't illegal. I can't say there wasn't some intrigue connected to the fact that this was forbidden where I came from, but that's not why I was attracted to these girls—I liked them because they were really pretty girls. And I ain't saying those girls wasn't plucky, all those years ago. Then again, I was cute. I was gorgeous as a little pimp!

On Miss Ida's, everyone paired off. I was getting older and it was natural for me to want my old lady, too. When I was fourteen we got a girl out of St. Louis, Claudia Oliver. She was seventeen. Claudia and I sat together and smooched, and I was crazy about her. And maybe she was stringing me along, because she fell for a trumpet player named Horace McFerrin and just broke my heart.

They had this bad, tough cop in St. Louis, Tom Brooks—someone from St. Louis would know who I'm talking about. Tom Brooks had a beautiful daughter named Shirley, and man, the first time I got a dose of clap it was from Shirley Brooks.

My mother sent me to Reggie Grant to find out what to do.

"Oh Lord, Mustard is a man now!" he said, and died laughing. He said to buy Harlem Oil Capsules, they had some kind of something that fights infection. Damned if they didn't clear it up. But it took time and those pills were horrible tasting, just like taking garlic.

Do you know, I think my best memories of the road come from right around the time I got that dose of clap. I sensed a turning point in my mother: I realized she considered me almost grown now. And though I stayed with the show a few more years, I was getting more and more anxious to be on my own. I stayed home and worked little jobs: busboy at the Fairmont, cleaning bathrooms at the Whitney Bank, plucking chickens at the French Market. I told my grandma I had a job in Slidell and stowed away to Cuba. The captain wasn't very pissed, I think this was something he was used to. Do you realize Havana, Cuba, in 1941 was one of the wildest places on earth?—gambling and prostitution and dope all over, and music hipper than anything I'd heard to that day.

I never saw Miss Ida after I left the *Scandals.* I thought of her often, thought about how strong she was and how she seemed to recognize the worth of my mother. I remember her kindly for that, and for how nice she was to me. When my mother found tobacco stains in my shirt pockets and raised hell, I'd run to Miss Ida. She was the boss and I thought sure she'd tell my mother what to do with me. She never did. She might pretend to—I remember her saying, "Thelma, leave the boy alone, he didn't do anything so bad." But it was always with what I later understood was a wink behind my back. She may have been Thelma's boss, but not when it came to Thelma's son.

The years with Miss Ida were my schooling in life. That was an education, man. How many kids get to do that?—meeting diverse people in diverse cities, seeing ways of life you'd never see staying home. New Orleans is a very difficult city to get out of, man. After a while you don't want to get out. I was lucky. I left.

3

NO KIND OF HERO
CALIFORNIA AND EUROPE, 1942–1945

As an individual the negro is docile, tractable, lighthearted, carefree and good natured. If unjustly treated he is likely to become surly and stubborn, though this is usually a temporary phase. He is careless, shiftless, irresponsible and secretive. He resents censure and is best handled with praise and by ridicule. He is unmoral, untruthful and his sense of right doing is relatively inferior. Crimes and convictions involving moral turpitude are nearly five to one as compared to convictions of whites on similar charges. —Army War College memo, November 1936

On October 9, 1940, President Roosevelt signed an order that remained in effect throughout the war: "The policy of the War Department is not to intermingle colored and white enlisted personnel. . . . This policy has been proven satisfactory over a long period of years, and to make changes now would produce situations destructive to morale and detrimental to the preparation for national defense." Segregation in our World War II armed forces wasn't merely de facto, it was official.

As usual, separate meant unequal. Negro soldiers constantly complained of unfair treatment and inferior facilities. "The way we are sleeping and eating sir, I just wish there was a way that I could snap a picture and send it to you," wrote a GI stationed in Florida to the Baltimore *Afro-American*. "[W]e do not have any running latrines. They have a group of colored troops who go around every morning and clean out the used bucket. . . . [T]hat is the way your boys who are somebody's sons are treated here in this Army, and we are supposed to be fighting for Democracy."

Most Negro recruits were assigned to noncombatant service troops: work gangs in uniform. "They didn't want no niggers carrying guns," says Earl; they carried shovels and garbage cans instead. Earl's job, loading and handling ammunition, was relatively technical, but his duty was clear: to serve white infantrymen.

Black GIs "represented the physical backbone of the armed forces," writes historian Phillip McGuire, "bridge builders, ditch diggers, latrine cleaners, potato peelers, cooks, dock workers, trash collectors, shoeshine boys, housekeepers, dishwashers, truck drivers, etc." Negro correspondents did their best to romanticize the unlovely work—"the inside story of this greatest blitz of all time," reads a typical dispatch, "is the story of the stevedores loading ships in British docks . . . of the truck driver, leering with fatigue over his steering wheel"—but as every laundryman knew, his job was dull, inglorious, and invisible. "All this build-up for something to respect," wrote one soldier, a biochemist in civilian life, "only to be treated like a brainless gorilla fit for nothing more than a posthole digger and a stringer of wire, a yardbird."

The War Department decided that Southern whites, since they knew blacks best, were best equipped to lead them. The practice backfired. "Major Sheriden is a rough dried, leather neck Negro hating cracker from Louisiana," wrote three black troopers about their commander. "Calls our women everything but women. Misuse soldiers, treat us as if we were in a forced labor camp or chain gang." Most bases were in the South, where civilians joined white soldiers in Negro-baiting and worse. "Now right at this moment the woods surrounding the camp are swarming with Louisiana hoogies armed with rifles and shot guns even the little kids have 22 cal. rifles and B & B guns filled with anxiety to shoot a Negro soldier," wrote "a disgusted Negro Trooper" from Camp Claiborne in Alexandria, Louisiana. The situation was especially painful for Northern blacks, accustomed to a measure of freedom. "There is a town down here called Bracketville," wrote a Philadelphian stationed in Texas, "and let me tell you it couldn't be any worse than hell itself."

Interracial violence flared often, whether up North—a riot at Fort Dix, New Jersey, killed five black soldiers and one white—or in the

South, where the total of lynched black soldiers will never be known. Some traveling-show chorus girls were picking berries in the South Georgia woods. "All of a sudden," recalled one, Mattie Sloan, "I looked up and saw these soldiers hanging in the trees. God, it was awful." When the troops moved overseas, the barely submerged race war went with them: "If the invasion doesn't occur soon," said an American officer in pre–D-Day England, "trouble will."

But it would be a mistake to see the war as merely one more episode of American racism. Just as Earl acknowledges that his army stint forced him to grow up—"When I went in, I thought I was a man. I came out a man, I'll tell you that"—the war ushered in epochal, positive changes for the nation. World War II was the pivotal event in twentieth-century American race relations, the dividing line between the bad old days of legal segregation and a more hopeful time.

By requiring Negroes to serve, in some cases to die for, a nation that refused them rights, Roosevelt and the War Department did what generations of valiant early civil rights leaders had been unable to do: publicize the conflict between America's democratic ideals and its treatment of blacks to the point where mainstream America recognized the need for change. Suddenly, "the Negro problem" was on everyone's mind.

Streaming to defense plants all over the country, blacks became a truly national presence, no longer tucked away in the South. The war economy lifted millions of Negroes out of agricultural peonage for the first time, fueling their expectations. More than two hundred local, regional, and national civil rights groups sprang up during the war years, and the NAACP jumped from fifty thousand members in 1940 to half a million in 1946. The Negro press, previously ignored by mainstream opinion makers, began pricking the latter's conscience (*Time* magazine's July 1944 complaint about "the thin-skinned and irritable Negro press, which has seldom missed a report of injustice to Negro troops and has played it for all it would stand" was a sure sign of black editorialists' newfound clout).

Successful Negro combat troops like the 761st Tank Battalion generated enormous goodwill back home, among whites as well as blacks; with Negro soldiers fighting, dying, and winning battles, it became harder and harder to shut blacks out of American democracy. "For the first time since the end of the Civil War," writes historian Neil Wynn, "federal policy, if not practice, was clearly stated as being opposed to both discrimination and segregation. . . . [T]he war made it possible for many Negroes to conceive of first-class citizenship for the first time."

Without World War II and the climate it created, there would have been no *Brown* v. *Board of Education,* no Montgomery sit-ins, no civil rights movement. Little Richard, Chuck Berry, and Fats Domino would never have become brown-skinned pied pipers to that virtually brand-new postwar species, the teenager. Earl Palmer would have been a jazz musician in New Orleans, his craft impeccable, his impact nonexistent.

I went down to the Customs House with my friend Jimmy Narcisse to enlist; we thought they'd put us together, but I never saw him again in my life. I just wanted to get away from home and be on my own, I didn't apply for no special branch. In situations like that, they sent you where they wanted, especially if you were a young black from Louisiana. Sent you where they wanted. That very day I went to Camp Claiborne, one of three or four camps near Alexandria, Louisiana. Camp Claiborne, Camp Livingston, Camp Polk, and Camp Something Lee. Whenever I'm trying to line them I always leave one out.

From Camp Claiborne I went to the Sierra Ordnance Depot in Herlong, California, near Reno. It was very cold. Plenty of guys on that train had never been out of the South. When we got up near Sacramento I heard somebody say, "Man, they gots cotton way up here too!"

"That ain't cotton," I said, "it's snow." Well, I'd been away, you know. Long enough to learn the difference between cotton and snow.

I was nowhere but California until I went overseas. I was acting corporal, then corporal, then buck sergeant, and the highest I made was staff sergeant. They made me a squad leader damn quick. I had something that was very much needed: the ability to be a hell of a drill sergeant. Forty-eight guys to a platoon, four lines of twelve, call them to attention: "Tench-*hut!* Right face! Forward march!" "Column left, march!" Being a dancer, I learned that stuff quick. Some guys didn't know their left foot from their right, they be turning all different directions, bumping into each other: "You going the wrong way!" "No, *you* going the wrong way!"

"Tench-*hut!*" I did a lot of that, boy. "Count off *one* two, *count* off *one* two, *one* two *three* four, *one* two *three* four. . . . *Count off!*" In the beginning of a

"It wasn't but shortly after I got in that I said, 'What the hell did I do this for?'"
Private Palmer, California, 1943–44.

company, they looking for people that got some kind of initiative. Certain few
guys like myself had the ambition to get some stripes on their shoulder so we
could tell other people what to do as opposed to constantly being ordered
around. "Hey Sergeant! Tell the corporal to tell the PFC private first class to

tell the private to clean up that dirt over there!" That's what the army is, they relegate authority all the way down the line.

It wasn't but shortly after I got in that I said, "What the hell did I do this for?" Most people who enlisted were young and thought this would be a salvation. They were sorely disappointed. Any black person with his eyes open, the feeling was the same: "What am I here for?" You was always running into stuff you didn't like. At first you took it. After two years you ready to hurt somebody.

I was ordnance ammunition, which means you serviced the infantry with small arms. You don't just go up and hand them the bullets, you get as close to the fighting as it's safe to get. Mile, mile and a half. When the infantry advances, you move the ammunition up and camouflage it. We had to learn about bombs and shells and gunpowder—you can't give a soldier no ammunition that's going to blow up in his face.

Every outfit I was in was all-black, with white officers. Most service troops were black: ordnance, laundry, graves registration, mess personnel, truck driver, cook. You had white service troops, but they were more or less specialists. They were the ones they let handle bomb fuses and such, build bridges, the more sophisticated stuff.

They had a few black fighting divisions—had some very old, heroic ones, man, like the 369th out of New York—but you got to understand, the army wasn't integrated. We had nothing to do with white troops. The only thing we had to do with white troops was service them. Over there, because there was a war going on, you had a little bit less feeling of being a servant. Over there you a man, you in a war, you didn't get fucked with as much. In general. Except for instances.

When we first got to Herlong, a cadre of seven black noncommissioned officers came into our company. These guys were all from New York. They spoke very good and they were friendly with the officers and there were some real tense feelings at first, because we were all from Texas, Louisiana, Mississippi. We used to say, "Man, these dudes think they're white." But I started talking with them because I had that drill shit right down and I think they figured me to be extremely intelligent compared to the others. The conversation always drifted to prejudice. They were more incensed than I was. I was used to being the underdog. They asked me how could I live under them conditions in Louisiana and I said, "Same way you living under them now."

Our company was 175, 180 guys. There was Alex Litman from Wichita Falls, Texas, who was some kind of track star. There was the Mitchells, Frank and I don't remember the other Mitchell's name, great big guy with a big wide nose. They weren't brothers but they were both from Detroit. So was Alex

Brundage. Fulton McFarland from Camden, New Jersey, was a little bitty short dude with a lisp, and black as my shoes. Brilliant dude. He had a good buddy from home, George Shannon, they came in buddies and was buddies all the way through.

Alex Brundage was the funniest of the lot, comedy right off the top of his head. A guy was showing us a picture of his wife: "This is my old lady! See, that's her with my sister-in-law and my sister-in-law's boyfriend!" Brundage says, "Hmm, I wonder who took the picture."

Another fellow's wife came out to visit and was making it with all the soldiers. This guy was dense. Brundage tells him, "Man, ain't you never heard about knocking on the front door and running round the back?" After the guy figured out what Brundage meant, he tried it. Ran around the back and sure enough, a guy jumped right out the window, landed on him and dislocated his shoulder. The guy that jumped was Brundage.

Aubrey Leacock was a fuckup little dude from Astoria, Long Island, always bucking for Section Eight. That's the discharge for being nuts. Leacock worked hard at acting crazy. The reason everybody figured he *was* a little crazy was he was always threatening some great big guy. We used to tell him, "You don't know but one of these sumbitches going to punch a hole in you before they realize you acting." Had another guy used to fall out with fits by the side of the mess hall. Come out the mess hall, look around, and have a fit. Did that for over a year and never got his Section Eight. Last time I saw him was right before I went overseas and he was still trying.

I got to sharpshooter in target practice. Not expert. Expert, a sumbitch bust the bull's eye wide open; I hit it two out of five times. When we were still up in Herlong, the Golden Gloves came to Reno and I went all the way to the finals, won two fights before I got knocked out. I was either bantamweight or flyweight. I don't remember who I fought in the first two fights, but I know exactly who I fought in the third: Clarence DeGarmo, an Indian kid. Knocked the shit out of me.

I'd made it to staff sergeant, 642d Ordnance Ammunition Company, when I got busted. We were on maneuvers at Hunter-Liggett Military Reservation near San Simeon. The whole of San Simeon then was just a motel, a couple homes, a filling station, and a few warehouses for stuff they had no room for in the Hearst castle. Anyway, they had these Southern white infantry guys up in the mountains. Our guys were bringing them supplies and they started taking potshots at us. Our guys came back and said, "These sumbitches are shooting at us!"

I issued everyone live ammunition. That night the officers called a flash inspection—they knew live ammo had been issued. Everyone had hid their ammo but me—I'd gone into town on pass. They tore through my belongings and found my ammo stash. When I reported in later that night, the lieutenant said, "Sergeant Palmer, this will cost you your stripes."

"I'm aware of that, sir."

If they were going to court-martial me, I was damn sure going to let people know why. Them officers were trying to keep incidents like this from getting around, so I wasn't court-martialed. But the next thing I knew I'd been transferred and demoted. I was pissed, but I was pretty carefree a sumbitch back then and it didn't make a hell of a lot of difference to me. I thought I'd just go on and get my rank back.

They sent me to the coastal artillery in Salinas. Coastal artillery was going obsolete—wasn't no ship going to come in close enough for you to shoot it with no artillery! My job was plotting shell trajectories. I went with Pretty Girl, little part-white Filipino whose husband was a pimp. Filipino dude. Used to beat the hell out of her. He knew I was screwing her but we hung out, because I had access to weed. He and Pretty Girl lived with his sister Marge, who was going with another friend of mine, little guy named Bobby Aikens, tap dancer and a cousin of Earl Hines.

I enjoyed that stay. We didn't have nothing to do but play baseball and spend lots of time on the beach, catching them big Pismo clams. Salinas was a hot little town, lot of soldier action. I was going with a chick in Carmel that had a lot of money and lived out on the beach under them banyan trees. I went AWOL with her and flew to Chicago and Philadelphia. No shit. Oh, they disciplined me, shit yeah, put me in the stockade a few days. I didn't have no rank anymore so they couldn't bust me. Ned Faveret, whose sister was Ophelia Bennett from back home, got busted with me. Ned was a bad character anyhow. Probably looking for something to get in for and I was it.

I was at Fort Ord when orders come down that we were going to the Pacific. I didn't want to go to no Pacific, things were hot over there. So I wangled a transfer to another ordnance ammo company, the 640th, that came east to Plymouth, Massachusetts, to embark.

Just as we got to the East Coast, I tried to go AWOL. I just walked out. I wanted to see my mother in Buffalo. Frankly, I didn't know if I'd be going back once I saw her. I wasn't thinking, "I'm going to desert," I wasn't thinking anything—just "I've got to see my mama." I didn't even know the way to Buffalo. I got caught before I'd hardly started and sent right back to my company. "Forget putting him in jail, that's what the sumbitch wants." They wanted soldiers, not prisoners. "Put his ass on that ship."

Nobody knew when we were embarking. It wasn't like you could just catch

the boat and say, "I'm going overseas, see y'all later!" Hell no, this was top secret, clockwork shit, a thousand guys sent here one moment, thousand there
the next. You're a tiny ball bearing in all this, man—you can't imagine what
it's like to a young guy who's never seen this kind of operation before! I saw
this giant of a ship and said, "Look at this sumbitch! How does something that
big sit on the water?" They had thousands of troops on that ship. Below deck
as far as you could see—hammocks and bunks. And this mother could move,
faster than the submarines.

We sailed on a bright clear summer's day, 1944. The second night out we hit
a storm and that keel raised up—POW! Man! The waves they got out in that
rough North Atlantic sea, we talking about maybe a mountain of water—wave
like that come under the front of the ship, pushes the bow right up, and when
that sumbitch hits the water—BAM! Hundred-fifty guys ran up on deck. The
marines said, "Where you going?"

"We want to get off this boat!"

"Be my fucking guest, y'all."

Next thing you know, you hear *KrrrAAHHH*—you never heard the pro-
pellers when they were *in* the water! Naturally we all thought, "Torpedo!"

Next day the water was still rough. I spent the day leaning over the rail like
everyone else. It looked like a Japanese commuter train at rush hour. That
ship was two blocks long, which is a lot of guys puking! Guys went staggering
away from the rail to keep from getting puke blown in their faces, but the MPs
grabbed them and said, "Get back on that rail!"

We disembarked in Liverpool and it was like a fairyland, a whole culture
you'd never seen before. The buildings looked different, the people even
looked a little different. We rode to Birmingham across meadows and fields
that were so beautiful, man, and came to a place called Ringwood in Stafford-
shire County. A whole army laying there in the forest and you couldn't see it
from the air.

I'd met a dude on the ship, Joe Britto—a dark, kind of Portuguese person
from New Bedford, Massachusetts. Feisty. Very emotional little dude. Cry at
the drop of a hat. Me and Britto met two girls in the village. There was a park
where the trees were sunk into holes, so there was a beautiful little grassy pit
with a tree trunk down the center. We took these two girls there, or they took
us. Now, all over England they had the Home Guards, these mostly old people
went around making sure nobody's flashing lights at night. The four of us were
laying there smoking, me and my chick under one tree, Britto and his under
another, and all of a sudden this Home Guard guy comes up to Britto's tree.

"All right lad, I see ya in there. Come on out."

Britto, the motherfucker, yells, "Earl, they got us!" Us! I'm way off under another tree!

He starts marching us back to camp. Me and Britto is thinking, "They going to court-martial us!" This was a war zone! They were going to put us before the firing squad!

Britto kept a knife in his boots. He whispers, "Man, we're in trouble. I think we should kill him."

"No, Britto, no! They'll surely shoot us then!"

"Let's kill him."

Britto keeps turning around to look at this poor old man whose only job is to see that nobody has any lights on. Got his little white helmet, his flashlight with a dimmer. There's some sumbitches I will never understand. I really think Britto would have done it if I'd said, "Okay, Joe." We were both real young, and Britto was young and crazy.

The sergeant at the gate said, "Confined to quarters." Oh Lord! They were going to put us in jail and execute us! But nothing happened. We were back on duty the next day.

The last time I saw Joe Britto, V-E Day had come and gone. I was an MP in Marseille directing traffic when my whole old company, which I'd left in Germany, came through. I saw Britto on one of those trucks, I saw all the guys, and I stopped traffic in every direction.

"Wait a minute, let these boys through!" I stood there laughing. "Whaah, you sumbitches!"

"Look at Palmer, he's an MP!"

"Yeah, and I'm going to stick your ass in jail!"

"Please, please! Pull me off!" Because they knew they were going to the Pacific. How I got out of that is another story, but I hope them guys made it through.

We embarked from Southampton, where you could look out over that channel and as far and wide as you could see was ships. Oh, it was majestic! You'd think all them ships would break the waves, but I never was on a rougher body of water in my life. That English Channel, man, that thing was rough. God-*damn* it. All that water rushing through—that sumbitch is little more than a huge canal that runs from northern Europe right on down to France.

We went ashore at Omaha Beach and took a month getting across France, following in the wake of the Allied invasion. In movies you see the victorious troops coming in town, girls hanging off their necks. That didn't happen. We had kids run by, pull up your coat to see if you got a tail. The white troops told them, "All niggers got tails." But that began to break down very fast, because we got the reputation of being far more generous than the white soldiers. And don't forget, the service troops was mostly black dudes. We had the supplies, and the connections with the guys who had more.

The first good time I had, I met some girls in a little village. I still didn't get no pussy but I had a good time thinking I was about to. I didn't get any the whole time I was in France. The language barrier was a sumbitch. First thing you get that looks like an overture, you pursue it. I did that many times and was wrong. Walk on eggs and find you're talking to a housewife. You had to go slow. I met a chick in a market who spoke a little English. She said something I laughed at. I said, "Parlez-vous avec moi un petit?" and we started talking. She asked me about my town in America and I said I was from New York City. Now she was curious. Looked promising, but when I asked her, "Do you drink?" her face changed right away. "No drink, no drink, no drink!" She thought I was trying to get her drunk. I didn't go no further; you could tell when you'd fucked up. I said something like, "Maybe I'll see you tomorrow."

"No tomorrow!" She left me standing there thinking, "What got into me?" *Man*, was I horny.

We crossed into Holland by November. I met a little guy about my age, turned out to be in the Dutch resistance. I was fascinated by this cat, first dude I'd ever met from the underground. Those guys did some hell of a job before we even got there. His name was Johann Dohmen and he was actually a hero in that town, the city of Heerlen. We had a couple drinks and he asked if I'd like to meet his family and I said I'd love to.

They were delightful, a mother and two grown sisters and the littlest sister, Josi—I'll never forget that Josi; I taught her how to sing "Pistol Packing Mama, Lay That Pistol Down." She'd shout, "Arl! Arl! I sing!" The father was an invalid who stayed in his room. The older sisters, Berti and Kati, worked in a mill. Johann himself was a criminology student.

Maybe it's because this was my first experience being around a family again, but I was really smitten with Berti. I was at the Dohmens' all the time. I ate with them, brought them salt and K rations from the mess hall. I know it was just wishful thinking, but I came to feel almost like I was Johann's brother and Berti's husband.

Berti and I talked a lot of times about her coming to America. I don't know if she was serious, but I really intended to return for her. She was so happy when the subject came up. I asked her if she'd ever had a yen to come to the USA and she said, "Not like now."

I cried the day I left. We was all crying, man—me, her, the whole family. I went there for dinner and nobody ate. It was just kind of a sad day. You got used to good-byes over there. Even if you had nobody to say good-bye to, you always had a little regret about going. You was always coming somewhere and leaving.

We wound up in the thick of shit. Do you remember when the Germans mounted that, what did they call it, that wedge? The object was to get back to the English Channel and restart this whole damn thing right over. For the first time there was a little doubt about the power of the Allies. Germany was fighting every damn body over there and suddenly, man, they were steaming. The Allies was aghast until they woke up and said, "Hey, we need to stop these motherfuckers." Germany *was* a motherfucker. That von Rundstedt was a hero to the German people, like that great general in the desert war, Rommel. Von Rundstedt was *the* general in Europe.

I spent Christmas of '44 in a foxhole near Malmédy, under shell fire. I got a touch of frostbite and had a tetanus shot—they said it was tetanus, but God knows they put something else in them shots; I don't even remember sneezing. Pinned down in a puddle of ice water, listening to buzz bombs overhead. They were noisy, them V-2s. God*damn*, they were noisy. You only worried if you heard the motor stop. Long as you heard that son going *rrraaaahhhh*, it was on its way to England. Hear the motor cut off, you got in that hole.

Most times up to then we weren't carrying no guns; they wanted to keep you subservient and not a factor in the war, a fighting man. But now anyone with combat basic training was thrown into the breach. The first time I saw action we were carrying ammunition, looked up, and saw three Germans. All I thought was, "They want to shoot me so I better shoot them first," and a bunch of us took aim and fired and one of the Germans went limp. It was the most sickening thing I'd ever seen, a fully controlled person and all of a sudden he was a dishrag. I wasn't any infantryman, I wasn't no hard dyed-in-the-wool killer. I wasn't shitting in my pants but I was scared.

During that time guys I knew died every day. Ammunition dumps blew up from somebody fucking up with a fuse. Two of our guys got killed that way, caught between two exploding stacks of ammo. I heard one of them scream. Afterwards I couldn't go over and look. All they found was parts of those guys.

When that Bulge was over, I was relieved but a little disappointed. I'd had a chance to fight and wasn't deathly afraid anymore, so I started thinking stuff like, "That might have been my chance to be a hero." You're a cocky sumbitch, afterwards.

All of a sudden there was a German name: München-Gladbach. As we crossed the border, the people tried to give you the impression they wasn't

Nazis: applauding us and shouting and trying to get over as slaves we were lib-
erating. Standing in their doorways: "Hey! Amerikanisch!" When you get into
Germany, we used to say, you can't find any Nazis at all. "Nazi—oh no, no!
Jair-man, no Nazi!" Nobody was a Nazi but Hitler. Bullshit. They'd been out
there waving for years.

The enemy was just about wiped out by the time we got to the town of
Bielefeld, which was as far east as we went. We lived in a huge shed where
there were a lot of Russian refugees; we was fucking their chicks because if we
went in town we'd get blamed for all kind of things. That was the first time I
ever drank vodka—I got bombed off homemade vodka and fucked one of the
only broads that wasn't big and fat.

I got a soft job mail-orderlying—everybody was looking for a job like that,
everybody that wasn't a hero. The black troops took over Bielefeld's distillery
and sold schnapps to the white troops, hundreds and hundreds of boxes of
schnapps, sell it for two-three dollars a bottle, big earthenware bottles, almost
a liter. Could have been high-quality schnapps for all I knew, I never had no
schnapps before in my life. Seemed good to me, man, got you bombed in a
minute.

A bunch of us were shooting at a German plane and damned if it didn't
crash. There was a pile of ammunition hidden under the trees and we were
sure the plane was going to hit it, so we ran like hell. Then we all ran back and
took each other's pictures by the plane, shouting "Yeah! Yeah! Yeah!" and bullshitting to everyone about how we'd done it. They ran those pictures in *Stars
and Stripes*—"Ordnance Men Down German Plane." I'm positive we didn't.

The only problem we had was with our own troops, your white Southern
troops. Whenever race wasn't on your mind over there, it got put on your
mind. Get caught after dark, you were fair game for a Saturday night beating,
whale away on your ass just for sport. As if to say, "You came on over here and
did all this, you going to kiss our ass anyway. Thank you, we don't appreciate
it." I heard of a case where black dudes ambushed and killed some whites
who'd beaten a black soldier. It wasn't publicized in *Stars and Stripes*. They
didn't talk about it when blacks fought back.

All over Germany white dudes were disguising themselves as blacks and
raping German girls. It came down that the MPs were bringing a girl to pick
one of us out of a lineup. I told the sergeant, "Not me. Uh-uh. You can do
whatever you want with me, but I ain't standing there for some frightened girl
to point out by mistake."

They put me in confinement, me and five or six others. Now, it turned out
every company was having the same problem: guys saying, "I don't want no

more of this. I can't get out of the army, but send me somewhere else or I'm *always* going to give you trouble." They made up their mind to ship us out, two truckloads, forty guys, send us where we'd be somebody else's problem.

They shipped us to what's called a staging area, where you got picked up for duty in the Pacific. We were supposed to go to Callas, in the south of France, but they made a mistake and wrote "Calais." The sumbitches sent us to northern France! We had a vacation at the army's expense, a leisurely trip down through Germany and across Belgium and into France. We avoided big cities; we didn't want no investigation that might disrupt the party, and we *had* a party. Drew supplies everywhere we went, gave them to chicks and drew some more, forty horny guys swapping food for pussy. We had a sergeant in charge, black guy, mean, but a good cat. He'd taken one look at them orders and knew they was wrong. He knew we were doing something we could be court-martialed for. He told us, "When I say go, we go. Anybody who isn't back on this truck, I will personally shoot his ass." He meant it.

When we got up to Calais, the cliffs of Dover was one of the most beautiful sights I've ever seen. In the morning when the sun hit them, they looked like snow. Wasn't nobody in Calais but British troops. They couldn't figure out what the hell we was doing there. They finally straightened it out: "Man, y'all supposed to be at the other end of the country!" So we got back in our trucks and took another couple of weeks, partying all the way, stopping where we thought it might be a nice situation and spending the night. One or two places we spent more than the night. Remember, we were dissidents who'd gotten an opportunity to fuck the army. We took it. I'd never been very obedient. I wasn't a badass through and through, just a sumbitch come to understand.

What parts of France wasn't shot to shit was beautiful. We stopped at Saint-Tropez, which was nothing but a couple of little buildings and a beautiful beach; Bardot hadn't made it famous yet.

At Callas soldiers were streaming in from all over Europe. They had all these Senegalese natives who stole your clothes right off the line. I was conking a guy's hair one day and one of them came in.

"Fix mine!" Had one of them huge mats of hair.

"Okay, I'll fix it." I conked his hair and didn't take the paste out. Next thing you knew, he was running through the encampment screaming and looking for me with a machete and I was laying under a bunk with my rifle trained on his ass. You could almost hear his scalp cooking: *Sssssssss* . . . I don't know what happened to him, he ran off screaming.

I came this close to being taken by a company headed for the Pacific, and it was staring me in the face: I could be gone, shipped out. I ran into a guy in a bar, a sergeant with the military police. We got drinking and talking, getting drunker and drunker. Next day I went to see him.

"Well, here I am."

"What do you mean here I am?"

"Man, you said you was going to take care of this!" I reminded him all about how he'd promised to get me transferred to the MPs. Which he hadn't. I made it up. But he couldn't deny it, because he couldn't remember a thing we'd talked about.

"You promised, man. This ain't right! Why you doing this to me?"

"Okay, okay. I'll see what I can do."

And that's how I got in the 292d MP Battalion, where I spent the last few months of my time directing traffic, patrolling the streets of Marseille, going in and out of clubs on La Canebière, the main street round there. Prostitution was legal but a madame had to have papers saying the girls in her house was examined. If they didn't let the MPs in, you knew something was wrong. Lot of the houses had Senegalese guards. You could get in terrible battles with those sumbitches, man. Chop you with machetes. I never tangled with them. I sent somebody else to tangle with them and stayed in the jeep.

A guy had to really do something for me to arrest him; I was having too much fun hanging out in clubs, partying, drinking that pastis. Lots of black market stuff came into Marseille. We knew when a sumbitch had a hot truck-load, and they had to give us kickback if they wanted to get off that dock. So they paid us off and we spent their money on women and booze down in the south of France and had a ball spending it.

I went to hear two guys play in a club on La Canebière. Guitar player playing his ass off, hardly any fingers on his hand. Violin player wasn't there all the time but the guitar was almost always there. I'd talk to him, tell him how good him and his buddy sounded. It wasn't till much later that I realized who they were: Django Reinhardt, of course, and Stéphane Grappelli.

Who turned up in Marseille but my friend from home, Steve Angrum! I'd heard he was there and went around looking, but I couldn't find him.

"Steve Angrum around?"

"Yeah, he's right over there."

I'd look, and no Steve. Go somewhere else.

"Steve Angrum here?"

"Yeah, but he went over there." I'd have never found him if I hadn't run into Paul Martin, another boy from New Orleans.

"T-Paul, what the hell you doing here? Man, I'm looking for Steve Angrum. Everywhere I go they say he was there but he's gone."

T-Paul looks at me. "It's that brassard on your arm!" He shouts, "Steve, come on out, it's all right!" And up from behind a wall peeps Steve. He'd been selling stolen meat and thought the MPs was after him!

I got a number that said I was in the rotation to go home, and not too far in the future. When the day finally came, there wasn't much to do by way of preparing, just throw your things in your duffel bag and get your ass to the boat. On my way I got a splinter that went way up under my fingernail. It was hurting its ass off and they wanted to take me to the hospital and keep me there.

"Hell no! I'm fine! Take me to the ship!" I got on that ship and didn't relax until it pulled away. Once I got that splinter out I went to drinking with two white guys, a captain and a master sergeant. Both of them were from Kansas City and I told them all about tap-dancing there. That was one of the few times I felt a real equality with white soldiers.

You wonder what makes a man of a sumbitch? Being out on his own for the first time — no mama, no family, nobody. When I went in, I thought I was a man. I came out a man, I'll tell you that. To live through a war, that's one of the greatest experiences in the world. Living that close to death, and seeing all that, and coming through it, that's a hell of a feeling. It was quite an experience. It was the damndest experience in my life. I sensed that even then.

Not that I was feeling sentimental, hell no! During that trip back, they came around asking if we wanted to join the reserves.

I said, "No thank you. No fucking thank you."

4

RUNNIN' WILD IN THIS BIG OLD TOWN
NEW ORLEANS, 1945–1957

You can dance with a lot of things besides your feet. —Duke Ellington

"What's happening?" wondered *Louisiana Weekly*'s Scoop Jones during Lent, 1947. "[A]t the season of the year when night life is supposed to be at its lowest ebb it's really in the peak of condition. Even the guys who operate the town's spots are 'treed.'"

After a long, slow fade, nighttown in black New Orleans had come alive. A new wave of entertainers—Roy Brown, Annie Laurie, Paul Gayten, Dave Bartholomew—seemed poised for national stardom. "Their story," wrote Jones, "is really the story of New Orleans's postwar night life. New Orleans's pre-war night life can best be remembered as an array of honky tonk clubs, underpaid musicians and entertainers. With the war it became revolutionized and birthed glamorous showplaces in the form of nightclubs and restaurants. A powerful musicians' union has been organized, giving the boys who beat out the boogie a decent wage."

Negroes had more money to spend but still weren't free to choose where to spend it. The late forties brought a final, nationwide flowering of Jim Crow culture: Harlem's Theresa Hotel and its 125th Street environs, Central Avenue in Los Angeles, Chicago's South Side blues joints, and the less famous but equally exciting whirl that revolved around New Orleans's black nightspots. "Ya shoulda seen those shingle straw hats, and those blouses made of handkerchief

linen," wrote *Louisiana Weekly*'s "Brown Eyes," "and ah! those
bolero jackets and those grosgrain skirts . . . 'twas fine, Jackson; fine
as dollar wine."

What was the sound of the Dew Drop, the Caldonia, the Club
Rocket, the TiaJuana? In mid-to-late-forties America, one particular
strain of earlier, swing-era jazz—the jump music of Basie and other
Southwest bands—blended with sanctified church music and
down-home blues to produce a sound that fit the day's quickened
pulse. Swing's sophisticated lilt belonged to an earlier, more inhib-
ited period, when sex was encrusted with ceremony. Prewar social
dancing was a ritual of courtship, but postwar dances were uninhib-
ited get-downs to a new and urgent soundtrack. Although it had an
unmistakable local flavor, the sound of postwar black New Orleans
was the sound of postwar black communities everywhere. Triggered
by two developments—the rise of black radio and an explosion of in-
dependent record labels—the moribund "race music" industry transformed itself into a thriving, nationwide genre: rhythm and blues.

In 1947 the best R&B band in town belonged to a young trumpeter named Dave Bartholomew. Although he had a sterling background in traditional jazz and big band swing, Bartholomew was a
clever businessman who tailored his music to the day's fashions.
Driving the band (and singing ballads) was a prodigy who, though
he'd played seriously for less than two years when Bartholomew
hired him, was already known as the most exciting young drummer
in New Orleans: "the new sensation on the tubs," as the *Louisiana
Weekly* called twenty-two-year-old Earl on March 15, 1947. "Earl was
better than any other drummer they had in New Orleans," says
Dave Bartholomew today. "He was the talk of the town. We had a
lot of good ones, but they all of them admired Earl."

He made a good living with Bartholomew, but Earl's first love
was jazz. A lively bebop subculture arose in mid- and late-forties
New Orleans; again, the city merely mirrored the national picture.
Young black musicians across America were captivated by Parker's
and Gillespie's new sound. "The hell bebop wasn't a mass movement!" says Earl, who decided to become a drummer the night he
heard two bop-inflected big bands, Billy Eckstine's and Dookie
Chase's.

The Dookie Chase Band was a group of talented local young-
sters—Vernel Fournier, future Ellingtonian Emery Thompson,

future Basie-ite Benny Powell, and others. Its alto sax star, Warren Bell, still remembers hearing his first Charlie Parker record: "I was captivated, inspired, the whole gamut—this was what music was supposed to be!" Young Bell learned every Parker solo he could: "inside out, wrong side up, I knew them all. Still do."

"We used to haunt the record shops," says Bell's contemporary Harold Battiste, "waiting for the next Charlie Parker record. It was like waiting for the news." Cosimo Matassa, a young French Quarter native whose father sold jukeboxes, opened the Bop Shop, a record store at 302 Rampart Street. "It looked to me like bop was the coming thing," Cosimo says today. "But I'll tell you what happened. A guy would come in, take two records in the listening booth, listen for an hour, say 'Thank you baby,' and leave. Bebop was not very commercial. *I* couldn't make any money with it, I'll tell you that."

The city's bebop subculture remained just that: an all-but-unrecorded coterie (though Earl made his first album, *New Orleans Suite*, with a group of New Orleans boppers in 1955). "Maybe once in a while some adventurous entrepreneur would let us play," says Harold Battiste, "but our steadiest gig was in somebody's living room." It wasn't simply that the city's postwar traditional-jazz renaissance was siphoning off potential bop fans. Bebop's biggest problem, in New Orleans and elsewhere, was its own thorny nature. It made demands. "To appreciate jazz, there has to be a little thought involved," says Earl, "but people just want to go somewhere they can pat their foot and shake their ass." After a blaze of late-forties publicity, bebop was always and everywhere a cult affair. In New Orleans, where it was overshadowed by old-time jazz, it had even less of a presence.

The city's beboppers did have a commercial impact—but not as jazzmen. Almost offhandedly, while looking forward to their late-night jam sessions, a group of them—Earl Palmer, Red Tyler, Ernest McLean, and others—would become the first great rock-and-roll recording-session band and change the listening habits of America. But that's getting ahead of the story.

I got out on November 10th, 1945. When we disembarked in Newport News, the Red Cross workers on the dock wouldn't give the black soldiers coffee until the whites got theirs. "Wait, boy!"—that's what a Red Cross woman said to me. I was so hurt I cried like a baby.

They kept me in Camp Shelby, Mississippi, a few nights and sent me home. When that train pulled into the L & N station where my grandpa used to work, I was so damn glad! My little cousin George was there to meet me, and my Uncle Freddy, and my Uncle Papa took me home in his car.

My mama wasn't in town. She'd been going out with different troupes, whatever she could get. By the time the war ended, man, vaudeville had trickled away. Oh, a few clubs in New Orleans still had floor shows. My mama and Nita worked. They went to Panama, they went to Cuba with Joe Robichaux. But things wasn't like they used to be. There was even less to be made than before, because vaudeville was dying a horrible death.

I moved back into 918 Claiborne, did a lot of jobs and a little bit of dancing. The army paid you twenty dollars a week for a year after you got out; fifty-two-twenty we called it. The Chattard brothers still had their barbershop and the merchant seamen came into the shop at night, bringing Noel Chattard coke from Cuba. Everyone still hung out by Big Al Dennis's shoeshine stand, kibitzing and watching the girls get off the Claiborne Avenue streetcar. Big Al's son Albert Jr. played football at Grambling now, so I talked football with Big Al, boxing with Big Lo, and tap dancing with little Haree, Harry Wilson, little midget who came up dancing on Bourbon Street just like me. I played football and paddle tennis at Lemann Playground, even won my division in city paddle tennis. In football I played end, baseball I played first base, basketball I played forward, all the time. Tulane was my school in football. I always liked the best of shit, and Xavier, the big black college, just wasn't.

I boxed at the San Jacinto Club on Dumaine and trained for a while with Joe Brown, who became lightweight world champ. Big Lo had brought Joe from Baton Rouge. When Joe beat Ike Williams, the champ, in a nontitle fight, the gangsters came to Big Lo.

"We want Brown's contract."

"Over my dead body," said Big Lo.

"We could arrange that," said the gangsters.

So Big Lo had to sell Joe's contract to Blinky Palermo and Joe became champion on him. I hear Joe's got a shoeshine stand now, on the corner of North Broad and Bayou Road.

When I came out of the service, they were starting to think about getting black policemen. They saw I'd been in the MPs and asked did I want to be a cop. "Shit no, are you out of your mind?" We already had Milton Bienamee. Before he was a cop he was Milton the Fink. They'll kill a fink today, neighborhood guy or not; back then you just avoided them. But Milton *liked* to hang out. Milton came up with us, he wanted to be friendly! We all knew him as a fink, so he never got any big information. Wasn't any big information

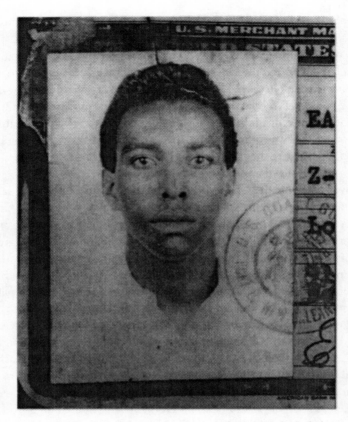

"I moved back into 918 Claiborne, did a lot of jobs and a little bit of dancing." Merchant Marines ID card, 1946. Earl signed up but never shipped out.

around there anyway, people just sold weed or stole from the grocery. Milton had a brother that was known around New Orleans as on the verge of being a good dancer, on the verge of being a good singer, but a stone natural comedian named Good Lord the Liftin'.

I took a job as a traveling salesman's driver, mostly so I could revisit the places I'd gone with Miss Ida. I drove this man to Montgomery, Birmingham, Helena, Texarkana, and then I got fed up with his ass and stranded him in Memphis. He was a mean motherfucker. Sold some type of trinket, I don't know.

I plucked chickens and did some bullshit house painting with Steve Angrum. I was a terrible house painter. Steve put me on ceilings and I didn't think to use a drop cloth. We painted old man Alphonse Picou's house and Mr. Picou came home and told Steve, "Get that boy out of here!"

Steve and I weren't that close before the war but we just kind of gravitated to each other now. His mannerisms were so funny, so different from mine. Steve was easygoing. By God, I wish you could have heard that sumbitch talk —typical New Orleans Tremé, man, with that lazy, lazy voice: "All right, cool it, Palmmm . . ."

Steve was levelheaded. When you fly off the handle like me, a guy like Steve is a steadying influence.

"Lemme tell you something, Palmmm, you don't need this shit. Let's get out of here."

I don't know why I have such a temper. I wish I knew. I knew plenty of people had worse, back in New Orleans. Everybody got in fights. Back then you didn't stab and cut and shoot each other, you bare-knuckle fought and I knew how.

Steve's father, Mr. Steve, was a clarinet player, born on the Fourth of July, 1895. Nice quiet sweet man. Steve's mama was just like mine, a loudmouth. Miss Babe. Little bitty woman about this big. Steve himself played good piano. Later on, his wife Ida Mae probably curtailed his musical career.

"Why don't you get a real job?"

"Okay Ida Mae, whatever you say, Ida Mae."

I guess there was a portion of laziness there, too. Steve was one of those people you couldn't think about getting out of New Orleans. Steve could hardly get out of bed! Little later, I'd ask him to drive me to a gig.

"I'd take you, man, but I ain't got no gaass. . . . You gotta buy some gaaaassss . . ."

I'd buy the gas and Steve drives me. Sits around all night.

"Steve, you want to play?"

"Aw I can't play with you guys."

"Come on man."

"Nawwww . . ."

He always thought he wasn't good enough. Steve was always kind of introverted, always thought he was no good. That was a drag because Steve could play.

He was a good friend. We'd sit and die laughing about the same things ten, twenty times. The last time I ever saw Steve he was sick with cancer but we sat there and laughed until we cried.

"He was a good friend. We'd sit and die laughing about the same things ten, twenty times." Earl with Steve Angrum, New Orleans, mid-fifties.

So Steve and I hung out and smoked weed and walked the streets all night, just be talking and chewing that strip, those Benzedrine inhalers you bought at the drugstore, broke off the top, took out a piece of pasteboard and chewed it. Bitter as gall but talk about uppers! Energy like a dog, walk until you foaming at the mouth. Chewing that strip, couldn't sleep, called it chewing that strip. Don't know what you're talking about, just talk plenty.

We always dressed nice, in nice clean slacks and sport shirt. Used to be all over town, we didn't have no trouble getting around. Nothing to do but walk around, get loaded, talk. Walk out to the French Quarter where you could buy weed cheaper than in the Tremé, two joints for a quarter instead of fifteen cent apiece. If we met girls we met girls; we didn't particularly go out looking. Just go out, have a beer and be talking about things. Talk about boxing, talk about music, talk about the situation of me and Walter Fats Pichon.

I hardly ever thought about the idea of father, but Fats Pichon, it's been ru-mored he may have been my dad. He was a fine pianist and a hell of a enter-

"It's been rumored [Fats Pichon] may have been my dad. He was a fine pianist and a hell of a entertainer . . . had a great orchestra back before the war." Walter Fats Pichon with his band aboard the steamship *Capitol*, 1938. Fifth from right is a teenaged Dave Bartholomew, future Rock and Roll Hall of Fame member, New Orleans music legend, and Earl Palmer's boss from 1947 to 1952. (Frank Driggs Archive)

tainer; we always thought Fats Waller had caught him someplace and learned an awful lot from him. Pichon had a great orchestra back before the war, but then he went to work on Bourbon Street and stayed for years and years and years. I never saw him all that much, but I took for granted that he might be my daddy. I called him Pops. He used to sport some beautiful, expensive ties and I went up to him once and said, "I like that." He took it off and gave it to me, just like that. I said, "Thanks, Dad," and he just smiled.

In the Tremé they had bars on every corner. They had the Crystal Club on Dumaine and Robertson, the Keno on Dumaine and Claiborne, the Struggle Inn and the Gypsy Tea Room on St. Ann, Joe Provenzano on St. Peter and Villere, Sidney Brown's on Orleans and Villere, Toni Heisser's on St. Philip and Claiborne, the Orange Room on St. Ann and Galvez, the Orange Liquor

Store on St. Philip and Claiborne, and Roland's on St. Ann and Derbigny. Rampart Street—thriving. They took all them places down. People don't go to nightclubs now, they stay home. Rampart Street is nothing.

We'd go in a bar and tease Me-Love, a stone fucking drunk who was around as far back as I can remember. I never heard nobody use her real name, never knew her by nothing but Me-Love. She liked to flirt with us younger guys. Say: "Come to Me-Love, you little dawlin, little essence of the rose. Come to Me-Love, Me-Love gonna teach you about *looovve*, you sweet little t'ing you. Look at you, you so fine!" We teased her until we died laughing.

"Me-Love, you going give us some? We going buy you a drink."

"Me-Love give you *all you want* you little lily of the valley. You going to buy me a drink baby?"

Buy her a drink, she say, "Well come on!"

You say, "Well, we don't want to go nowhere, we just want to talk." She get mad and start cussing.

"Ain't none of you all going to come fuck Me-Love?"

"Me-Love, we going to, but we got to get some more to drink."

She'd say, "I done had enough to drink, come *on!*"

This woman was a phenomenon. How could she be so drunk and stay so spotlessly clean? That crisp white uniform, never a wrinkle. You'd sit there staring: "How she do that?" Smell her breath this far away, and her eyes was bloodshot red. Me-Love was jet black. Yeah, she was kind of ugly. I'll tell you who she looked just like: Papa Celestin.

So I worked around, played some pool—I was kind of a little pool hustler— and drew my fifty-two-twenty and started playing drums. Pretty quickly I came to be not bad. I walked into a job with Harold Dejan at the Old Opera House where I made good money playing for strippers. I was sneaking round with Stormy—Stacy Lawrence, a famous white stripper. Stormy scared me to death. She wasn't no hooker, she was a glamorous stripper, the number one stripper in New Orleans except for Little Christine and the Cat Girl and the ones from out of town. She was absolutely gorgeous, man. Ohhh! I mean in every way. Big blue-green eyes and jet, jet black hair down to her ass. Being an exotic dancer in those days, she wore it like that.

Stormy lived with a dyke named Tommy who was furious at me. She also had a white guy, Monty, an executive for the L & N Railroad that bought her anything she wanted, cars and pianos and piano lessons from Paul Gayten.

Stormy came on to me—you didn't come on to no white woman in those days. One night she just said, "I want to talk to you."

"Okay, Miss Stormy." I thought I'd played something wrong. I went in her dressing room and she lit a joint. I thought, "Uh-oh, what's going on here?" But we just talked. She wanted to know where I lived. Harold Dejan saw me coming out and said, "Be careful now."

Then she asked me to her house and oh, that was something! It went on damn near a year between us. She'd pick me up and we'd do it in her car. That was before Monty gave her a white Packard. When she got that, I wouldn't go with her—here she was, man, looking like Vampira, pale, with black hair and red lips and a body out of this world, driving through New Orleans in a white Packard. The first night she pulled up, I hid behind the stoop.

I had the GI schooling coming to me and was trying to decide how to use it. Liking to dress, I thought about tailoring school. Not to be a professional. I just thought I was paying a lot for clothes and wanted to make my own.

My friend Red Tyler said, "Tailoring? You thinking too small. Make enough money and you can buy any clothes you want. Why don't you go to music school?"

"What am I going to learn? I'm already the best drummer in town." Everybody said so.

"You don't even know what you're doing," Red said.

I started to say, "Well fuck you!" But for him to say that, when I knew he liked my playing—I had to stop and think what he meant. It dawned on me right away: He was right, I *didn't* know what I was doing.

"Red, that's very fucking true." And I went and signed up at Grunewald's Music School.

It was two schools actually—whites downstairs, blacks upstairs—in a old warehouse building on Camp Street. Around the corner was a little grocery where you could get po'boy sandwiches, drink a beer. Class started at ten in the morning. Might've been nine and everyone was always late. I was working every night at the Opera House; I'm sure there were times I didn't go to sleep and went right to school. You could not miss school. Miss too many classes they dropped your ass.

Most of the guys at Grunewald was already performing musicians. There was Quentin Batiste, a great pianist that became a good arranger, and Bull Giant, a big dude that did a lot of weed, hung out at Dumaine and Robertson and played trombone, not reading good but just naturally playing his ass off. But wasn't serious about it, just going to collect that GI check. Old Johnny St. Cyr, the Dixieland guitarist, had a son there. Another guy that used to be the weed turn man around there: Rudy, big tall dude with gold in his mouth. Freddy Crane was a white pianist and a great arranger who became very big in Dallas doing commercial writing. He used to be with Al Hirt's group until he died.

Sometimes Freddy came upstairs with an arrangement because we had a better big band than them. That was all right with us, if we didn't have none of our own charts to play. Freddy Crane, Jack Martin, these were white guys we knew and liked and joked with. "How you read that music, man? They got *black* dots on there!" Another nice white guy used to come upstairs and play tenor with us was Cheeks. He had little bitty lips and big round cheeks; that tenor mouthpiece looked like a pencil in his mouth. Cheeks! Put a derby on the sumbitch, you'd swear he was Oliver Hardy.

You had private lessons on your instrument. My drum teacher was Bob Barbarin, Paul's brother. Bob was the formal drummer—see, Paul didn't read or anything like that, he just was a great player. Bob was the one that was able to teach. Willie Humphrey was my best teacher. He took special pains with me and taught me all about my favorite subject, harmony. Willie always said he was surprised I'd come to Grunewald when I already played so good and knew all the New Orleans styles. He had known me as a kid, and I think he was proud that here I was, a dancer and a musician that wanted to formally learn what I'd been doing. Willie was a nice man.

Some of these old musicians knew much theory. I didn't know what theory was! They had a German bass teacher so old he was bent over. Pants up his chest. We brought him the music to Ray Brown playing Dizzy's "One Bass Hit."

"Can you play this, Mr. ——— ?" What was his name? Funk? Finck? That's it, Otto Finck. He looks at the music. "Hmm . . ." And then played it, *dut duhh, dippidy dippidy doom.* Played it corny and very strict, but every note, and right on the time.

"This old motherfucker!" we said. We brought him "Two Bass Hit."

"Ahh! Much easier!" He walked through that.

Once you doing well at something you say, "Shit, I can learn more of this." I wrote my first arrangement after six or seven months. Real simple, "Amenon" or "Pennies from Heaven." You don't know how good that sounds the first time you hear it: four horns playing a harmony you thought up out of your head! That's my clearest memory from music school. Man, that's a hell of a feeling, a damn good feeling, like making your own man. It lives, it lives! Then you begin to disseminate how fucking difficult it really is.

Soon I was arranging harder things, like Kenton's "Tale of an African Lobster." Me, Tyler, Ernest McLean, Edward Frank, and Salvador Doucette began putting on concerts at the Y on South Claiborne so we could hear our arrangements outside of school. We got a lot of people and made a little money, too. I felt like a finished musician, though of course I was nowhere near that, man, nowhere near.

Dave Bartholomew was just a guy with a band that wasn't really doing anything, but musicians considered it the best band in New Orleans. Dave came from Edgard, out in the country. His folks had a little money, they were fancy blacks for those days; some were doctors and stuff.

My Uncle Dave Oxley was Dave Bartholomew's drummer, so when Bartholomew tried to hire me I said, "I can't do that, my Uncle Dave's in the band."

"No he ain't, I just fired him."

I called Uncle Dave. He said, "Go ahead on, you go ahead on, I ain't never working for the sumbitch again." My Uncle Dave was a big, big man that didn't take shit off no one. Dave Bartholomew could get mean sometime and I guess he'd went over the line with Uncle Dave.

Dave Bartholomew was a hell of a trumpet player. I called him Leather Lungs. Remember that growling sound Earl Bostic got on alto? Dave played that way. They overblew the note, man, got a growl out of the horn. Dave was just strong. Powerful. But he was mainly a good showman, never ashamed of clowning. He had an awful lot of personality, hustled his ass off, and was a sumbitch that didn't take no for an answer.

I'd bought my first drums from Harold Dejan, I think he'd bought them from Big Foot Bill Phillips. Whatever I paid I'm sure was more than what Harold gave Big Bill. It was a big white set with a nude woman and a twenty-five-watt bulb inside. Horrible set, man. The cymbals sounded like garbage-can covers. When Dave hired me I went down to Morris Music Shop on Rampart Street to get some new cymbals. I didn't know nothing about cymbals. I said, "Give me those." I thought they were great because they were brand-new and shiny. Dave said, "If you don't get out of here with those, those—go get some cymbals, man!" I borrowed some from Placide Adams, and Dave said, "That's better." There was a lot of talk about them cymbals. New Orleans people—always making more out of something than it is. Do something dumb and they'll make it the dumbest thing they saw in their life.

But by the time you got in Dave's band, you knew you were a musician. Mr. Clarence Hall, Joe Harris, Meyer Kennedy was on saxophones, and later Red Tyler. Frank Fields on bass. Fred Land, "Pilou," on piano, then Salvador Doucette. Ernest McLean on guitar. Theard Johnson sang but Dave did more vocals than anyone. I sang, too—hell yeah! I'd sing a song like "Sunday Kind of Love," "Portrait of Jenny," ballads, tunes that had changes Theard couldn't hear. Theard sang your big black male vocalist songs, the Billy Eckstine, Roy Hamilton–type songs. Later on Tommy Ridgley replaced him.

Meyer Kennedy had been a wonderful alto player with Papa Celestin but this was his last hurrah. He considered himself Dave Bartholomew's adviser but he should have known Dave wasn't a person that listened to anybody. Meyer never came up with no ideas anyway, he just sat there like we was lucky to have him. Oh, Meyer thought his shit didn't stink!

Fields always had his mind in a book. Why is it always the bass player that's a scholarly sumbitch? Wears horn-rimmed glasses, takes correspondence courses. Fields learned how to repair televisions through a correspondence course. The shit he pulled! Got in people's way, like the time him and Pilou was rooming together in Houston. Pilou knocks on my door.

"Say Earl, can you get this dude out of my room?" Pilou had a woman he was trying to get into bed, but Fields was cracking the books. I went on over.

"Hey, Gus!" Fields calls out. He called me Gus too.

"Hey, Fields. Let me talk to you a moment."

"Well I'm doing something, Gus."

"I know, Frank. Come on out here, let me tell you something." We go in the hall.

"Man, Pilou got this woman there, they want to go to bed."

"Oh yeah? Oh!" He hadn't even noticed she was there, he was so busy with his books. I'll never forget that. "Earl, can you get this dude out of my room?" When Pilou was mad at you he called you dude. After that I started calling Fields dude, and that's what everybody calls him to this day.

Red Tyler I knew practically all my life. Red was with a bad bunch of guys, a gang called the Hip Cats. Yeah, Red Tyler was a little tush hog! Then all of a sudden he was playing music. I was already working at the Old Opera House when Red and I used to hang out by George the Greek's on St. Louis and Burgundy. Or at Grunewald's, where we'd go round the corner by the little shop and sit in there getting sandwich for lunch and drinking beer and coming back to class. Red and I were so close I used to be jealous of his brothers, not having one myself. He'd say, "Well, I got to go by my brother's," and I'd say, "Why? *Why* you got to go by your brother's?"

Dave kept that band very commercial. He didn't want no bebop rhythm section, the drummer dropping bombs—people were dancing out there. Our satisfaction came from our arrangements—we voiced the horns as modern as we could. I'd sneak in a bomb and Dave would flash me a dirty look and say, "Uh-uh, Chief." I knew I was doing wrong, but I was bending him.

Tyler and McLean and I always snuck in a little bebop. We was all trying to play bebop, playing it the best we could. The hell bebop wasn't a mass movement! Maybe not as popular as rock and roll, because it was too musical for the common lay ear. But young musicians all over the country was getting into bebop. I'm talking about black kids mostly—white kids' families didn't want them playing that nigger music. Bebop was nigger jazz.

I made much more of a name in the other music, but ask yourself: If I was one of the beginners of rhythm and blues, what was I playing before? I'm a jazz drummer. Jazz is all anybody played until we started making those records. The backbeat came about because the public wasn't buying jazz, so we put something in that was simpler and that's what made the difference.

Catherine Roy's mother was Odile, her father was dead. The family lived near us but the only one I knew was Catherine's brother Edward, who had a crush on Aunt Nita.

Catherine worked as a seamstress at Haspell's on St. Bernard, where they had a bunch of mostly black women making clothes. I met her through a girl-friend of Steve's and liked her right away. We had to sneak out a lot because her mother was very strict on her. Catherine couldn't be seen at a dance, nothing like that. We'd go way downtown, way far away from the neighborhood. Not so much dancing, just sitting talking. It was a long time before we were intimate because I had a lot of respect for Catherine. But it didn't take me long to decide: she was it. She was different. She was a good girl, a good woman, a respectable girl.

I was twenty-three when we married, she was eighteen. For years the only arguments we had were when she'd say, "You ought to get a real job." What's a real job? In a good week with Dave I made sixty-five, seventy dollars. That was good pay. There were times Dave said, "I'm sick of this shit, I'm joining somebody else's band." "Bull*shit*," I'd say. "This my only job!"

We played the San Jacinto, and Monday-night dances at the Catholic church halls: St. Katherine's, Blessed Sacrament, Holy Ghost. We could work on Bourbon Street—in certain clubs—but we couldn't play the balls for Rex, Comus, and Momus and we couldn't play the hotels, which were the real money gigs: the Blue Room at the Roosevelt, the Monteleone, the St. Charles. We played the Joy Tavern up in Gert Town, the Hideaway in the Ninth Ward, the Club Robin Hood on Jackson and Simon Bolivar. The Dew Drop, on LaSalle. The Two Sisters, Little Ferd's, and Al's Starlite Inn in the Seventh Ward, back on London and Dorgenois. Shadowland, a uptown club owned by a ritzy black family, college-educated high yaller people. We jammed at Toni Heisser's but that was more or less as a favor to Toni, a friend of Dave's. She didn't pay us much but we drank free and ate all the crawfish and crab we wanted.

We opened for Louis Armstrong in 1949, the year he came down to be King of the Zulus. It was Pops, Earl Hines, Jack Teagarden, Arvell Shaw, Barney Bigard, and Big Sid Catlett. Pops's mouth looked like somebody'd been slicing it with razor blades. Where did he put the mouthpiece without hurting his lip? I heard someone say, "Pops, how you feelin'?" Louis pointed to his horn and said, "That piece of iron is killing me!" When Teagarden got up onstage with us, Pops sent somebody back for his horn and came up playing. Dave shouted, "Ladies and gentlemen, Louis Armstrong!" It was hard to keep Dave away from Pops, he kept jumping up and playing too. I heard Earl Hines say to Armstrong, "You shouldn't be playin' with these guys, man," but Pops said, "Aw man, I'm home, I'm enjoying myself."

We played Xavier and Dillard and sometimes we'd go up to Baton Rouge and play Southern University. We played all the outlying cities: Shreveport, Lake Charles, New Iberia. Traveled downriver to Buras and Grand Isle, and across Mississippi to Mobile. Played the tourist towns along the Gulf: Biloxi, Bay Saint Louis, Pass Christian. Dave had an old station wagon and sometimes we used Mr. Hall's car, too. Me and Theard snickered about Mr. Hall, who was getting real old and cantankerous and corny. He was seventy-three years old even then.

"You all right, Mr. Hall? Can you see?"

"I'm all right."

"You all right?" Tee hee hee. Dave was laughing on the side but saying, "You ought to be ashamed of yourself!"

Bayou Barataria, that's the best oysters in the world. One day we going down there and saw people dredging up big and I mean *big* oysters. We say, "Goddamn man, is this where they get their oysters?" So Pilou tied a handkerchief round a twig and coming back, we stopped. We'd bought rakes and one guy stood by the car like he had to pee while the rest of us took off our shoes, rolled up our pants, and ran out there and raked in them oysters, two bulging sacks' worth. In and out of there, quick. Catch us messing with their oysters, they'd shoot us. Nobody ever find your ass, either. But at two o'clock in the morning who's out there? They home screwing or whatever they do.

We did that a lot. Then Mr. Hall said he knew a place on the way to Buras that had the biggest catfish you ever saw in your life. We all bought poles—you could buy a cane pole then for twenty-five, fifty cents—and that's the first time I ever went fishing. After some pretty good-sized catfish somebody pulled a fish out of there and we said, "GODDAMN, LOOK AT THAT THING!" Mouth like *that.* Look like a tarpon with whiskers. *"LOOK AT THAT FUCKING FISH!"* And we caught others that big or bigger. Pretty soon it got so we'd leave for a gig early so we had time to fish.

Dave called the people down there Freejacks, a word I never heard before or since, means part black, part white. We didn't interact with them too much, because they were known to be some funny-time people. Get nasty and turn on you. They had some sumbitches out there was huge, monstrous. Altercation break out, they dragged the two sumbitches outside and left them out. Whatever happened out there, they didn't come back in. They were country people down there, man, that whole area is country!

We played a white club in Arkansas where the part-owner was a magician who had himself put in a block of ice and escaped. We went to Bogalusa, where I met Bobby Bryant playing in a band called the Rhythm Aces. The tenor player was Jones, everyone called him Puddin'head; he went to work with a company in Chicago and became kind of a big shot. Willie "Hump" Manning was the leader and always tried to get me to join.

They had some fine broads out in the country, too, big legs, big asses, just walking by going about their business. George Miller, a bass player friend of mine, had a girl in Biloxi, a nice girl, housekeeper for some white people. She gave him money and he flirted right in front of her face. George was a good-looking pimp type of guy. I went in his room to get some weed and he was drunk asleep and this girl was straddling him with a two-by-four, about to bash his skull in. I reached out and caught the board—she'd have killed him. She ran out the room and I threw some water in George's face so he'd know what the hell I was telling him had just damn near happened.

"That crazy bitch! I'll kill her!"

"Man, you almost just died yourself!"

I saw two women fight with razors in a club in Pass Christian. At first you thought they were fistfighting but every time one hit the other, blood popped out. That's another time I thought I was about to see somebody die. We played a black club in Biloxi called the Big Apple—most black joints in them days was called the Big Apple. The owner's name was Booby Palmer and he used to kid me about he was my daddy because he knew I had a temper. I'd attack his big ass and he'd grab me while I was screaming, "You motherfucker you!" I wasn't laughing, I was pissed.

We traveled to Don Robey's Bronze Peacock in Houston and went over good. That was a beautiful, nicely appointed club, man, not a run-down joint with gingham tablecloths like the Dew Drop. It was late in 1947 and we stayed in the Crystal White Hotel, the nicest hotel for blacks in Houston. After we'd been in town a few nights, three girls came after me and Pilou and Theard saying, "Niggers think they cute just because they dressed nice." We'd heard about the girls from Texas and we were scared. They were known to cut your ass! Throw lye in your face! You always heard about them Texas women! Get in a fight and hold onto each other so they can't get away and then carve each other up. Boy, we were sharp, though. After the third or fourth night I was going with one, Eloise Harper. And then a girl came to Houston I'd been going with at the Dew Drop, Little Bit Brown. I said, "Little Bit, there's a girl I'm going with here, so if you're mad you and me can end things, it's all right. Because she'll hurt both of us, I think."

Little Bit said, "I don't care about the bitch!"

"Honey, if you want to get hurt I'll show you who she is. But don't have her hurting me." Eloise Harper—man! Tan-complected girl with freckles, sold tickets at the Peacock. She sold them and a guy named Vashti collected them, gave them back to her and she sold them all over again. Them two made a lot of money like that.

We played with T-Bone Walker, a nice cat but not much fun to play with; he just did the blues. I had more fun playing with the band, because we was at our very best then. Felt good about ourselves, looked good, were looked up to. Don Robey stood up and shouted, "How you all like this band?"

"Yeah, Don, yeah!"

"Well, we going to have them back!" Other than that, Robey was pretty low profile. He was a highly influential dude in Houston, everybody knew him, he was Mr. Black Houston. A fellow I saw around there a lot was a light-complected black guy named Dickerson. Wore overalls, but this sumbitch must have been a millionaire. At night you could look out the Peacock and see lights from another part of town; in between was an expanse of darkness. Somebody said all this was Dickerson's, all of it, almost as far as you could see. You know who Dickerson's friend was? Glenn McCarthy, the rich white oilman that built a lot of the buildings in Houston and had a hand in everything. From what I understand, Glenn McCarthy turned Dickerson on to stocks and stuff, and Dickerson had tons of money other than what you could visibly see. Dickerson's old lady Madeleine was a beautiful woman. Theard Johnson went after her. He didn't succeed. We all got the feeling he could have; by the time we were ready to leave she got very friendly with him, and then it was too late.

William Houston was the president of the musician's local. Charming, laughing, good pianist and singer, and everything he did was an illegal hustle.

They had such a thing called trust fund jobs, where record companies gave the union money for musicians who couldn't otherwise get work. It was mostly good for older musicians but we all did them. At one of these a lady standing right in front of us asked the hostess, "Where did you get this marvelous band?"

"Oh, Mr. Houston sent them to us."

"Oh! Are they expensive?"

The hostess quoted the price and it was way over the scale for a trust fund job. Houston must have pocketed the difference. Jesus, was he doing this to everybody? Me and Tyler and Joe Jones and Reynauld Richards went to the union to complain. They said, "I wouldn't worry about it."

"Uh-uh," we said. "It ain't right." We formed a club to have our meetings and make our protest and called it the Progressive Musicians Association. Houston and them others painted us as union busters trying to start our own young men's union. We wrote the AFM and they held an investigation and called a meeting in the summer of 1952. We went in and you know what happened? Houston suspended us and fined us five hundred dollars apiece.

I said, "What?"

Houston said, "This case is closed."

I looked at the board members—guys I knew as a little boy, Sidney Montague, Louis Cottrell. "You all going to sit there and let this man do this?" They just looked at the floor.

Me and Red took our last money, joined the longshoremen's union, and went to work on the riverfront cleaning out oil tankers. As light as Red was, he got so black I couldn't recognize him; I'd call out for him to go to lunch and he'd been standing next to me the whole time.

New Orleans was a town that was known for drummers. Stanley Williams, boy, he was a drumming sumbitch with Papa Celestin's band. Manuel Sims, who went on to play with Buddy Johnson—they called him Foots, because he *played* that bass drum. There was June Gardner and a little guy named Little Dibbs and Wilbert Hogan. Max Roach fell in love with Wilbert's playing, wanted him to come up to New York, said, "Man, I'll get you straight up here."

Vernel Fournier played with Dookie Chase's band and he was boiling. I heard Vernel and Art Blakey the same night just after I come out of the service and right then and there's what got me playing drums. Blakey always was strong, but he was younger then and that stamina was just—man! After hearing him romp through some of them big band arrangements—"I love the rhythm of the riff, riffin' on the mellow saxophone"—they'd do a ballad like "Cottage for Sal" and Art played brushes so beautifully. I heard Art and Vernel and said, "Goddamn boy."

Weedy Morris was another great drummer. Nervous guy, high all the time—I'm sure that's how he got his nickname. Weedy's brother was Leo, who became Idris Muhammad. A guy we called Hungry, Charlie Williams, was a mother on drums, a guy who never knew how good he was and died of an awful bone disease.

Ed Blackwell was an up-and-coming bebop drummer then, a very, very fine drummer. He could play New Orleans–style, too, but couldn't play much R&B, not really. Blackwell, Alvin Batiste, and Harold Battiste were together all the time, and Ornette Coleman too, when Ornette was around. Everybody else avoided Ornette. We said, "Uh-oh, here he comes." Ornette was a drag to play with, man, he sounded terrible. Whether he knew the right changes or not, he didn't play them. Played the bridge in the wrong places; sometimes he didn't even play the bridge. If Blackwell wasn't playing with Ornette he played like he was supposed to, with very good taste.

We avoided Ray Charles too. There was a time when Ray and Big Joe Turner and Al Hibbler was all hanging round the Dew Drop doing nothing. Well, Big Joe was working but he stayed in New Orleans for long stretches. When we come in after a gig, Ray would be waiting to jam with us. I thought he was good and played a hell of a lot of piano; it's just that all he wanted to do was his Nat Cole imitations and we'd played Nat Cole all night long. Came in the Drop, we were ready to play some bebop.

Ray and Al Hibbler got in a fight once; if I recall, it was about who was going to get up and sing first. They both said, "I'm going to kick you in the ass!" and we cracked up laughing. "We don't doubt you'd do it, but we just wondering: How you going to *find* his ass?"

Big Joe Turner was a big fat drunk. Big Joe! A man with hollow legs. How did that man live so long? Guitar Slim was another character that hung around waiting for us. One of the stunts he'd do, he had a long cord where he'd run out on the sidewalk and keep playing. While he was outside we'd unplug his amp. Came back in, we were playing bebop.

"Who pulled my cord out! I'll cut his throat!" Kind of a wild guy, Slim; when he said, "I'll cut his throat," he looked like he meant it.

Earl King didn't really come to the forefront until after I left. Earl recently told me I was the first person he ever heard use the term *funky* about music. We had a guy in the Tremé, old Foley. Called him Drag Nasty, which means just what it sounds like, it means you're draggy and drunk and nasty. You stink.

You could smell Foley coming, if the wind was right. He'd fall in a gutter of stagnant water by Roland's Bar and sit there, drunk. So I told these guys at a record date, "Think about Foley, how funky and dirty he stinks and smells. Think about playing the music just like that."

George Miller and the Midriffs—oh yeah! *Good* jazz trio. George Miller on bass, Lester Millier, you said it "Meelyay," on drums, and Alec "Duke" Burrell on piano. Everybody poured in to hear the Midriffs, musicians especially. Duke was a mother of a piano player, *ball* of fire, and George was a left-hand bass player that was terrific. Lester was an underrated drummer. He did some time—they found eight-, nine-foot bushes of weed in his yard. *Trees* of weed. Lester Millier.

Steve and I used to stand and watch Burnell Santiago play in that little bar-room behind the Donze brothers' grocery where they had this old upright. Stand there for hours watching this mother play. Burnell looked like a little Filipino. Fantastic! Man! Back when I was little, they said Paul Whiteman wanted to take him and he wouldn't go. He was a junkie and not a very brilliant kid. Playing for fun, making a little money. He was always taken care of by somebody—his brother, broads, Harold Dejan. I think he died of consumption. Goddamn, Burnell was something. We called his brother Black because he was the darker of the two. Black Santiago, Burnell and Black.

Professor Longhair? I never really thought of him as anything special. People got caught up in the excitement and never heard all the bad notes. A totally unschooled piano player and not a very intelligent person, didn't even know he was funny. He played at Caldonia's on Liberty and St. Philip, just a guy that played for nothing, for fun, for wine.

Frank Moliere, called him Little Daddy, was a piano player who went with Alma Purnell, a big broad that used to dance with my mama. He also had an old lady who bullied him all the time. Both them broads bullied him. Frank used to go all the way around the block to keep from coming past his house in the direction where his old lady would know he was coming from Alma's.

He'd tell us, "Man, sometimes I have to take off my shoes and tiptoe!"

"On the street?"

"My woman know my walk." Because Frank had one of those walks—the drop, they used to call it, that pimp limp. You'd say about someone, "He got that drop."

Snookum Russell played at the Paddock Lounge on Bourbon Street. He had a trio with Famous Lambert and Thomas Jefferson, a trumpet player who later got his own band and got popular. Thomas Jefferson was so dumb he believed it when Paul Gayten told him he rode a horse so he wouldn't spoil his Rolls.

"Man, how you get down here from Politeland without getting your car so messed up in the mud?"

"Well, Thomas, I get on my horse."

"You got a horse?"

"Sure do."

"Oh. Well, no wonder. I was just curious." Dumb!

Before he had his trio, Snookum Russell had a big band, one of them road bands like King Kolax, Lucky Millinder. Always traveling, working one-night stands. Barely getting by, but good. The raggedy bands, we called them, big raggedy road bands. Everybody knew Snookum's band. Ray Brown played with Snookum, which is where I first met Ray. I don't know where Snookum was from, not anywhere South, because he had a very clipped, Northern accent. Nice guy, but was he ugly! Wide, wide mouth, big teeth, flat face. Looked just like a catfish. He fell in love with Steve Angrum's sister Alice and she went on the road with him and learned to sing. But she'd never been out of New Orleans and wanted to come home, so Snookum broke up the band and went to work at the Paddock.

Nat Perillat was a terrific saxophone player, blew everyone's mind but he died so young. Jack Lamont, boy, there was a little guy could play some alto. Stepped out from behind a bus on Gentilly Highway and a car killed him. Warren Bell—awesome alto player! He's one of these really Creole kind of guys, had a wife like Steve's that kept his career standing in New Orleans. Wound up getting a day job, one of the best alto players you heard in your life.

Son Johnson was an alto player, just a natural strong-winded, strong-playing motherfucker—some nights on Bourbon Street you could hear him over every other horn out there. All the great bands tried to hire Son Johnson, Ellington, Lunceford. He didn't care. He wouldn't leave.

I'm telling you, a lot of famous cats loved the musicians from New Orleans. Sonny Stitt, the first thing he thought of when he came in town was jamming at the Dew Drop. I was doing an amateur show at the Carver Theater, me and Tyler. A little girl was singing "Pennies from Heaven" and down the aisle comes Stitt, right up onstage. Higher than a kite. Scared that little girl to death. She ran offstage.

Stitt leans right in on me.

"What time you get off, man?"

"Sonny, I'm playing!"

"What time you get off?"

"Sonny, you chased that poor child offstage!"

He looks over his shoulder. "Oh, I'm sorry. Hey, I'm get a drink, I'll be back."

Tyler said, "That motherfucker's crazy!" Me and Tyler talked about that incident a long time. We talked about it so much, Steve used to talk about it too, and he wasn't even there! Steve used to say, "Y'all remember when Stitt ran that poor little girl offstage?"

Charlie Parker's manager, Teddy Reig, heard me one time and introduced me to Bird, who was staying at a little hotel down from the Dew Drop. I don't remember if he was playing or passing through.

I said, "I've heard a lot about you, man. I heard you play with Jay McShann, twice." That was back around the time Bird made his pretty solo on "Confessing the Blues."

So we got to talking. He said, "Sure like to get high." Asked would I know where he could score.

"I don't make it a habit," I said, "but I'll do it for you."

"You don't have to, man."

"People find out you ain't from here they'll give you anything."

"Well, I appreciate it."

So I went and scored, wasn't no big deal, and gave it to him and he thanked me. We had a drink. We had a Jax beer, as a matter of fact. He mentioned a drummer he liked, Ike Day out of Chicago, said I'd be lucky to hear him sometime, he was a bitch.

And that's the last I ever saw of Bird. He never paid me back for the dope— I'm sure he did a lot of that. I bought it from Porky Pig, a little tough from uptown, little round fat dude. Carried a pistol. If he ain't dead by now he's a big fat old man.

When the pulse of rock and roll grabs you and won't let go, it becomes the Big Beat. That's how it was when Earl Palmer laid into Little Richard's "Lucille," sounding as if he were using baseball bats and kicking a thirty-foot bass drum.—Max Weinberg (with Robert Santelli), *The Big Beat*

If there was a way to bottle and sell ignorance, you could get rich here. There really are no swift thinkers, no fast lanes, and people who have some get-up-and-go about them, they get up and leave. Like Earl did.
—Ellis Marsalis, New Orleans musician, 1997

The race and hillbilly record businesses, which turned into today's pop-music industry, began with the Southern expeditions of a few Northern record men. Pulling into town with portable gear, intrepid twenties and thirties pioneers like Victor's Ralph Peer and Columbia's Art Satherly auditioned and recorded the locals. It was a brusquely efficient method: Southern towns provided the raw material, the record men harvested it.

Although the burst of recording activity in postwar New Orleans began in the old-fashioned way (the Braun brothers of New Jersey's DeLuxe Records arrived in town in 1947, set up shop in a high school auditorium and recorded local stars Roy Brown, Paul Gayten, and Annie Laurie), it soon grew into something more. New Orleans had its own recording studio, manned by a self-taught but talented engineer. More to the point, it had a group of sophisticated, capable musicians. Unlike the old race-records artists, many of whom only knew three or four songs, inflexibly rendered, the members of New Orleans's so-called Studio Band were clever, versatile, opinionated professionals. They brokered the music; middlemen, they actively shaped it. Early-fifties label owners streamed to New Orleans not only for the local singing talent, they came for the Studio Band, who in large part forged the musical vocabulary of rock and roll. It's richly ironic, of course, that most of them were devoted jazz musicians who couldn't have cared less about the music of Elvis, Chuck Berry, or even the homey they catapulted to fame, Fats Domino.

Cosimo Matassa sold records, radios, TVs, washing machines, and refrigerators in the front of J&M Music on Rampart and Dumaine. In the back was a tiny recording studio. "The uptown folks," says Cosimo—polite society, that is—"thought of me as 'the nigger studio.' Even though I did people like Pete Fountain and Al Hirt, what stuck was that I worked with blacks. The studio was never in the newspaper, there were no tea *dansants* for me. An Italian was kind of an outcast down here, too."

Sessions at J&M were informal. Nobody punched a time clock, which wasn't always to the musicians' advantage: they were paid for a three-hour session, but with artists like Fats Domino, known in his early days to interrupt a take and ask, "How does that sound?" a session could last all day.

"Some of that quote talent was pretty difficult to get stuff out of," says Cosimo. "Ernest McLean was playing a guitar solo on a Smiley Lewis song, just eating that guitar up. Smiley ran over, grabbed the neck of the guitar, and yelled, 'Cut that out! I gotta go on the road and play that!' And Smiley was one of the savvier artists!

"So the quote Studio Band, other guys called them 'the clique,' but they were chosen because they were *contributors*. When you hired an Earl Palmer or a Red Tyler, you didn't just get a sideman, you got an assistant producer."

In Earl Palmer you also got an innovator who rewrote the book on rhythm in popular music. Earl may or may not have been literally the first, but he was easily the first widely heard drummer to streamline the shuffle beat of rhythm and blues into the prototypical rock-and-roll beat. As Earl says, he was only trying to match Little Richard's frenetic right hand (the Latin rhythms popular in the early fifties and always an undercurrent in New Orleans music undoubtedly affected him, too). Regardless, his achievement was to overhaul pop music's rhythmic foundation, discarding an "old-fashioned," jazz-based sound for something new: the headlong thrust of rock and roll. The best place to hear the rock-and-roll beat emerge is on Little Richard's "Lucille," "Slippin' and Slidin'," and "The Girl Can't Help It," where Earl's playing is a surging, exhilarating breakthrough.

Earl's manner was as exuberant as his playing. Harold Battiste remembers his first encounter with the drummer. A fledgling arranger, Battiste had been asked to contribute a big band chart to a radio broadcast. "Earl was playing drums. I wrote an arrangement of 'Day by Day' and I guess Earl thought it was pretty hip, because when the band finished, he jumped down off the bandstand, ran over, and kissed me!" "Earl?" says Warren Bell, "that's probably the most outgoing person I've ever met."

In New Orleans in the early and mid-fifties, an ambitious and self-assertive young black man was a threat to the social order. Anxiously trying to shore up Jim Crow, the postwar Louisiana legislature passed one discriminatory measure after another. A 1956 law forbade public social contact between the races, resulting in musicians' arrests like the one Earl mentions. Bolstering the old antimiscegenation code, a 1950 statute explicitly outlawed "marriage or habitual cohabitation" between "a person of the Caucasian or white race and a person of the colored or Negro race."

Both laws affected Earl directly. Not only did he often play music

with whites, but in 1954 he fell in love with a transplanted New
Yorker named Susan Weidenpesch. As their relationship deepened,
the sotto voce chorus grew. "Beware, brother, beware," said Earl's
friends. From across the city's racial divide came equally significant
remarks and glances, not all of them hostile. A friendly white cop
warned Earl to think about leaving town. He *had* been thinking
about it. Whether the main impetus was Susan or that lucrative session work in California, by late 1956 Earl's bags were packed.

ow, Freddie Martin, who had Martin's Dry Cleaners, opened a club across
from the Llopis Funeral Home on Dumaine. Sunday evenings when the
football game was over, everyone went to the Crystal Club.

Martin says to me one night, "Man, you in that music business" — "that music business," he called it. "After the game people come in here, drink a beer
and they gone. I need me some music. Sunday nights be dead."

"I know a guy that's just what you need," I said. "Plays boogie-woogie piano
down in the Ninth Ward. Get him in here. He won't cost you much."

So Martin went and hired Fats Domino. Fats played by himself a few weeks,
then one by one he got together a little band: his brother-in-law Harrison Ver-
ret on guitar, Charles Burbank on sax, Robert Stevens on drums. To tell you
the truth, I never really hung around to hear him play. All his tunes was the
same, and so simple. Too simple for me. He was just playing boogie-woogie piano, which is what everyone played that wasn't an accomplished pianist, boogie-
woogie and blues.

But I guess Dave must have heard differently, because when Dave got the
job of talent scouting for Imperial Records, Fats was one of the first people he
signed. We all thought, "That's nice. He can play pretty good, maybe he'll
make a little money."

The first record I ever made was Dave's first record, "I'm a little old country
boy, running wild in this big old town." It was at Cosimo Matassa's place,
J&M's, a record store that had a recording studio in the back. J&M's was the
only place I ever recorded in New Orleans. As a matter of fact, it was the only
studio in New Orleans.

That little room was hardly bigger than a bedroom. Picturing it, I see Lee
Allen and Red Tyler in the middle, the piano and me on opposite sides, and
the singer by the horns, near the piano. Everyone faced Cos, who was in the
little bitty booth. Cos never had an assistant; he came in and out and set them
mikes himself.

Earl (center) at his social club, the Crystal, Dumaine and Robertson Streets, ca. 1949.

As unsophisticated as he was, I think Cosimo was a genius. I've seen engineers use two dozen mikes to get the sound he got with three. He knew how to position mikes and he knew each mike like it was a person. Didn't even have no mike on the drums, just a mike on the bass and piano, one on the vocal, and the one that Tyler and Lee used was pointed at the drums. Cosimo knew that room, see. Today they put a dozen mikes on the goddamn drums alone! They put drums in a separate room now, or behind a baffle, but Cos never had no baffles in that studio—you couldn't fit one.

Union scale was $41.25 for a session. If I had a gig at night, I wasn't doing bad at all for 1955, damn right. Though it wasn't like I was in the studio every day—we might not do a recording for a couple weeks.

I'd go to a session at one, finish about five or six. We'd cut three songs. Take our time. Stop and go eat, come back and finish. Smoke a joint, perk up our sense a little bit. Cosimo didn't particularly like us smoking weed, so we didn't do it unless he wasn't around. Take a break and walk down Dumaine Street, get high, come on back.

I wore slacks, sport shirt, and sandals—I don't care if it was winter, it was hot in that little tight room. Dave dressed nice—we all dressed nice. Nowadays you see a six-piece band, five are slobs. None of us were slobs.

The core of the Studio Band was whoever was in Dave's, mostly: me, Fields,

McLean, Red. We could take directions better than other guys. A few guys had nothing to do with Dave's: Edgar Blanchard, Roy Montrell, Justin Adams, Lee Allen. Roy was a great all-around guitar player, good jazz, good blues, good rock and roll. He died, he was a junkie. Justin Adams was never in Dave's band; he played with his mother and his brothers Placide and Gerald. Edgar Blanchard was a quasi-proper dude. That was his humor, to appear proper, though he wasn't and you knew it. He'd raise one eyebrow and say, "Earl, you *are* full of shit."

Lee Allen wasn't in Dave's, but he was a honking tenor player. Lee was from Denver, he came to New Orleans to play football and basketball at Xavier. He played the shit out of the blues; any other tunes, he had trouble with the chords. He didn't have the knowledge of chords to be a first-rate bebop player. He didn't read music very good.

Frankly, man, nobody considered what we were doing a big thing. "There that drummin'-ass nigger playing on them records"—that's what my old friend Butsy said when he saw me around the Tremé. "Man, he think he cute. Gimme dollar, nigger, or I'll whip your ass." People figured, what's so big about making records as opposed to playing down at the San Jacinto? Me and my friend Freddy Pierre always went to a place called Steve's on Claiborne Street. Freddy went with Nora, the waitress. He said to her, "Nora, do you know Slack is on that record we listening to?"

"Yeah, I know, Fred."

Freddy turns to this other guy that's sitting at the bar.

"That man there is playing on this record we hearing now."

"Who gives a fuck?" says the guy.

Freddy says, "I give a fuck, you motherfucker. Want to step outside?"

A lot of people didn't even know records were being made here; they thought records came from New York. Andrew MacRoyal was a friend of mine didn't know anything about records or nothing. We listening to a Fats Domino record one night in an oyster place on Orleans and Claiborne.

"You hear that?" I said.

"Yeah."

"You like it?"

"It's good. It's good music, man."

"That's me playing."

"No!" He jumps up and starts shouting to everybody, "Guess what!" I'm pulling on him: "Aw man, I didn't tell you to do that!"

We was just going on the job, looking forward to when it was over so we could hang out. Oh, I enjoyed going to the studio—I knew I'd make more money in six hours than in a week of gigs. But we didn't realize how popular that stuff was getting. What was rock and roll to me? I lived in a jazz world. I was not interested in Little Richard or Fats Domino. That's difficult for you to understand, because you come from a generation that is. I don't. It's something we did that was not important to us musically. Anyway, Fats Domino was a bigger star everywhere else in the world than New Orleans, because everybody knew him at home. If Fats was on TV and it even got shown in New Orleans, I think his family and his good friends would be about the only people watched it.

"Hey, Fats on TV."

"Yeah?" Very blasé. People from New Orleans are crazy. They're the least appreciative of their music. They take it for granted. People in New Orleans didn't mob stars, they did that in California.

Fats was a very shy guy, man, shy and insecure a lot. Came from one of those real country little places out on the edge of town, never been out of New Orleans. Ate a lot of that country food, coon and possum and chitlings, them kind of wild foods like that. Fats has a cousin named Cowain, which is Creole for turtle; whenever I go home Cowain is always giving me turtle soup, which I hate. Fats himself makes the best gumbo you ever had. When we played live behind Fats, Dave announced the tunes, like Fats was just a member of the band. Sessions, the same. Dave ran the show. Told Fats what to do, how to do it, everything.

We made a tour with Fats that went to Kansas City, Las Vegas, and Los Angeles. Fats didn't want to go. We had three days of chasing Fats from place to place. Every time we came for him he was at this or that cousin's. Dave finally caught him and said, "Man, you can do what you want. But if you don't come out of there, Imperial Records is going to sue your ass." The stars were supposed to be Fats and Jewel King, but Jewel wouldn't go. You know who we got? Fess. And he *killed* them. That tour bombed except for Professor Longhair. Fess was a hit out there, even if the club owner in Kansas City wouldn't pay us because Fess kicked a hole in the piano. I don't know who the hell booked that tour. I guess Lew Chudd at Imperial wanted to see how Fats drew on the road. Didn't draw shit. We ended up playing behind a shake dancer in Kansas City named Rose, the club owner's daughter; her costumes was hanging all over the dressing room and she didn't smell like no rose, I'll tell you that.

The first time I felt like a page was being turned was Little Richard. I hadn't heard anything like this before. He went into that *ding-ding-ding-ding* at the piano and I thought, "This sumbitch is wild!"

Richard wasn't a star when he met us but I *thought* he was. He walked into J&M like he was coming offstage: that thick, thick powder makeup and the eye liner and the lipstick and the hair everywhere in big, big waves. Walked in there like something you'd never seen. And meeting him all them times since, I still get the same feeling.

I don't remember exactly what I said; something like, "What the fuck is this?" Not who, *what*. "Gus," I said to Tyler, "what the fuck is this?"

And Red said, "Wow! Go on in there, child!" That was a New Orleans term—you'd put your hand on your hip, stick out your little finger and bend it a little. It meant, "He's round the bend, this is a fag." But Richard was so infectious and so unhiding with his flamboyancy, he sucked us right in. We got laughing with him instead of at him. I never thought Richard was crazy, never thought he didn't know exactly what he was doing. I just thought, "What the fuck is this?"

I'd go anywhere with Richard now, but at that time everybody was a little concerned about being seen with somebody that looked and acted so gay. He didn't need us anyway, he had his own entourage. Young black guys, all nice-looking younger dudes. We'd be joking: "Which of them's gonna fuck him tonight?" Richard liked to record right after a show, when he was wired. Came in the studio with a briefcase full of bills and set it up on the piano. I remember Lee Allen dipping his fingers in it and pulling bills out and laughing. Richard looked at Lee and say, "Lee, will you get *out* of that bag!" I said, "Play your cards right, Lee, and you could walk away with the whole bag," and Richard said, "Shut up, Earl!"

Dave didn't produce any of Richard's sessions, Bumps Blackwell did, and I usually led the band. Bumps's job was not very difficult. Richard always knew just what he wanted to do, and we knew how to do it. Bumps had kind of a slick L.A.-cat attitude in the beginning. We cut that real short, curbed it right away.

Bumps and Richard argued all the time, which we attributed to the fact that Richard was a temperamental gay dude and Bumps was kind of overbearing. Bumps was afraid of Art Rupe, too. "Pappy," him and Richard called Rupe. "I don't know how Pappy's going to like this." That was Bumps. "*Fuck* Pappy." That would be Richard.

What I remember about those sessions is how physical they were. You got to remember how Richard played—can you imagine matching that? I'll tell you, the only reason I started playing what they come to call a rock-and-roll beat came from trying to match Richard's right hand. *Ding-ding-ding-ding!* Most everything I had done before was a shuffle or slow triplets. Fats Domino's early things were shuffles. Smiley Lewis's things were shuffles. But Little Richard moved from a shuffle to that straight eighth-note feeling. I don't know who played that way first, Richard or Chuck Berry. Even if Chuck Berry played straight eights on guitar, his band still played a shuffle behind him. But with Richard pounding the piano with all ten fingers, you couldn't so very well go against that. I did at first—on "Tutti Frutti" you can hear me playing a shuffle. Listening to it now, it's easy to hear I should have been playing that rock beat.

Richard's music was exciting as a sumbitch. I'm not talking about the quality of it. It wasn't quality music. It wasn't no chords, it was just blues. "Slippin' and Slidin'" sounded like "Good Golly Miss Molly" and they both sounded like "Lucille." It was exciting because he was exciting. Richard is one of the few people I've ever recorded with that was just as exciting to watch in the studio as he was in performance. He was just that kind of personality, on edge all the time, and full of energy. But I never remember him angry with anyone. He was a sweet-tempered guy. Still is. Whenever I'm around that way, I stop at the Continental Hotel where he lives, go up and see him, sit down and talk a while. Always come away with a pocketful of little Bible booklets.

Smiley! That nasal, bluesy voice! The man had this big blues-sounding voice, a natural blues-sounding voice. You ought to have heard Smiley Lewis in person—he made the walls rattle! Sumbitch never needed no microphone. Heavy voice. Heavy-handed attitude, but nice. We got along great. Smiley's stuff felt good to play; you didn't have to do much but just get in the pocket and make it swing. You gleaned that right away. You didn't want to overdo nothing, because Smiley did that blues so good, that easy slow blues.

Smiley liked to go to the Struggle Inn. They had a chick behind the bar, a big fat light-complected chick, big high yaller. She knew Smiley liked her. I didn't see any evidence they had anything going—he just liked to compliment her. He'd say, "Man, all of her is fine." I liked Smiley not only as an artist; he was a hell of a man. He was all man. That's somebody you'd look at and say, this ain't somebody I'm going to mess with, boy, I ain't going to mess with Smiley Lewis, because he's muscular. Short and stocky but not fat. A *knot*—you know what I mean?

You want to hear that song "Since I Fell for You" in its rawest, best form? Annie Laurie could sing. She was a female Smiley Lewis. We used to call her Big Dick Annie. It's a shame to talk about Annie like that! She wasn't a good-looking chick, man, looked like she could have had a few bouts in the ring.

Lloyd Price, there was a go-getting kid. "You gotta listen to me, I know what I'm doing," that type. Came from Shrewsbury, out by the Airline Highway, and it dawned on me when we did "Lawdy Miss Clawdy" that this was the same guy I'd seen in a little joint out there. They had a couple of clubs up around Shrewsbury; Tommy Ridgley was the king of these places, man, didn't have to play anywhere else.

Shirley and Lee weren't terribly talented. Shirley was nasal and tinny and high-pitched. *Off*-pitch. When Shirley sang, you felt around to see if you was cut—that girl sang sharp! Lee always sounded like he was trying to compensate by singing flat. She sang sharp, he sang flat. It's amazing they had any hits at all, which wasn't many.

Of all the owners, I thought Lew Chudd was pretty honest. Fats thought he wasn't, but I understand from Dave that Lew saved a lot of money for Fats when Fats was losing big in Vegas. I used to talk to Lew a lot, used to call him a has-been ballplayer because he'd once been in the Cardinals farm system.

The owners were mostly based out in California—Chudd, Art Rupe, the Bihari brothers, the Mesners from Aladdin. Chess was in Chicago; Leonard Chess came down all the time. Syd Nathan came down a couple times from King in Cincinnati, little pear-shaped man with a gravelly voice and thick, thick glasses. Ahmet Ertegun came down from New York. He was a nice guy. Jerry Wexler I always thought was a little sneaky. Certain look in a guy's eyes, man. I ain't saying I'm right about people all the time, but when you find you been right more than wrong, you don't have any reason to think you wrong when you see that look. I didn't like him. I always had the impression he was trying to save money that wasn't even going to him. He wanted to hire me for nothing, for expenses, as a talent scout. Of course, maybe it was Ahmet's idea. Maybe so.

The whole time I was in New Orleans, the only bands I played with were Harold Dejan, Dave, and the Earl Williams Quintet. I knew Earl long before I worked with him. I'd *been* knowing him. Dave liked being a novelty, which means that Earl worked more. Earl played more jazz, too, so when he asked me to join—he kept asking me, again and again—I finally went with him.

Three of us in that group were the best jazz players in New Orleans at the time: Edward Frank, Red, and me. Sam Mooney never became well known but he was a good guitar player. Ellis Marsalis used to sub for Frank and sometimes for Tyler; sometimes he'd even play Earl's bass. We welcomed that, because Earl couldn't play. We used to cheer every time he hit a note that was actually in the chord. The people thought we were crazy. Earl had never gone near a bass, he just didn't want to hire a bass player.

Earl never left New Orleans. The last time I saw him, maybe ten years ago, he'd had a stroke. Didn't know who I was. I was about to leave and he started to cry. He'd recognized me, and I started crying too, and hugged him.

"Three of us in that group were the best jazz players in New Orleans at the time: Edward Frank, Red, and me." The Earl Williams Quintet at Natal's, ca. 1953. *Left to right*: Red Tyler, Earl, Earl Williams, Sam Mooney, Edward Frank.

We worked at the Sho-Bar and the Texas Lounge and Natal's out on Gentilly Highway. The Sho-Bar was a well-known strip joint with white bands; after hours they brought in black musicians for jam sessions that might go till nine, ten in the morning. That's when the police busted us for intermingling, so we started jamming in Benny Clements's apartment, 912 Toulouse. Jammed anywhere we could in those days. "Well, let's go over there, little June and them is playing, let's sit in." But most of my jamming was at the Dew Drop, because that's where the musicians hung out.

The Dew Drop was the best place in town. It was our hangout, *the* club for blacks. We called it the Drop. "You going over to the Drop?" Most local musicians came in every night after work, and it was where out-of-town musicians came when they wanted to hear some music, some black music.

Four, five, six, daybreak in the morning, still roaring. It was a sit-down place but they had a little area in the back for dancing. They had some rooms upstairs, maybe ten at the most, where different people stayed. I had a little fling there with a shake dancer named Markee.

Charles Brown, Amos Milburn—those kind of big out-of-town acts would headline. There'd be a comedian: Sweetie Walker or Lollipop Jones. Both them cats was from the old days, both had worked the Palace with my mother.

Bobby Marchan was one of the emcees, a little AC/DC guy. There was a gay who'd been in show business with my mother, flaming, and that was Patsy Valdalia. He was a fixture. Had another gay emcee there, Chalida. Esquerita hung around the Dew Drop too. He dressed like Richard, all that flash. Another flaming gay who was a terrific singer was Larry Darnell. Dressed very sharp. Pretty guy, really pretty, women was crazy about him even though everybody knew he was gay. He was very dramatic. The one big tune he had, "I'll Get Along Somehow," he used to sing the shit out of. He did a dissertation in the middle about "I have here in my hand some letters you wrote" and he moaned about how deceived he was by this girl, and when he was just about to go back into the song, he'd tear up the letters and throw them up in the air and the place always went nuts.

I don't mean to give the impression that running gay was a popular thing. Gays were still in the closet, so this was the attraction of people like Esquerita: they were outright raging faggots so they were entertaining as hell. The only place you'd see three and four gays going down the street together was the French Quarter and they were white.

Lot of white people wanted to come to the Dew Drop. Most were turned away, but they let a few in. Every time the cowboy actor Lash LaRue came in town, he came by. He played a hell of a guitar and was a regular guy that people liked. Leon Kelner, who played the Roosevelt Hotel, came around, nice quiet man, had a little fifteen-minute TV show. Milt Bernhart—I knew him because he sat in with us at the Texas Lounge—he came to the Drop, had a good time. White musicians who were in town at the Roosevelt came down. It wasn't their fault they couldn't take you downtown; you knew they couldn't do a damn thing about it.

I saw a white guy get thrown off a city bus once for sitting in the black section. "Can't sit there, it's the black section."

"I can sit anywhere I want."

"Not with niggers you can't." Threw him off the bus. One time Mike Serpas, a white trumpet player we called Cheese, painted himself green. Got on the bus and said, "Where do you want me to sit, I'm green!" Threw him off, too.

If a black person tried to go to a white nightclub, he could get his ass kicked, his brains beat out. I don't know of any time that happened—the era we talking about, blacks knew where they could and couldn't go. I saw black employees get beat up for insubordination. I saw a black guy try to quit the Safari, a club I played at. They wouldn't let his ass. They said, "You ain't leaving until after tonight." He said, "I quit, you can keep my money. I'm leaving now." Took him out in the parking lot and beat him up.

It was different if you were a star. The Safari rented a big beautiful trailer for Dinah Washington. She said she'd rather be in the storeroom with us.

"Miss Washington, we got this nice place for you!"

She said, "I want to be inside."

They said, "Miss Washington, *this* is your place."

She said, "The queen has laryngitis." Meant she was on strike.

It wasn't illegal for blacks to back up a white headliner, as long as the band was all-black. Lot of times, if blacks was backing up a white girl, they put the band behind a screen. Isn't that something?

Of course, there was lots of intermingling; Stormy and me weren't the only ones. By the fifties it was pretty flagrant. Joe August, a blues singer they called Mr. Google Eyes, was known to fool with white chicks. Sugar Boy Crawford was always flirtating with white women. He got beat up about that, the police beat him up. One Sunday morning the police found Lee Allen and a white girl named Patty Driscoll drunk and half-dressed in a parked car with the door wide open. Right on Canal Street, people streaming past going to church. The cops like to have killed Lee, beat him every time a new shift came on until they finally let him go. You didn't want to go to jail in New Orleans, you might never come out. You don't know how those days were. They could kill you if they wanted and say you'd committed suicide. Who was going to argue? Who was going to investigate?

You always had run-ins with cops. You couldn't call them run-ins. You got run out. At Municipal Auditorium I went to hear Shelly Manne, who was on his last tour with Stan Kenton. I just wanted to meet him and talk, so I waited outside after the show. Every time the stage door opened, I started—I was scared I'd miss him—and the cop kept saying, "Boy, get back!" Finally Shelly came out with some other guys and headed off real quick.

"Mr. Manne!" I shouted.

"Nigger, didn't I tell you get back?"

Shelly heard that and turned around. He said, "Oh, there you are! I was waiting for you, man. Come on." He'd never seen me before in his life. That's the kind of man he was. We got to talking, and I took him to the TiaJuana where I could sit in. That's a tough area, man, a bad neighborhood for dudes. It could have turned into a terrible thing, bringing Shelly there. He stayed long enough to hear me play. "When you get to California," he said, "get in touch." Shelly Manne. Now you know who my daughter Shelly is named after.

I'm sure there was people in New Orleans celibate, I just didn't know them. And I was the most rotten of all. Catherine knew my reputation—New Orleans women were a little more accepting of that kind of thing, know what I'm saying? Catherine never came to the Dew Drop, just didn't fancy going out. She hadn't even a favorite tune, that I knew of. And we had Earl Jr., Donald, Ronald, and Pat pretty quick, and Catherine became a great mother and stayed home. That's what allowed me to be the philanderer I was.

I was good at jitterbugging and frequented dances. They had a pair of twin sisters, Evelyn Catherine Walker and Catherine Evelyn Walker, who loved to show off with a sissy named Al. He jitterbugged with both of them. Like bookends. Spin one, grab the other and throw her up in the air and before she come down, grab the first and throw her in the air. They rehearsed all day. Talk about pretty girls! Tyler went with Evelyn and I went with Catherine. We'd sneak in the window while their father was ossified in the back. Their bedroom had a window on each end and their beds were by the windows. After a while they thought they'd pull some stuff on us. They switched beds. We knew it all the while, you know how? They wore different perfumes.

I said to Tyler, "Hey Gus, you hip?"

"Uh-huh."

"Well, which window you going in tonight?" We heard a voice from inside: "What did you say?" That's when we told them we knew. "Tricking us"—that's what they called what they'd been doing.

Red and I were out another time with Frances Cobble, a white girl who later married Edward Blackwell, and Lucy Fatita, a girl from Kenner. We were parked way out in Camp Plauche, a deserted army barracks up around Shrewsbury, and we saw a police car coming. Lucy and I jumped out and hid. As light-skinned as Red was, he stayed in the car with Frances. We heard the cops tell them, "It's dangerous being out here, they got a lot of niggers out this way."

"Okay, thank you, officer," Red said, and the sumbitch drove away.

Them same two girls were with us in a motel out on Gentilly Highway where we rented rooms for assignations, as they say. Bajoom parlors, we called them, for what you used them for: ba*joom*. We were in adjoining rooms smoking weed.

"Gus," I called out, "did you just hear a siren out on the highway?" We pushed them girls right out the window and their clothes after them. The siren went on down the road after someone else. We cracked up laughing. When you're doing something wrong, boy, you always think they're coming right after *you*.

"Can you see the headlines?" Frances said. "'Musicians Caught in Love Tryst'!"

Red said, "I don't care what the papers said—if those cops had broken in, I'd have grabbed Earl and been tongue-kissing him!"

When I wasn't philandering, I was at Dumaine and Claiborne hanging out with Shack and Lo and Larry the weed seller and little Harry Wilson, Haree the midget. Haree worked as a waiter at the Boston Club, a rich white guys' club, and made a lot of money from tips because he was funny. He was a lovable little dude. Tough, too. Didn't step for nobody. Smoked a lot of weed, had a lot of fun, loved women, give you the heart out of his body, fight for you, risk his life for you, and you couldn't forget him because like I said, he was only about this goddamn high. He'd get up on a chair and punch a sumbitch out. Had a brother that was full-size, a big tough guy named Freddy. *Loved* Haree. He'd get mad with Haree when Haree got drunk and women took advantage out of him. Freddy slapped the hell out of him but he couldn't hurt him. Haree was a tough little knot. Had an uncanny knack for betting horses. When he died we had a parade for him all through the Tremé. "To Haree!" "Haree!" Everybody crying, oh yeah. Everybody loved Haree. Even people uptown knew him. They said, "That poor little midget died." Didn't know his name but they knew that midget. I can't remember a time I didn't know Haree. He was another guy that had never lived outside of the Tremé.

I met her in '54, at a Dave Brubeck concert at Tulane. She was beautiful and very, very aloof. She was with Bill Kelsey, a white friend of mine and Tyler's.

Afterwards I said to Bill, "Kelsey, don't ever introduce me to nobody that's prejudiced like that, man. That was embarrassing."

"Who are you talking about?"

"That girl Susan."

"She's not prejudiced, man, she was just high on pills. She grew up with colored people!"

So when I saw her, I said, "I owe you an apology."

"For what?"

"Well, I thought you were kind of funny time."

"Oh, Bill told me about that." She laughed and we struck up a friendship. It wasn't the beginning of anything; she was going with Benny Clements.

When she showed me some childhood pictures, something strange came

"She was here to take an art course at Sophie Newcomb College." A twenty-year-old Susan Weidenpesch, several years before meeting Earl.

back to me. When I was a boy stranded in Philly, I'd gone in Father Divine's restaurant every day, because you could eat all you wanted for a quarter. I always noticed a girl that served bread and set tables. Didn't think nothing in particular about her, but I remembered her. And who knows, maybe fifteen years later I was just trying to talk myself into something, but I could swear that this was that very girl.

You see, Susan's grandfather was an executive from a big midwestern company. When he died, his wife took the whole fortune and gave it to Father Divine. Took her daughter and granddaughter out of Cedar Rapids to a Father Divine mission in Philadelphia. Susan didn't get away from Father Divine's until she went to Hunter College. With a background like that, she was as black as I was.

She was here to take an art course at Sophie Newcomb College. Pretty soon she started coming in the Sho-Bar, sending me her phone number in a dollar bill with a tip to play such and such a song. I was coming off the bandstand and she was coming from the ladies' room and turned around and kissed me and walked on by. She was showing me she could take as much of a chance as me. Dangerous stuff, and was it ever a turn-on!

When the band moved out to Natal's, she got a job there waitressing. Lot of winking and waving, though you had to be careful about that shit because people were always looking for it. She and I both liked "Funny Valentine" and I'd tell Earl Williams, "Say, Earl . . ."

"I am not singing 'My Funny Valentine' to save my life!"

"Lady out there wants to give you twenty dollars."

"My funny valentine . . ."

It began getting serious with us when I realized I was going to leave New Orleans. My ambition was to go to L.A. and get in that studio work. I'd asked Catherine a long time ago to come with me. She wouldn't. Our relationship was stranded.

Very few people knew about me and Susan. Frank, Earl Williams, Tyler, Sam Mooney. Steve Angrum and Freddy Pierre. No one tried to talk me out of it; all they ever said was, "Be careful." I stopped going to the Dew Drop, and guys said, "Where you been?" But they knew. Gordon Natal knew, and he said, "If they ever stop you, you were driving her home for me."

She lived at 916 Dauphin Street. There was a black bar on the corner but it was a white neighborhood. After work I'd drop her off around the corner. After I parked, I'd walk by and she'd have left the door open. If nobody was around I went in. If they were, I circled back. A drummer called Joe Fox used to stand on the corner by the bar and say, "Goin' home, huh?" That was another guy that knew, Joe Fox.

The trouble with Susan's was once I got in, it wasn't easy getting out. You had to plan carefully. Might walk out and run right into a cop. I left in the dark of night or very early. Whenever I saw Tyler, I'd just kind of laugh and hum that song, "Living double in a world of trouble."

Susan didn't have to go through this with me. That has to tell you something about how a person feels about you, and it's got to make you feel something extra for them. I learned so much from Susan. About things I knew nothing about—what wine to drink with what foods, what fork to use at the table. Susan went places like Antoine's and Arnaud's, famous restaurants I couldn't go, and she'd bring the food home or get the recipes and cook them for us. If I was wrong, she had a way of telling me without hurting my feelings: "No, here's the way it is."

We'd go down in the Seventh Ward where there's lots of *passe a blanc* Creole girls and she'd put on dark pancake makeup and nobody would be the wiser, thought she was just some light-complected Creole girl from St. Bernard Street. Once in a while someone noticed them blue, blue eyes—*that* made them look twice!

There were times I got scared, but I never considered breaking it off. I just thought, "We going to have to leave." When I started talking to Susan about California, she said, "Yes, sure." Later, when we set the date, she said, "I have to go see my mother." I later found out why: she didn't know if she'd ever see her mother again, because her mother objected to us.

I tried every way I could to get my wife to go with me, but she chose to stay. I'd wanted Catherine to go to California long before I knew of any Susan. Susan was just one more reason to leave, and leaving New Orleans was the best thing I ever did.

5
THE POWER AND THE GROOVE
LOS ANGELES, 1957–

Nation's No. 1 Rock and Roll Drummer Bows on Capitol—New Orleans'
contribution to the world of rock and roll is the fabulous drummer, Earl
Palmer, who has made his home in Hollywood the past year, with his
family. Capitol introduces Palmer, who has recorded hits with Fats
Domino, Little Richard, Roy Brown, Ernie Freeman and Ricky Nelson,
on "Drum Village," Parts I and II (#3899). Both sides are instrumental
and feature the fabulous percussionist for the first time as a band leader.
. . . When Palmer isn't busy recording, he likes to collaborate on creating tunes and raising Pomeranians with his New York–born missus.
—*The Capitol Record*, March 3, 1958

When Earl arrived in February 1957, Los Angeles was alive with
rhythm and blues. The city's black population had skyrocketed
during and after World War II, nightclubs, radio stations, and record
labels cropping up like mushrooms after a rain. Aladdin, Modern,
Class, Dootone, Specialty, Imperial, Flash—"That was a *secret
world*," recalled songwriter Jerry Leiber in 1995, relishing the raffish-
ness of label owners like Modern's Bihari brothers, Aladdin's Eddie
and Leo Mesner, Specialty's Art Rupe, Imperial's Lew Chudd.
Rhythm-and-blues singer Joe Liggins is more matter-of-fact: "Los
Angeles had more record companies than anywhere in the U.S.
Some would pay royalties, others wouldn't."

Most of these labels had a Negro sergeant-at-arms, a music man
who functioned as the owner's ears. "In almost every region of the

United States where they had small labels," said Leiber, "there was a Maxwell Davis, Bumps Blackwell, Dave Bartholomew." Today these men would be rich off their creativity; in the fifties they were wage earners, their pay ill-reflecting the profits they generated (the savvy Bartholomew, who staked out his own miniturf, was an exception).

Earl joined this number in 1957, hired by Aladdin Records as an A and R man ("producer" had hardly emerged as a job description). When he met Eddie Mesner in New Orleans, Earl was quick to let the record man know that he wasn't just a drummer but a music-school graduate who could compose, arrange, and supervise a recording session.

He was as good as his word. His arrangement of Thurston Harris's "Little Bitty Pretty One" leapt to number 6 on *Billboard*'s pop chart, a million-seller. It wasn't the first time Earl made money for the Mesners; while still in New Orleans, he had arranged Shirley and Lee's "Let the Good Times Roll," a 1956 smash hit, the first Aladdin record to cross over to the pop charts.

If Specialty's Art Rupe remained quixotically loyal to Negro artists, other businessmen were waking up to the commercial wisdom of feeding blues-based material to young white singers. The teen market was out there, a still-slumbering leviathan, and another wave of independents appeared, targeting white buyers this time, intent on retooling Chuck Berry into surf music, rhythm and blues into rock and roll. Having barely touched down in Los Angeles, Earl was hired to duplicate his infectious "I'm Walkin'" groove for Ricky Nelson's cover version of the Fats Domino tune. He was playing both sides of the fence now, the original tunes *and* their paler simulacra, but the notion that he was "selling out" would have struck him as bizarre—this was what he'd come here for, why he'd fled New Orleans, where talent went begging.

The moment rock's fabulous profitability was no longer possible to ignore, more muscular players moved in on the independents. RCA (which had initiated the corporate takeover of rock by buying Elvis's contract from tiny Sun) lured Sam Cooke and Jesse Belvin from fly-by-night L.A. labels. Capitol signed Gene Vincent; Liberty, Eddie Cochran; MGM, Connie Francis; Mercury, the Big Bopper. In 1959 Liberty brought in producer Snuff Garrett, who had the good sense to hire the talented black arranger Ernie Freeman; Free-

man in turn brought in Earl, who played on hundreds of early-
sixties Liberty releases by Buddy Holly imitator Bobby Vee,
Gene McDaniels, Timi Yuro, Jackie DeShannon, Willie Nelson,
and others.

The original rock and rollers—Chuck Berry and Bo Diddley;
Elvis and Jerry Lee Lewis and Buddy Holly and their ragtag backup
groups—were amateurs, inspired tinkerers: folk musicians, really.
By the late fifties, rock was too lucrative to be entrusted to untrained
labor. The manufacture of hit records required a new worker, hip
enough to understand the music, disciplined enough to crank out
an album a day. Talented musicians streamed into late-fifties L.A.,
sleeping on floors, looking for angles into the studios. "I was working at some of the terrible country dumps in the Valley with Glen
Campbell and Leon Russell," recalls Hal Blaine, Earl's great com-
petitor, "and we were doing these cheapo sessions we called twofers,
two songs for twenty-five bucks. Sooner or later some of these songs
got released and everybody wanted to know who the musicians
were. And that's how it all started for us." (New Orleans, by the way,
where musicians were bred for versatility, supplied more than its
share of L.A. session pros: Rene Hall, Plas Johnson, Earl Palmer,
Ernest McLean, Harold Battiste, who became Sonny and Cher's
music director, and Mac Rebennack, who became Dr. John.)

The best of the new hired guns—Palmer and Blaine; guitarists
Campbell, Tommy Tedesco, and Billy Strange; pianists Russell,
Don Randi, and Larry Knechtel; bassists Carol Kaye and Red
Callender; arranger Ernie Freeman and several others—became
rock and roll's backroom Wizards of Oz, unseen, unsung, and
essential to the evolution of the music. "It really was the studio musicians who created most of the Sixties golden oldies," Carol Kaye
told writer Mark Cunningham, "not only in our performances, but
[in] our creativity, creating instant arrangements or deviating from a
corny arrangement to create a hit."

"Earl and I produced our own drum parts," Blaine says. "Producers and arrangers wanted to pick our brains, and any time Earl did a
record, I'm sure he did as I did": provide the extra fillips—Blaine's
thunderous snare and bass drum on "California Dreaming,"
Palmer's contagious fills on Sam Cooke's "Shake"—that nudged a
song over the line into irresistibility.

The studio pros went even further, into ventriloquy. Neither the

Buckinghams, nor the Association, nor Paul Revere and the
Raiders, nor many, many sixties groups played their own instru-
ments on their hits. The only Byrd to play on "Mr. Tambourine
Man," the record that ushered in folk-rock, was guitarist Jim
McGuinn; the other "Byrds" were Blaine, Russell, and Knechtel
(Earl was a studio Byrd himself, on the band's first release, when
they'd been the Beefeaters). The Ventures, rock and roll's first
instrumental supergroup, were often augmented or replaced; the
famous guitar part on their "Hawaii Five-O" was played by
Tommy Tedesco.

Beyond its dozens of record dates per day, Los Angeles had another attraction for musicians: movies and TV. Until the mid-fifties,
the major studios—Warner Brothers, Fox, MGM, Paramount, and
others—had permanent staff orchestras; at about the time Earl arrived, the old contract system collapsed into a much more competi-
tive freelance network. The veteran Hollywood players—"the blue
blazers," Blaine calls them—regarded newcomers like Palmer and
Blaine with scorn and disdain but were rudely jolted when the
"wrecking crew" (as Blaine took to calling his colleagues; "the older
guys kept saying we were going to wreck the business") quickly
moved into film and TV.

"Earl was the first black drummer to break into the higher-class
work, the Sinatra dates and the films and TV," says Paul Humphrey,
a later studio drumming star. "There were other guys out here, they
did R&B dates, but they wasn't able to excel to a level what Earl had
achieved. Some guys are gifted but they don't know how to take advantage of the gift they have. Earl was smarter."

"Earl took over," says Carol Kaye. "I thought he was the greatest
drummer I'd ever heard." He played sophisticated big band pop
with Sinatra, rock and roll with Phil Spector; he raced through
Looney Tunes cartoon scores (always, he says, fiendishly difficult).
He could swing a splendid big band at the Monterey Jazz Festival
one day, back Johnny Cash the next. The critic Leonard Feather
called him "ubiquitous."

According to stereotype the successful studio musician is a soul-
dead individual who, in his rare moments of self-awareness, curses
the system that seduced him. The truth, as usual, is more compli-
cated. In the mid-sixties a young sociologist named Robert Faulkner
interviewed dozens of successful session players for a 1971 study,

Hollywood Studio Musicians. While many of Faulkner's interviewees were indeed jaded (usually string players with unrealized classical aspirations), most considered their work a stimulating challenge. As one respondent said, "I doubt whether symphony players or other guys really have all the things down, all the experience that comes with knowing every style, of having gone through the mill. . . . I have to be funny, be a clown, be serious, play jazz, there's all types of music and all types of challenges." The best of the session players, writes Faulkner, were "expected to face recording problems with nerve, technical brilliance, flexibility, and even cold contempt for these contingencies."

"When a session was over," says Earl, "and you walked out and the guys said, 'See you tomorrow, Earl, thanks, great job,' you felt good, man; you felt, 'I've made it, I've arrived.' Almost everyone I've talked to felt the same way. Especially in film work, which was higher prestige and paid better. There were a lot of symphony players constantly sending in résumés for film work. A concertmaster on a film score, he was one of those guys: a virtuoso player able to lead a string section in any kind of music.

"Now, Percy Faith is pure vanilla. But if you ever wrote and arranged music, and you heard this shit coming at you, that you wish you could've written and arranged — 'Tutti Frutti' was fun, but this was music. This was a lot more sophisticated. The L.A. Philharmonic with Lalo Schifrin — it was gratifying to know I could do this: me, a little nigger that started by playing Fats Domino records winding up a fine enough musician to play with the Philharmonic. Little Richard fans try to argue with me all the time. I tell them, 'You talking about music you like. I'm talking about from a musician's standpoint.'"

Those last two sentences, meant to end an argument, conceal more than they clarify. Probed, they bring us to the heart of one of the several contradictions Earl Palmer has so energetically lived out. As a technician, Earl reached the top of his game in Los Angeles. He could sight-read passages of frightening density, polish off a Henry Mancini or a Lalo Schifrin film score with aplomb and no rehearsals. But what will people remember in fifty years and laugh with pleasure to hear, Little Richard's "Rip It Up" or Lalo Schifrin's soundtracks? After a few hundred New Orleans rock-and-roll sessions, Earl was bored. There were too few difficulties to negotiate, too few challenges for an active mind. But the best of those old records resonate with joy; they represent a neon moment when the old—the rich traditions of New Orleans—intersected with the brand-new: the excitement of postwar black Americans at finding their own voice. To mainstream America, Little Richard's music was a revelation, a forbidden language exploding blandness and pretension. The music of Hollywood carried no such charge. It was the packaging of emotion, not its expression. *You talking about music you like. I'm talking about from a musician's standpoint.* Earl became a consummate professional, but he never caught lightning again. Nor is he the first creative spirit to misjudge his accomplishment, prizing craftsmanship over something ruder, and greater.

don't think Catherine thought I'd really leave until the day I went. That was a hell of a day, boy, I'm telling you, a hell of a jam. I'd sat down with the kids and told them why I was going, but they didn't understand. "Daddy, daddy, don't go, why you got to go, daddy, why?" They was all crying. Catherine got furious, then she got crying, begging me not to go, crying and pleading then cussing and raising hell. Her mother was in the kitchen sulking and cussing. "I always knew that so-and-so would leave you with these children." I was crying when I pulled off from the house, thinking if I could just get through that day I'd make it. And I got further and further away.

I always wanted to live in California, even as a kid. There was a guy out here named Willie Covan, who had a lot of kids in dancing schools and sponsored them in movies. I always thought this was what I'd do, study with Willie and be a dancer. But when I got fairly successful at music, everybody—Bumps Blackwell, Lew Chudd, Art Rupe—started saying, "Man, come to California." I knew I didn't have no future in New Orleans. I was the best drummer, had the best job, and what was that? I knew there were guys in L.A. making all kind of money playing movie scores and big record dates.

Well, Tyler and myself and Edward Frank started thinking, and we began putting aside a pot. In not too much time we got together some good money. I bought a Mercury Montclair on Canal Street, brand-new '56 Merc, white with orange stripes and orange chrome. A big beautiful car, man: orange-and-white upholstery, air conditioning, whitewalls, spoke wheels. Paid two-thirds down and still had money left.

But before our money got big enough, Frank had a stroke. Then Red decided he didn't want to go. Just when I was thinking, "I'll never get out of here," Aladdin Records offered me a job as an A and R guy. The idea was to get some New Orleans shit out of me but I'd work in California, and that's what afforded me to come out.

So I drove here in that new car, me and Hausmann and Reggie, two guys that wanted to go to California and I needed the help. Hausmann DePass was wild. Loud and boisterous and fun loving. Not an asshole, just a kid, excited the whole time, always wanting to go see this, go here, go there, let's do this, let's do that, let's go see. I don't know if Hausmann had ever been out of New Orleans. His friend Reggie Fleury's demeanor was far more mature. Reggie talked real slow. Very logical all the time. Made a lot of sense.

It was two-lane roads except Texas. They always had big highways in Texas, that's some of the greatest highways in the country. We drove straight through; usually one slept and one sat talking to the driver. Reggie and I did most of the driving because we noticed Hausmann kept squinting at the wheel.

"You all right, man? You falling asleep?"

"No, I'm nearsighted."

The only time we stopped overnight was when Hausmann got hauled in jail for speeding. Little small Texas burg with a little small-town jail in the town square, maybe three, four cells. Reggie and me went straight there.

"Hey Hausmann!"

"Reggie! Earl! Get me out of here!"

"Shut up you son of a bitch!" someone yelled. "People trying to sleep!"

"Don't worry, Hausmann, we going to find a way!" We went and slept in the car.

Next morning the cops brought all three of us to a little liquor store on the highway. The judge owned it, or the guy that said he was judge. The man we gave our money to.

"I understand you boys was speeding."

"Yes, sir," I said, "but we sure have a long way to travel and we wish you'd let our buddy go."

"Well, we might be able to do that. Where you all headed?"

"California, where our boss is waiting."

"How much money you carrying?"

Hausmann starts to say, "Well, we got about—" before I managed to interrupt, "All we got is forty-five dollars between the three of us." We had seven, eight hundred dollars.

"That'll do," said the judge. Nothing signed, no papers. I'm telling you, man, these little burgs did what they liked. Left us with what they thought was five dollars, and we got the hell out of there.

Hausmann fell in love in Juárez. We'd stopped in El Paso so I could show them where I'd stayed when my mother got hurt. I was a grown man now, I could go across to Juárez and party, but Hausmann went berserk and fell in love with a Mexican prostitute. We were in a bar in a good-time section and before we knew it, Hausmann had slipped off.

"Hey, where he went?"

The bartender pointed down the street where they had a little rooming house. We went and found him with this little hooker.

"Time to go, Hausmann."

"Man, I think I'll stay."

"You can't *stay* here!"

"Go ahead on, I'll catch up with you."

Reggie was slick, man, he was a bartender himself. He got the bartender to slip Hausmann a Mickey. We dragged him out of there and didn't stop nowhere else except for food and gas, even though Hausmann wanted to go see Palm Springs. "We ain't stopping at no Palm Springs!" said Reggie. "Ain't nothing there but rich people," and we drove on to L.A.

When we got there we all got busy going our different ways. Looking for work. Hausmann found a job in a hospital, did a little extra work in the movies. Reggie became a bartender and bought into a little business that lost money. They both stayed, although I hear Hausmann's back in New Orleans now. Last time I saw him he was working at UCLA and came over to my house with a jar full of alcohol. It had a black rock in it, like a piece of charcoal. Said, "Palmer, you know what that is?"

"What?"

"That's a lung."

"What!" It was smaller than my fist. I stopped smoking, but only for a month.

Susan came out two weeks after me. Our first apartment was on Forty-second and Kansas, four blocks from the Coliseum. Black-owned building, but white people were staying in it, white-owned businesses all around, right close. Today it's black and Mexican. Drive around there now and you'll see chain-link fences, bars on the windows, padlocks—boy, it wasn't so tough then. We stayed a month, which was longer than the owner said we could; Susan had brought her Pomeranians, and Pomeranians will bark at the wind.

But that first week or so—what a honeymoon! Not to have to hide! It was a fulfillment I had always wanted to experience. And to experience it with a woman I really wanted to be with, to feel like a man and have a measure of respect I didn't have in the place I'm from—it was a great relief.

We still had to deal with people's feelings about us. We drove to a restaurant down at the ocean, a nice place, a romantic place. Coming back, we saw a carful of white guys. They're looking at this orange-and-white Mercury Montclair, a pretty car in those days. They pulled alongside. Got to making comments, especially when they saw the Louisiana plates.

"Nigger, if you were home in Louisiana, do you know they'd be lynching your ass?"

I'd had a few drinks and was thinking, "This ain't supposed to happen here." I cussed back. Boy, I got furious. At every red light, all the way up Hawthorne Boulevard and LaBrea, I got out of my car and headed toward them, but by the time I got near, the light changed and they pull off laughing. They weren't afraid of me. I don't know what I'd have done except maybe get my brains beat out. Suddenly I said, "You know what, Sue? They're exactly right—they'd lynch the shit out of me in Louisiana," and we began laughing. She said, "Do you realize how stupid you look jumping out of the car, running to the red light and they pull off and you run back in the car?" They finally turned off. They had fun with me, they really had a ball.

I'd left where I was born and raised and gone along with things, knuckling under so many times, so to be going through shit here, where I'd wanted to come all my life—you can only take so much. Even today I still feel like I could jump up and fight a sumbitch.

Those guys didn't say nothing near as dirty as another guy. We were stuck in traffic on Fairfax and Beverly when a guy in a little Mercedes convertible pulls up alongside and says, "Is that your pimp, whore?"

Oh boy. I got out and headed for him. I tried to lift his car. I wanted to turn that car over. He rolled up his window and his eyes got this big. I thought I had superhuman strength, thought I could lift that sumbitch off the ground and I guess he thought so too. I felt good scaring him. Susan was really worried; she figured if I got to this guy I'd hurt him.

"Come on, Earl, stop. Earl!"

She got out and tried to pull me back in the car. There was an older, white couple there, they knew something was wrong and kept asking, "What did he say to you? What did he say?" I wish to this day I would have thanked them for their concern. They sounded like they knew I wouldn't be out there unless this man had said something very insulting.

It dawned on me Susan was going through an awful lot of abuse. Here she was, working and scuffling, and whatever we made I was sending to another woman's children. If Susan had said, "I'm tired of this shit, I'm going back to New York," I can't say I'd have had any right to say she shouldn't. She dug in

Early days in Los Angeles.

there and worked, man. Took a lot of insults. Heard a lot of things I didn't. Knowing my temper, she kept a lot to herself, "niggerloving bitch" and shit like that. Susan was very, very strong, had a sense of humor, and she was wild. Susan was feisty. She was cussable. Fuck with her, you found out she had a mouth.

Eddie Mesner was slow moving and deliberate and a little bit sinister. His brother Leo was a tall bald-headed man, pleasant smile, moved fast. Nervous type. Eddie took care of Aladdin's music, Leo took care of the money. They

"Susan was very, very strong, had a sense of humor, and she was wild. Susan was feisty. She was cussable." Susan, late fifties.

were a little sleazy. Well, Leo wasn't, but Eddie was. He played the horses, sported with women, drank. Borrowed money from me because Leo wouldn't give him none. I liked Eddie, really, I just knew him to be crooked if he got a chance. He'd get Jesse Belvin to write songs and put his own name on them. Buy them outright from Jesse, who was a junkie, for fifty dollars. Eddie was always trying to finagle somebody.

They put me on salary when I came. Wasn't much, but I got a royalty—a very small royalty—on everything I produced. That's the first I ever heard of points, know what I'm saying? Thurston Harris's "Little Bitty Pretty One" was my arrangement and I got points on that. Not a hell of a lot, but I was surprised to get any.

I was making more than in New Orleans—two, three hundred a week—but I wasn't playing nearly as much. They had other people here they had to wean out, Jesse Sayles and Sharkey Hall and Charlie Blackwell, Bumps's brother, and Ray Martinez, who was a big fat drummer, a fat kind of guy mixed with black and Latino. Jackie Mills was a white drummer who worked a lot with black musicians; of all the white players, he was the one that played with the most black groups. Johnny Otis was okay, but Jackie Mills was better.

Wasn't a month after I got here, I had to go right back to New Orleans for a session. By this time everybody in town knew I'd left. "Earl ran off with a white woman! Left his wife and children!" New Orleans is the gossip center of the world. "Back already. . . . Must have not worked out, huh boy? Got a lot of nerve coming back here, son, they going lynch your ass."

"Hey Paaalmer man, good to see ya!" That was one person I was happy to see—first thing I did was I went by the Sears where Steve worked. He had on that big grin, with his gold tooth in front. I went to the studio and Cosimo gave me a big hug. I don't know if he knew anything about Susan but it wouldn't have mattered to him. Cosimo is a wonderful man.

That's the last time I went to the house on St. Ann. My kids were on the stoop, they didn't even know I was coming. All their little friends started shouting, "Mr. Earl is back, Mr. Earl is back." It was hard to hold back tears; I knew I was only going to leave again. I went inside and said, "Hey, Cat." It was just like I was talking to myself, explaining why I'd come back, this or that session. I think she may have thought I was coming back to her. At the risk of sounding egotistic, I know one thing: she loved me. It wasn't until I was in California a while that she finally got furious. She was furious for years. She's furious today.

That first year was rough. Many times I was comforted by Susan, crying over my kids. There must have been days when she wasn't sure I wasn't going to turn right around and go back.

And then things got better. Lew Chudd told his guys, "Earl's here and I want him on every record we do." Imperial started hiring me, Modern started hiring me. When I left Aladdin—I was only with them about a year—I really got busy, and that's when the pain started going away.

The first studio I worked at out here was Bunny Robyn's, 535 Fairfax. Universal was another, on Cahuenga. The Soul Stirrers recorded there. It had nothing to do with Universal Films, just a little room and a little old Russian

Earl and Ricky Nelson, 1957 or 1958. Sessions with Ricky Nelson tended to be drawn-out affairs; Ozzie, the rocker's father and manager, was an old-time bandleader fond of reminiscing. Earl remembered Ozzie "from when I was at the Roosevelt as a busboy. We'd get to talking about New Orleans and Judd DeNaught the bass player would say, 'Get him talking, man, and we'll go into overtime!' Ricky sat there quiet as a mouse, never argue with his father in any kind of way."

engineer named Boris. I never knew his last name. Boris. We did Ketty Lester's "Love Letters" at Armin Steiner's studio in back of his house. Ted Brinson, who was a bass player and a mailman, had a studio in his garage. Modern used Ted's studio. Class used Ted's some—that's Leon René and his son Googie. Leon René was old even then; he was from New Orleans and wrote "Sleepy

Time Down South." I remember talking with him about Alcide Pavageaux and Alphonse Picou and all them cats who played before I was born.

Radio Recorders was on Santa Monica and Orange, that's where I did my first big-time stuff, Doris Day's "Everybody Loves a Lover," things like that. Thorn Nogar built it. Owned it. Big, *big* man. Drank. When Radio Recorders got popular, Thorn got a staff and went and drank in the Formosa all day; only dates he worked is when the big shots came in, then he'd go right off and get drunk. The one engineer with a bigger name at the time than Thorn was a guy named Adolf at Warner Brothers, supposed to be the dean of recording engineers. But he didn't do no records, just film.

When the music got so they started using smaller bands, Gold Star became the most popular studio in town. Everybody around that place was great: Stan Ross and Dave Gold, who owned it; Larry Levine, the head engineer. I started working there a lot in '58, '59, just when they was getting busy. I did "Chanson d'amour" there with Art and Dotty Todd, who argued and cussed each other out all day long and sang together wonderfully. Eddie Cochran, we recorded him there. I remember the Teddy Bears from there too, though I'm not sure I worked with them: Spector and Carol Connors and Marshall Leib. Spector was about as big as a bar of soap after six weeks' washing. Their music was amateurish and very vanilla, but the harmony was nice and clean and young sounding.

We did a demo of "La Bamba" at Bob Keane's garage in Silver Lake and cut it again at Gold Star. That was the version they used. Buddy Clark was the bass player and Rene Hall played guitar. I did "Donna," too, and "Come On, Let's Go"—I think I played on everything Ritchie Valens did, which wasn't but six or eight songs. He was such a withdrawn, quiet kid. Maybe he was scared, little Latino kid from Pacoima in a big-time studio. Short, stocky boy, Mexican-looking right down to the little curl in front. He started in with that "Mr. Palmer" shit, and I said, "Don't be making with that. We're going to sing, you and me" and I sang "Cielito Lindo," the song I learned from those two boys in El Paso back when I was a kid, and Ritchie shouted, "Okay, Mr. Palmer! Ah yeah!"

Cochran was a good-looking blond kid. When I say he was impressive what I mean is, most of these kids were real rank beginners but this boy wasn't. He took control, even to the extent of rewriting what Rene Hall arranged. He was friendly and warm and respectful—when I went to shake hands he put his arm around me and said, "Man, it's nice to have you on my session. I appreciate it a lot."

By the end of '58, beginning of '59, my career zoomed. I took over the black

"That was good days, with Buddy's group. . . . That was my jazz peak." In the studio with Buddy Collette's combo, late fifties. *Left to right:* Eddie Beal (piano), Earl, Red Callender (bass). (Albert Murray)

recording thing from Jesse Sayles and Sharkey Hall. Shelly Manne introduced me around and gave me a TV show to work in his place. It wasn't too long until I was turning down record dates for film and TV; it really wasn't too long, because I was always striving for that. I did "Kookie, Lend Me Your Comb" with Edd Byrnes, couldn't carry a tune in a basket but he was handsome. That led to 77 *Sunset Strip*, which he starred in, and *Bourbon Street Beat* and *Hawaiian Eye* and *M Squad* with Lee Marvin—Benny Carter did the music to that.

There was no time I wasn't playing jazz, and that's when I was happiest. When Buddy Collette left Chico Hamilton to start his own group, he got me. We played the Jazz Cellar on Hollywood Boulevard and Jazz Central down at Hollywood and Western; we played a couple nights a week at the Ash Grove, which was mostly folk. That was good days, with Buddy's group. When you talking about my own playing, that was my jazz peak.

About '58, '59, I made a lot of little weekend trips with Earl Bostic. That's a guy looked just like an accountant. Wore thick, thick glasses. Always on a diet but ate banana splits. "Don't put no whipped cream on that, I'm dieting." Called everybody Pardno. Go ask some of the older musicians, they'll tell you: Earl Bostic was a technical genius. Wasn't as hip and modern as Bird, and he had a sound that wasn't the most pleasing, a growl almost, grating, *rrrrrrgh*, but as far as playing that alto goes, Earl Bostic's facility was a sumbitch.

Bostic's bass player was Adolphus Alsbrook, who had the sleeping sickness. He'd tell you something and you'd go, "Then what happened?" Snoring away. Never fell asleep on the job, though. Bill Jones was the singer. He's not singing now, he's a big old guy who's retired. He and I rode together all the time because we smoked weed; Pardno would say, "Y'all want to ride together so you can smoke them things." We might play San Francisco, have a gig the next day down in San Diego. Bill and I would pull away behind Bostic, turn round and party all night at Slim Gaillard's, get on the road and drive straight through, get to San Diego two, three hours ahead of the band and say, "Man, we *been* here." In Tucson once, they wouldn't let me and Bill swim in the motel pool. Just as we were leaving, the whole damn hotel burned down, and Bill and I still look at each other today and say, "When you had the time to do that?"

When Bostic called me, I told him, "Only the gigs out here." You didn't want to go out any longer than weekends — them girls at the answering services had musicians for boyfriends and every one of them was after your job. Them chicks be very quick to tell a contractor, "Oh, he's out on the road." So Phoenix was as far east as I went. A lot of guys could have done better, but they went on the road and that was the kiss of death.

Me and Rene Hall and Plas Johnson always talked about how we could make some money and not leave the studio. One day I said, "Let's do a rock version of 'In the Mood.'"

"'In the Mood'?"

Bought my house on it.

You see, back in New Orleans millions of old white guys always said, "By God, do you boys know 'In the Mood'?" If they liked it so much, why wouldn't their kids, if we put a rock-and-roll beat to it? Rene and Plas said, "Okay, write an arrangement," so I did. We put it under Ernie Fields, an old bandleader wasn't doing nothing. It was a big, *big* hit. It went to number 4 — that's pop, not no R&B chart. We never did another thing, but it worked once. I'm telling you, "In the Mood."

I was doing five times as many dates in a year as I did my whole time in New Orleans. I got involved with Ernie Freeman at Liberty and pretty soon I was doing three dates a day. Album a day, man, Ernie Freeman arranging, Snuff

"Album a day, man, Ernie Freeman arranging, Snuff Garrett producing." Earl
listening to playbacks, early sixties. *Left to right*: Ernie Freeman, Snuff Garrett, Earl.

Garrett producing. Gene McDaniels, Vikki Carr, Bobby Vee, Vic Dana,
Petula Clark, Charles Boyer, Walter Brennan. Sure, sometimes I felt like I was
prostituting myself. I didn't blow my brains out. Back when I was doing Fats
Domino, that's when I was really depressed. Out here I could say, "Look what
I'm getting back." Ain't just talking about the money, it was a professional job
to me now and I took pride in being able to do this, that, and the other. Dis-
liking the music was not a problem of mine. Like it or not, I took pride in playing it and I tried to play it, all of it, like it was my favorite.

By '61 I was getting calls for dates with no rock and roll on them at all. Neal
Hefti hired me for *Sinatra and Swingin' Brass*, which was strictly top-call players, and I come to understand that I was a finished musician. That's when it
don't matter what they throw in front of you, you ain't worried. People always
ask, "How long did you rehearse that?" You never saw it before! You think they

Earl (playing congas) on-screen in the 1961 Tony Curtis picture *The Outsider*, a melodrama based on the life of Ira Hayes, World War II hero and Native American. In a luridly racist scene, the drunken Hayes (Curtis) jams with an Afro-Cuban combo (Earl, pianist Ray Johnson, trumpeter Gerald Wilson, and trap drummer Leon Pettis), and the band's deafening music and leering faces trigger the weak-willed Indian's moral collapse.

send it home for you to practice? You go in in the morning, the music's on your stand. Take off your hat, light your cigarette, and sit back and open that page. They give you the downbeat and you read that thing right down the line.

When it really dawned on me that I could do this was when I had to play cartoon music, the hardest music I ever had to play. That's easy to determine right off the bat. Tom and Jerry fucking cartoons. I'd think to myself, "Here I am playing music I used to be scared to listen to, let alone play!" At one time I was doing damn near all the cartoons Warners made. That music looked like fly shit, notes all over. If you fucked up, you fucked up. I didn't worry so much about that. I took pride in trying to do it as fast and as good as I could. Lot of guys worried about making mistakes and losing their jobs. That was their motivation. In my case it was just force of habit that made me want to do it right.

I was good. I was goddamn full of energy, man, and I needed it. I had two families to take care of, three, including my mama and them. In my peak years I brought in more than a hundred thousand a year. That was the mid-sixties, when people was not doing sessions until they could get me. I was above the competition, Hal Blaine and me. The guys coming along under us, the Jim Gordons and Paul Humphreys, they battled it out. I didn't need to.

I hardly went anywhere in those days, I had everything I needed right here. I took Susan to New York once or twice on vacation and we stayed at the Plaza. Went in a fine restaurant and I asked to compliment the chef; he came out and it was Pete Robertson! Pete and Louis Henry were still partners but Louie's health had failed him. Pete brought me to see him, and Louis Henry was just a sick old man. I was grown now, making a lot of money, and I was happy to reach in my pocket and give Louis Henry five hundred dollars.

The period we talking about, I don't remember going four or five days without seeing Tommy Tedesco, Carol Kaye, Red Callender, Buddy Collette, Ernie Freeman, Rene Hall, Plas Johnson. Red or Lyle Ritz on acoustic bass, occasionally Jimmy Bond. When things went to the Fender bass, you had Carol, Bill Pittman, or Ray Pohlman. Ernie Freeman, Larry Knechtel, Don Randi, and Leon Russell played piano. For a brief period, Dr. John. On guitar you had Barney Kessel, Tedesco, Herb Ellis, Howard Roberts, Billy Strange, and a nervy little guy, Jerry Kole, the type of show-off who'd walk in, take the first-guitar part off Barney Kessel's stand, and go, "Say, Barney, how would you interpret that?" Kessel would say, "I don't give guitar lessons on record dates." The other drummers were Jimmy Gordon and Richie Frost and Hal. That's on records—the hotshot film drummers were Alvin Stoller, Frank Carson, Larry Bunker, Jack Sperling, Irv Cottler, and later Shelly Manne.

"I hardly went anywhere in those days, I had everything I needed right here." Earl with daughters Pamela (left) and Shelly, 1960–61.

(Left to right) Susan, Earl, and Thelma Theophile at the Ambassador Hotel, Los Angeles, late fifties.

Billy Strange—son of a gun! We used to call him the Billy Strange doll, wind him up and he'll take over the session. Me and Hal did that too, except Strange forgot about being helpful. Southern boy. Bitching guitar player.

Leon Russell didn't last too long, he went off on his own. I called him Jesus. Look at his face—you see a very quiet-looking guy? That's exactly how he was. Hell of a piano player, always more country flavor than anything.

Carol Kaye was a guitarist who became the top Fender bass player. I think she realized she'd always be one of a thousand good guitarists, but this could be her specialty. We always said Carol was high on air, she was so effervescent and right in the middle of things. Tedesco gave her a hard time, say, "Go sit in the back and be quiet." She'd say, "The hell with you, Cheech!"

That's what everybody called Tedesco, "Cheech." Tommy was just a big fat funny Italian dude. Came from a strictly Italian neighborhood back in Buffalo or Rochester or somewhere back that way, had that very brusque blue-collar approach but when it came to music Tommy was not crude, no way at all. He played the best gut-string guitar of any sumbitch out here. Wonderful guitarist, and I mean great. Jazz, I didn't consider him on a par with Barney Kessel or

(Left to right) Susan, Pamela, Constance Weidenpesch (Susan's mother), Shelly, and Earl attending a show by comedian Alan Sherman at the Chi-Chi Club in Palm Springs, mid-sixties.

Howard Roberts, but Tommy played it all: classical gut string, flamenco, rock, jazz, Fender bass if he had to. That's why I call him the best studio guitarist ever. At least for the years I was there, and I played with all them guys, from Kessel to Larry Carlton.

Rene Hall arranged everyone's records. His stuff wasn't my favorite but I admired one thing, the simplicity of it. "You Send Me," that's a perfect example of simplicity, I can't think of any arrangement that could have been better for that tune. Just a very good commercial arranger, busy until he died. Rene came from New Orleans. When I was little, my mother used to scream at him, "Put my baby down!" because Rene used to toss me up in the air. He played calliope on those Streckfus Company boats, always used to say that thing put off so much steam you had to wear a raincoat to play it.

There was an engineer out there, I won't call his name; somebody must have asked him what he thought once, and from then on he had to assert himself. Come a time he picked the wrongest thing in the world to say to the wrongest person and boy, when he said it the studio got to where you could hear a mouse piss on cotton. Because Red Callender was very, very particular about tuning his bass. Red was known to have great pitch, he was known to hit the note. So this engineer, sounding very authoritative, says to Red one day, "By the way, Red, I think you're a little out of tune."

Everybody say, "Oh shit."

Red leans way down over his mike. The mike went about this high on him — Red was a big man.

"Out of tune, you say?"

"Yeah, Red, little bit."

Red looks at the cat like he's staring at an ant.

"And how in the *fuck* would you know?"

The really funny thing about it, even better than Red's reaction, was that when that engineer opened his mouth, you could hear everybody in the room just freeze. *Uh-oh! Wrong guy!* He could have said, "Earl, you're hitting the snare a little hard." That could have happened. But to tell Red Callender his bass was out of tune?

Red and Rene were the guys I was closest to. The white guys, I liked them and we became friends, but it was a different kind of closeness. We mixed like a sumbitch during the day. When we went to lunch, there was total socializing. But I didn't go to their homes on Sunday, I didn't go to the country club with them. I was over in the black community and they was in Canoga Park, Woodland Hills. So no, I didn't socialize with any whites to speak of; you worked with those guys but you didn't hang out.

I ain't gay or nothing but Hal Blaine was a good-looking guy. I'm sorry but Hal had pretty eyes. His real name was Belsky, which is what I called him: "Hey, Belsky!" Hal was a hustling type of guy, hustling jobs and making impressions. He had a personality for being very funny. Good storyteller, tell you one after another, right off the bat. Could have been a stand-up comic.

When I met him, he was drumming on the road for the Diamonds and I did the session. He came over and said, "Mind if I sit by?" He was very nice and paid good attention, read the part over my shoulder while I played, thanked me and I said, "Aw no, man, it's a pleasure." Somewhere or other I heard him play and knew I could recommend him. I wasn't Jesus but I wasn't worried about nobody taking my job.

Hal and I were competitors, not enemies. That made him prominent in my life, as I'm sure I was in his, unseen but prominent. A lot of people said, "Aw, Hal's nothing compared to you." I said, "You telling me I can't evaluate a good drummer." Hal never had real good jazz chops but that don't make him not a hell of a drummer for what he did.

They say Buddy Collette was one of the only people Charles Mingus didn't fuck with. Those two went to school together at Jordan, very famous L.A. high school. Buddy was one of the guys helped me get started here. He and Red Callender were the first blacks doing network TV and film; Jerry Fielding broke the color bar by getting them on the *Groucho Marx Show*.

Joe Maini was an alto player and a crazy, funny sumbitch. They tried to get him and his wife to reconcile and Joe told the judge, "I'll stop fucking chicks if she stops fucking chicks." You know what Joe Maini died of? Blew his brains out playing Russian roulette. Another cat blew his brains out: Frank Rosolino, one of the best trombone players I ever heard. Killed himself and one of his sons, crippled the other. Last person in the world you'd think would blow his brains out. Laughing, joking, comical all the time. The day he did it, he was laughing in the back room of Maurie Stein's music store, where everybody got high, all of us, the musicians in this town that liked having a good time.

Maurie Stein! There's a world I could tell about Maurie Stein! He'd been a woodwind player back in New York in the pit bands, and his brother Jule Styne was the big songwriter. Maurie used to tell stories about how tight Jule was. He'd call him up: "Hello, Jule? It's Maurie. Your *brother* Maurie. How you doing? Oh, another show? Another two hundred thousand? And your horse came in? No stuff! You're contracted for two more shows? That's wonderful! Me? I just got a little problem—I owe about thirty dollars on the light bill. Hello? Hello, Jule?"

Maurie died sometime in the eighties. In the garden of Parliament in Jerusalem you can buy a tree and plant it in somebody's name. I bought one and had it say, "Long live Maurie Stein," and I wrote that down on a piece of paper and stuck it in the Wailing Wall.

Curt Wolf had the thickest German accent you could ever hear. I used to say, "Curt, man, when you going to speak English?" He'd say, "I *em* spicking Engglish, Airl!" He was the contractor at Warner Brothers. That's a powerful position, contractor. Tell me! The producer doesn't hire you, the composer doesn't hire you—the contractor does. Composer says, "I need this, this, and this instrument" and the contractor goes and gets the players. Dave Klein was *the* contractor, and afterwards came his sons Solly Klein, the family dark sheep, and Manny Klein, the younger brother and a great trumpet player, and their sister Viola who took the phone calls, and Manny's wife Marian, we called her Dopey. That's the Klein contracting dynasty. These are big-money jobs, so that shit stayed in the family. Today it's Marian's son Gus.

Ben Barrett was strong all through there, but his thing became pretty much almost exclusively Motown. He was an ex-cellist; before that he'd been a prizefighter and we talked along those lines a lot. Another powerful contractor was Bobby Helfer, a stone bigot but a fair-minded bigot—he didn't like me but he'd hire me. Helfer tried to commit suicide with pills, changed his mind and started making calls but it was too late, nobody could get to him.

A lot of musicians became contractors—that was a gig everybody wanted, double-scale gig without having to pound your ass off—man, guys tried to rook each other out of that job. I was the first black to contract a network TV show, *Cassie and Company*. J. J. Johnson did the music and went over budget every week. I kept warning him, and he kept going over.

Quincy Jones was a brain-picker. He'd ask you, "What would you play on this?"

"Well, I'd play such and such."

"Good, play it." Brain-picker or not, I don't know anything he wrote that didn't sound great. Just good music, everything falling right in place. He had the knack, like Neal Hefti and Billy Byers, where if you just played his notes, you swung. It was written that way.

But I'd have to say Ernie Freeman was the greatest arranger I knew in the studios. Composed, arranged, played a hell of a piano. Had music so strong in his mind, he could sit down, no piano, and write a score like he was writing a letter.

Ernie was a sad case. Drunk all the time, and I hate to say it, but Ernie was a Tom. We had a push going about too few blacks in the studios and we formed an organization called MUSE, Musicians United to Stop Exclusion. Ernie flat-out refused to join. He was a guy that wouldn't speak up.

But it didn't matter if he was drunk or not; he could hear a wrong note in the last row of the orchestra. He'd wave his arms for the music to stop: "*Someone* is playing a wrong note." Stroll around and roll his eyes, grinning like a fool. Strolls all the way back to the fourth violin.

"*Mmm.* Played an E-natural, didn't we?"

"Yeah, Ernie."

"What's our part say?"

Guy looks at the music. "Oh, I'm sorry, Ernie. E-flat."

"Aha! *Hahaha!*" That crazy laugh. It was all part of his little game. *I'm roaring drunk but you still can't get nothing past me. I can hear a gnat piss!* He only clowned like that when he was lit. When he was sober, perfect decorum. "Bill, that's E-flat, not E-natural." Drunk, the act went on.

Ernie was an undersung genius. He was no big band arranger like Neal Hefti or Benny Carter, no film-score arranger like Hank Mancini. But neither could those guys write a good rock arrangement. Or as good a pop arrangement as "Strangers in the Night." That's one of the biggest hits Sinatra ever had. Ernie Freeman arranged it.

> **That's what tees me off about that Rock and Roll Hall of Fame—how many instrumentalists you see in it? Not myself, not Jamerson, not Benny Benjamin. These guys started sounds, man. These guys locked singers in, singers that had some little song, couldn't carry a tune in a basket or swing if you tied a rope around their neck.** —Earl Palmer, 1991

A photograph shows him sitting at his drums thoughtfully and a little menacingly, half-hidden in a cloud of smoke from a Sherman cigarette, a figure to strike fear and dismay in the younger cats' hearts — the man to beat, as if that were possible. Jim Keltner, a member of the next drumming generation, remembers watching him work. "The power, groove and taste—'God,' I thought, 'that feels so good!' Earl had a mysterious sophistication that was so different from the rock drumming I'd heard at the time."

Finally a man of means, with baseball stars for neighbors, he could survey L.A.'s sprawl from his hilltop house. He and Susan had two pretty little daughters now, Shelly and Pamela. Susan spent her time at the ice rink with Shelly, a promising figure skater.

To ensure his upward mobility, he put in fourteen- and sixteen-hour workdays, racing from studio to studio, leapfrogging the fellow he paid to haul his three drum kits. Not only was he supporting his second family and sending money back to his first (and to his mother and his aunt), he was a big spender who liked nothing more than setting everyone up at the bar. Apt to run out to Vegas or down to Tijuana, or just to roam L.A. after-hours joints all night long, he did his best not to let work dull the pace of his socializing.

The fat days didn't last. It's hard for anyone who wasn't a musically inclined youth in the sixties to comprehend the speed with which, in the *immediate* wake of the Beatles, kids picked up electric guitars. The first of two death knells tolled for studio musicians: self-contained bands that recorded their own material. In 1966 Beach Boy Brian Wilson took six months to create one song, "Good Vibrations"; two years earlier, hired guns had spat out entire Beach Boys albums in two or three days. Abbreviated now to distinguish it from

rock and roll, its presumably less artistic predecessor, rock was serious work, the domain of *auteurs*.

Scorning the bands' pretentiousness and lack of chops didn't put
any more money into a studio player's pocket. Luckily for the L.A.
session musicians, a countervailing trend had developed. By the late
sixties, jazz and rock had seeped into film and TV scoring. "[Jazz] is
no longer a dirty word in the film industry," reported *Down Beat* in
March 1969. The visual content of *Easy Rider* and *Zabriskie Point*
was inseparable from their rock soundtracks; a treacly pop-rock,
meanwhile, was becoming a staple of TV scores. As the seventies
began, Earl was working more soundtracks than record dates; for
the time being the film and TV calls had picked up the slack.

A second bombshell hit at the end of the decade, when Earl says
he truly saw "the handwriting on the wall." Digital electronics made
it possible for one musician to impersonate an orchestra. "Everything
changed," says session musician Paul Humphrey. "Today the cat who
scores the music has got him a module, an MT-32 or a D-110 with a
little eight-track or some ADAT. He can play the piano part, play
the bass line, play the drum track at home and then take it into the
studio and they transfer it to twenty-four- or forty-eight-track. In the
old days the contractor had his Rolodex. Now you don't even need
the contractor because you don't need musicians."

Earl's income plummeted to barely $20,000 in 1980. There was
still room for a few drummers, but a working knowledge of samplers
and drum machines was almost mandatory. "I didn't have eyes for
that," says Earl. "Harvey Mason told me, 'Use my electronic stuff if I
ain't using it.' I played it a little. Never did buy any." It's hard to
imagine Earl, his bony frame molded to the dimensions of a big
drum kit, hunched over a lunchbox-sized alphanumeric pad, tapping out space-age sounds. Time had finally passed him by.

Or had it? What Earl supplied, brown-skinned soul, remains at
the root of every major pop music style to wash over America since
1955. The rock-and-roll backbeat is a signature sound of this half
century; still uncredited, Earl is one of the true composers of contemporary America's soundtrack, the joy and might he poured into
records now forty years old as infectious as ever.

In March 1996 the following item appeared in *Addicted to Noise*,
one of the many rock magazines to have sprung up on the Internet:

In preparation for a world tour that will follow the April release of their awesome new album, *The Golden Age,* Cracker are rehearsing at a desert hideaway near Palm Springs. The first single off the album is the explosive "I
Hate My Generation," which is a kind of Roxy Music meets the Clash an-
them for the mid-'90s. The video, which was shot in L.A., features some
rather elderly musicians, including the great Earl Palmer, who played on
Sam Cooke and Little Richard sessions in the '50s. According to Cracker
leader David Lowery, when Palmer was asked if he would be able to play
along with the songs, he gave Lowery a look and said, "I invented this shit."

We had a saying: the whites in L.A. moved west until their hats floated. Baldwin Hills is professional blacks: doctors, lawyers, musicians, ballplayers.
Maury Wills was one of the early blacks in there. He didn't have any trouble
from the neighbors, just didn't get invited for dinner.

I built a house there, overlooking the Los Angeles Basin from West L.A. all
the way downtown. I used to sit outside and listen the city come to life. It's all
quiet until you hear a faint hum. Automobiles hitting the freeways. A soft hum
that builds, never loud, until you notice it ain't quiet and silent like it was an
hour before. At first I looked down on the smog, just a brown haze. After a few
years I didn't see it anymore, which told you what? You in it.

My house wasn't fancy. I built what I needed and left room on the side for
a vegetable garden and a pool. Earl Bostic lived behind me. He said, "Pardno,
you just cut off my view!" I said, "You ain't had none to start with. Why didn't
you buy my lot?"

Two houses down from Bostic was Paul Robi from the Platters, whose
daughter married Lynn Swann and Sugar Ray Leonard. Next to Robi was Red
Callender, whose ex-wife Toni is still there. To my left was Mr. and Mrs.
Marple. He owned Nutone—you know, the intercoms you put in the house so
you can hear the baby. White couple, one of the few that didn't leave.

The times I was out here as a kid, this city right here was pretty bigoted.
Come 1960 it still was. Far more subtle, but there. Aw, there's none of that in
the music business, you think, until you make it to the big-money echelon.
Then you realize why you wasn't there before—*because* it's the big-money
echelon.

In Los Angeles you couldn't expect any help and didn't get it. I got myself
to blame for not making no decent investments, but there was people, man,
leaned right across you as if you wasn't there and told another guy to buy a
stock. One day at Capitol me and Ernie Freeman were the only blacks on the
gig, as usual. A guy went around the room and invited everybody except us to

his daughter's wedding. I know we didn't know him as well as the others, but mister, say *something*. During a coffee break the subject came up about Orval Faubus, the segregationist in Arkansas. This same guy's opinion was, "Segregation is a terrible thing, but those people," meaning us, "have to be patient. Things like that don't change overnight."

He turned to me and said, "Do you or don't you agree with me?"

I said, "Man, that's a rough question." I kept scratching my head. He didn't notice I was stepping on his toe, harder and harder.

"Hey, you're hurting my toe!" he finally yells.

"Have a little patience, man. I'll get off in a minute."

He got my point. We became good friends.

At first I was just looking for work, it wasn't until later that I felt like a pioneer. You begin to notice, "Jesus, ain't nobody else but me doing big-time film calls." Until the mid-sixties me and Red and Buddy were the only blacks working steady in film studios and network TV and high-prestige record dates. There was others spasmodically—Bill Green on tenor, Jimmy Bond on bass— but I'm not talking about every now and then, I'm talking about day in, day out.

On a typical workday I'd get up at seven, leave the house at twenty-five to eight. I was driving a Florentine Mists olive, sparkle-finished Cadillac that was gorgeous. I'd get in the studio, give my drums a little tilt here and there, play a lick to see I'm reaching everything all right. Then get up and have a coffee and smoke a cigarette and talk to whoever's there. Guys would be on the phone calling their service. Tedesco and Snuff Garrett might be playing cards.

"Let's run it down, guys."

The first downbeat you got was to rehearse the tune. Just making sure you got the notes. Then you might start interpreting. Producer says, "Give me little more of that New Orleans bass drum, Earl." You didn't want to tinker too much, though—why keep playing it and playing it, lose the fight in the gym?

On the other hand, if somebody fucked up, you had to start all over again. Ain't like today, where you just edit a mistake out. So we had a challenge: make the thirty-seventh damn take sound just as fresh as the first.

Sessions went nine to twelve, two to five, and eight to eleven. Plenty of times I worked all three *and* squeezed in a jingle. I'd tear out of the morning session late, as often as not. I'd have already called the next date: "Sorry, I'm going overtime here. I'll be a half hour late if you still want me." Sometime, but seldom, they'd call someone else.

I'd call Susan, see how she's doing. "What's for dinner?" You'd run down to Brewer's on a break, have a drink, run right back. They had a bartender called Ray, drunk all day long, exactly the kind of guy who gets liver cirrhosis, them

The Man: a figure to strike fear and dismay in the younger cats' hearts, 1966.
(Michael Ochs Archive)

beady drunken eyes and a boiling complexion, but that man knew what everybody drank and he set it up before your ass hit the chair.

If the afternoon session didn't go over I'd visit Erickson's, a Swedish steam
bath where you could lay out. After you'd had a steam bath and a rubdown, you

took a nap—man, talk about sleep good! Steam bath, rubdown, shower, nap—*mwahh!* Just feel great. Then a nice big dinner and go to your night date.

I was just so busy and active, man, I kept going. I might stop at the Parisian Room on the way home, or Bostic's Flying Fox, or Spider's after-hours joint. I crashed in the studio plenty times, lay down on the floor just like back with Miss Ida's in them old theater lobbies. Stay out all night, get some coke to perk me up, and go right back to work.

You picked up your check at the union; that's where the record company sent them. They used to say about me and Hal Blaine that we'd go down to the union, throw a briefcase on the counter, and say, "Fill 'er up."

Back in the sixties the union had power—oh yeah. If you a record label or film studio, musicians would not work with your ass without a union contract. First thing I did when I got out here was join the union. It ain't that way now. Places weren't hiring scabs then. Unions were strong all over the country. But the handwriting went on the wall when those controllers went out and Reagan said, "Fuck you, you can't strike." I'm talking about the handwriting on the wall. The Republicans has denutted all unions.

As I was coming into my supposed glory years, the main studios I worked at was Radio Recorders, Master Recorders, United, Ocean Way, Western Recorders, Gold Star, Sunset Sound, Wally Heider's, RCA, Capitol, and TTG.

We cut "You've Lost That Lovin' Feelin'" at Gold Star. I hardly had anything to do but play tom-toms and tune my snare drum real loose and they echoed it. Played a big old heavy afterbeat on the snare and tom-tom. As a matter of fact, Spector rarely told me what to do at all.

He took two days to get eight measures the way he wanted them. Right before the pause where Bill Medley comes in for the second verse, Phil wanted the tempo to stay constant but sound like it's slowing down. I'm glad I wasn't playing on that part. He kept shaking his head. "Nope. Nope. Nope." Not angry and nutty, just not satisfied. In fact, he was very patient. Each beat had to be a little behind where it would normally land, about a thirty-second note behind. Not knowing much about notation, he couldn't explain it very well. He should have had somebody write it out: put the first note right on the beat, next note a thirty-second note behind the beat, and so on. That would have been exactly the way to get what he wanted to hear, but he wasn't enough musician to explain it. Nobody knew what he was talking about, though they appreciated it when it finally came off.

Something about this little motherfucker, you could tell right away he knew what he wanted and wouldn't compromise. That's what impressed me, not the music. It was different, but I'd heard things different and unique and nothing ever happened to them. Everything this guy touched turned to gold, until that "River Deep—Mountain High" that he thought was going to be a gold mine in itself.

Spector wasn't an arranger of notes; I don't know if he could write no notes at all. He was an arranger of ideas, of the elements that make a hit record. If there is any genius in him, that's where it was. He had his finger on what other producers would die for: he knew what the kids wanted to hear. But you ain't getting me to accept him as no musician. Who are people going to listen to a hundred years from now? Who? Phil Spector or Duke Ellington? Ellington is on a goddamn stamp, what's Phil Spector on? The world knows Duke Ellington, the world don't know Phil Spector. The rock world knows Phil Spector.

Let me tell you, Sam Cooke was a stylist. I enjoyed doing Sam Cooke, I tried to do it as well as I could. But I don't put Sam Cooke on the same scale as Sarah Vaughan, nowhere near. I'd have to call out fifteen singers. Sarah Vaughan, Ella Fitzgerald, Nat Cole, Billy Eckstine—*then* I'd get to Sam Cooke.

Ain't a lot memorable happened on those Sam Cooke dates. I wasn't looking at these songs as magic. It was another song you did that day. "You Send Me," that was very simple. I remember the stop-time in the bridge made me think of tap dancing. You know, that may have been my idea. I sort of remember suggesting that. The triplet fill on "Twistin' the Night Away," that's just something I was doing around those days on a lot of different things—you can hear it on the record with Dizzy at Monterey.

I hung with Sam sometime, not too often. He hung with J. W. Alexander always, Bobby Womack a lot, at the Gaiety Delicatessen on Sunset next to Lou Adler's Roxy. You'd meet a lot of girls up there. They went gaga over Sam. I was there with him not long before he got shot. Six of us: J. W., the Simms Twins, Sam and me and Cliff White, Sam's guitar player. We were talking about Jesse Belvin and this kid Mel Carter, whose singing Sam liked, and about Zelda Sands, who was this Mel's manager and had I mean a gorgeous body. Everybody talked about Zelda. God*damn* it! I asked Sam about his gig at the Copa, and he laughed and said, "A little nigger in the Copa!"

Aw, Sam was nice to hang with, a very classy type of dude. But if you going to ask me about singers, the most talented I ever worked with were two: Sarah Vaughan and Nat Cole.

The only date I did with Nat, my favorite male singer, was "Ramblin' Rose" and whatever else was on that session. Here's a man who had a beautiful voice, always masculine, but tender and warm. His portrayal of a song had such understanding; it was like he wrote everything he sang. His diction was exquisite but it never sounded contrived. When Nat wasn't singing, he'd cuss like everybody else. Scratch his chin when he was thinking: ". . . son of a bitch. . . ."

I met Nat in New Orleans, long before I worked with him. He was friends with Paul Gayten, who brought me to Nat's hotel room on Bienville Street. I had written a song to give him, "Kitty"—remember that twin I went with, Catherine Evelyn Walker?

Nat said, "I don't take nothing on the road, send it to my manager."

I never did. I thought he was fluffing me off. And years later this man says to me: "You never sent me your song."

"Man, I thought you was bullshitting!"

"I don't bullshit, I deal with everything everybody sends me. I just don't read nothing on the road."

"Shit, I didn't know that."

"That's because you stupid." I liked him. He was one of these people come into the studio seemed like they already knew the arrangement. Listen to it once and cut it, zap.

Sarah Vaughan was a chick that liked to hang. She was the Hang Out Queen, outhang anybody, drinking and getting high, day and night, talking and laughing and joking. I did a date with Sass, we couldn't finish it for being high and hung over. We all just quit and went home. She had a mouth, too. Guys got furious at her but they took a swing at *you*. Anytime you was with her, you ran the risk of getting punched.

Sass always sounded to me like someone was playing an instrument that sounded a little like a voice. She could sound like any horn, man, saxophone, trumpet. She could make her voice sound like a cello. Sometimes to show her range, she'd sing very low. That's the only distasteful thing I heard Sass do; I guess I looked on a woman singing that deep as freakish. Sarah *was* a freak. Her voice was an extension of her brain: if she thought of it, she could sing it.

That *Explosive Side of Sarah Vaughan* might be my favorite of all the albums I made, but the greatest time I heard Sarah sing was informal. She came over to the house one night and said, "I don't want nobody to ask me to sing." Well, we got to feeling good. We were all standing around the piano: Harold Battiste, me, my aunts Josephine and Nita, my cousins Gus and Verdell, Harold and Lydia Land, Buddy Montgomery. And I could've told you Sass would start singing. She knew every song and what she didn't know, she'd scat her ass off. I just remember being in heaven.

There were times me and Susan had troubles. Susan had a temper and she was very jealous. I gave her reason, too: for lack of a better word, let's say I was a dog. But not all our fights were about women. At one time she was becoming an alcoholic. She backed off, thank God, when she got busy around the ice rink with Shelly, who turned out to be a hell of a figure skater.

I've slapped Susan. I never beat her up—I have a bad temper, but you're a wife beater or you're not. I pushed her down. She knocked the shit out of me, too. Framed me with a painting. I'd met some Australian guys in a topless bar in Hollywood, real nice guys, and we piled into Susan's brand-new Falcon to go to another joint. I was supposed to be home long, long before. Anyway, I had to take a pee in the bushes. Being pretty drunk, I got turned around, and me and the Australians never got back together. So I found some Mexican guys at a parking lot who said they'd take me home when they left off work. I got in their car and fell asleep, thinking, "Those Australians stole my car!" The Mexicans drove me home. They had to help me out of the car and up the walk. I open the door and Susan screams, "Don't bring your drunken friends in here, you son of a bitch!"—*bang*. Over the head with a painting. "You drunken bastard!" *Bang*. I was wearing that painting around my neck, pissed off like mad, but I kept laughing because all I could think was, "I've been framed!"

Next day was Easter and I was supposed to go egg hunting with the children. I said to Susan, "I ain't feeling so good."

"I don't care how you're feeling, we promised these children and we're going!"

First I had to find the car. I went back to the bar where I'd met the Australians and it was sitting right in the parking lot. Keys on the floor, windows rolled up. Nice cats! So we all went Easter egg hunting at Hank and Mary Anne Levine's up in Laurel Canyon. Hank was an arranger, Mary Anne taught dance. They had a dirt area where you parked, then you walked past the pool to the house. I threw up in the pool. Shelly and Pamela yelled, "Oh, Daddy!" Nobody swimming, thank God. I was so embarrassed, man, so embarrassed. Mary Anne said, "Earl, don't worry about it," and she put some cold rags on my head. Susan was furious. Poor Pamela was ashamed but Shelly laughed her ass off, because to Shelly I was a damn comedian.

When I look through my ledgers, I see so much I didn't even know I was on. Stuff that's gone out of my mind completely. Go in a session, you never knew who the artist was going to be. If I didn't get their name I'd write "boy," "girl," "group," which is no help to me now. I wish I remembered more of them dates, but I don't feel too bad about it because it's so damn long ago and there is so much of it.

JANUARY 28, 1966 — TINA TURNER, PHIL, CAPP, $303.34. I mean Spector had musicians all over Gold Star for this one. Strings in tiers, man. "River Deep Mountain High." Bombed its ass off. Came and went right fast. That shattered him. It would have shattered anybody.

I had never seen a woman had that kind of nervous energy. It was never a forced thing with her; when she wasn't singing she talked fast, moved fast, twitched. We were all hollering, "Dance, Tina, dance!" and she kept laughing. She was a very energetic little woman. They'd just started in with short skirts, wasn't up to real minis yet, but above the knees, man, and Tina was looking good. I've always been a leg man, and as you know, this woman had legs.

Ike wasn't there, which suited me. The first time I met Ike he'd just come in town. He wanted to pay everybody cash. I said I didn't work for no cash. He starts to cuss me out and opens a briefcase with stacks of cash and a gun. That's about what I expected. I'd heard he was a thug.

"Who the hell are you?" he says.

"I'm Palmer, and I don't work no cash dates. I'm a union musician."

"What I'm supposed to do, make out a contract just for you?"

"You going to have to do something like that, because I don't want no cash money. When I get fined fifteen hundred dollars by the union, are you gonna pay?" He wound up filing a contract for me alone.

That was my first memory of them. I got kind of an insight as to how he treated her when she was laughing and joking and he turned around saying, "I can't hear myself think, would you please be quiet?" I didn't talk to Tina that first time; tell the truth, I may have been a little intimidated of having a confrontation with this sumbitch if I looked at his woman wrong. But I looked that she was fine.

Ike himself looked like a mean son of a gun. Had his hair conked in big waves, little goatee under his lip. One guy in their band was from New Orleans: Nose, as we call him, Leo Nocentelli from the Meters. He was young and gangly then. We talked about New Orleans and I asked him how it was to work with Ike. Nose was pretty displeased.

I ran into Ike later on, around the time he was starting to get in trouble. I went to Bolic Sound on LaBrea, where he had a studio, to pick up a friend on the way to a Lakers game. He came in and I said, "Hello, Ike," and he said, "What's happening man?" that type of brusque thing. He was not the type who encouraged chitchat.

I saw her later, too. She used to rehearse in my friend Van's building and I'd stick my head in, say hello, and she'd stop and we'd talk about old days. She's a nice lady. I wasn't ignorant of the fact that this was still a fine woman, little more mature, maybe, but still fine. But there was kind of a genuine good feeling of seeing her and discussing around the old times. We didn't mention her troubles but I felt good she'd made it through. Because I never knew her to deserve the stuff that Ike done to her, in any kind of way. But I'll tell you something else: he made that girl's career.

SEVERAL DATES, MID-SIXTIES — MOTOWN RECORDS. Motown had two sisters called the Lewis Sisters. Nice friendly white girls. In fact, I had a little fling with one. We were recording them two, three times a week, and as far as I know, they never made one record for Motown. What was going on was Motown recorded these things and sent the tracks back to Detroit, where they put the real vocal on it. Rather than transport their artists out here, they used us and saved money on travel and overtime.

See, at that time, if you doing a session with vocals, the vocalist had to be there. Say you did a session with Diana Ross: you could not bring the musicians in and do tracks for her to sing over later. Other companies were willing to abide by that but Motown wanted to cheat. I don't know whose idea the scheme was; I assume it was the two guys that led those sessions, Frank Wilson and Hal Davis. It saved Motown money for a while, but as soon as the union found out, Motown had to pay up. But they couldn't possibly have reimbursed us all the money they'd saved.

We worked at Bob Ross's studio mostly, little place on Romaine south of Sunset. All of us did these things: me, Carol, Tedesco, Rene Hall, Bill Pittman, Ray Pohlman, Red Callender. I always figured it was Carol who blew the whistle. I can't think of anyone that had the balls but her.

Motown was a cold-blooded operation. Berry Gordy was a nervous little guy, always in a hurry. You know how some people don't turn their head to look at things, just shift their eyes sideways? That's him. We never really had a conversation, me and Gordy, he didn't talk to no side musicians.

NOVEMBER 11, 1966 — BOBBY DARIN, $130.07. I don't remember the date but I remember Darin. He was head above shoulders more professional than most of the little singers I was doing around then: Paul Anka, Fabian, Bobby Rydell. Wayne Newton was a long-legged short-torso kid but Darin struck me as professional right off the bat.

DATE UNKNOWN, JIMMY DURANTE, TTG STUDIO. Avi Hadani, who owned TTG, was an Israeli fighter pilot and a war ace. Every time one of them wars broke out, Avi had to go back. We made up a lot of jokes about that. He was kind of a hero to us. We waited two days on Jimmy Durante to do an AC spark plug jingle at TTG. They found him at some racetrack. He came in and it was just like you known him all your life. Come in making jokes, who's this guy, who's that guy? Cracked everybody up because we was glad to see him, we were finally going to get it over with—and he's Jimmy Durante! He's known to be funny, you're hanging on his every word. Bob Stone was leaning on his bass, had his arm around the neck and Durante looks at him and says, "You gonna marry that broad?"

JANUARY 28, 1967—PAUL REVERE AND THE RAIDERS, $250.58. That was Hal's client. I don't know what I was doing there.

JANUARY 2, 1968—PRIME MINISTERS, $81.25. These were young kids that came from New Orleans. The drummer was a guy named Skip or Chip. The cops beat him to death. Stopped him in traffic or something, but he was feisty and flamboyant and got in a discussion with them. Jim Gordon took his place—that's the first time I met Jimmy. They were a good band, young white kids who played rock but with a New Orleans flavor. Broke up and scattered.

JANUARY 3, 1968—JACKIE WILSON, COUNT BASIE, $81.25. Teddy Reig asked me to do *Manufacturers of Soul*, Basie's album with Jackie Wilson. Harold Jones, Basie's drummer at the time, didn't play rock, which is part of why Teddy hired me. At the session he asked me, "What can we do to make these charts a little more commercial?"

"One thing, we could try using a tambourine."

"Who can we get to play tambourine? Larry Bunker?" That made no sense—a top-notch percussionist, just to play tambourine?

"Man, let Harold play tambourine," I said.

"Can he?"

"All niggers play tambourine, Teddy." Harold Jones played tambourine and got paid for it. I still have a medallion he gave me for that.

Teddy once tried to hire me to join Basie. "There was a time I would have paid to join this band," I told him, "but I can't afford to now." Teddy said he understood. I said, "Man, I'm probably go home and get drunk after this."

SEPTEMBER 5, 1968—BUCK OWENS, $81.25. Buck Owens looked real sharp, like a German officer. He had his own drummer, who said, "Well, why don't you play washboard?" I said, "Okay." When I walked back in with a washboard, everyone looked at me kind of funny, but I don't remember any insults. And a bunch of country guys, that's where I would have expected it. I went in belligerently prepared.

I cut Tennessee Ernie Ford, Johnny Cash, Speedy West, all them country guys. Willie Nelson, Brenda Lee, Roy Lanham, the Sons of the Pioneers. The very first day Glen Campbell came in town, he crashed on my floor. Guy named Jerry wanted to do an old Ted Lewis number, "Me and My Shadow Strolling Down," and he wanted me to write a rock arrangement because of my success with "In the Mood." Glen drove this Jerry all the way from Albuquerque, New Mexico, and crashed on my rug while Jerry and I talked. My daughter Shelly was no more than two. She said, "Daddy, that man's sleeping on the floor," and she went and put a pillow under his head. Glen Campbell is no bigot but when he brought his father out here, the old man said right in my earshot, "Damn, Glen, you right! That's one good nigger!" Glen like to died, but I said, "Let him alone, Glen, that's just the way he's used to speaking."

OCTOBER 17, 1968 — NEIL YOUNG, $326.87. I'm telling you, man, I don't remember it.

NUMEROUS DATES, 1970–71 — DELLA REESE TV SHOW. Best big band I ever played with. Sweets Edison, Bob Brookmeyer, Bobby Bryant, Ray Brown, Herb Ellis, Joe Pass. Until the *Tonight Show* came out here, that was *the* big band on the coast.

AUGUST 1970 (SIX DATES) — *Zachariah*, MGM. That's the hardest session I ever did. They made a movie called *Zachariah*, a real hokey satire on cowboy days. Elvin Jones played a gunslinger. In his big scene, instead of saying "Draw," he says, "Gimme them drumsticks" and plays a big solo.

Jimmy Haskell was the composer. Jimmy's a guy that did a little bit garbage of anything. "Oh yeah, we can do that." Probably at a lesser price, too. That kind of guy works the shit out of you, because he's aiming to please. He'll go past breaks, rush you, come in with the score half-written and write the rest right there. One of the last times I worked for him, Jimmy was sitting there eating peanuts out of his pocket writing the score.

Anyway, somehow or other the sound got messed up. The drum solo had to be played all over again. Jimmy told the producers, "Oh yeah, we can do that."

I said, "Wait a minute. I'm not going to do this. I'm not going to fucking do this, man."

Haskell said, "Why?"

"Do you know who this is? I can't match Elvin, nobody can. The man is a genius." Finally I said, "All right. Give me two hours." I took my lunch and a Moviola machine and some music paper, went across the alley into a little room, and transcribed Elvin's whole solo. Took me two-and-a-half hours to write out a five-minute solo. Then I played it. I not only got paid overtime, I got a bonus when they realized how hard that was and how near it came to being perfect.

NUMEROUS DATES, 1970–74 — BAKED POTATO, SWEETS EDISON. Sunday nights, always a Sunday night. Never paid much, twenty bucks, but we drank for free and got a lot of coke. Don Randi, who owned the place, asked me about getting a group in there. I said, "Why don't you get Sweets? He's going to bring all the pimps and hookers in. Every musician that comes in town going to come by and see Sweets." Sure enough, the Basie band came through and they all sat in. Ellington band, same thing. Red Foxx came in to work out his nightclub routine; he'd get up there and stay an hour or more. The band was me, Sweets, Plas Johnson, Dolo Coker on piano, Larry Gales on bass. That's some of the best jazz I played here. Sweets is a stylist, a great stylist: the minute you hear him you know him.

JUNE–AUGUST 1973 (TWELVE DATES) — BONNIE RAITT (LOWELL GEORGE, PRODUCER). Lowell George was a fat short guy had this big old rustic beautiful house above a nudist colony in the Malibu hills. I did a session there once: Lowell, Freebo, and a little skinny blond kid, long nose, long hair. Real sweet little attitude. Wachtel, that's it, Waddy Wachtel! Little pinch-nez glasses. I remember him because I liked him. Them broads didn't hide or nothing, I guess they were used to being watched! Telling you, it's a shame I don't remember any of those Bonnie sessions.

JANUARY 18, 1973 — INAUGURATION, $1,500.00. Don Costa, Sinatra's man, was musical director of the thing. Sinatra was emcee. Now, Don wanted one drummer, me, to be available to all the acts. As it turned out, everybody brought their own band, so I wound up only playing with Roger Miller. All I had to do was walk around tasting hors d'oeuvres here and there. Since I was with Sinatra's man, they gave me a Secret Service button that let me go in any room I wanted. All the guests are wondering, *Who is he?* They didn't have many black Republicans then to speak of, so they all figure this is somebody they should know and don't. It dawns on me: they're worried. They don't know who this nigger Republican is that's big enough to be in this particular room.

Who is this nigger? That's exactly what they thinking. *Who is this nigger? For him to be in here, must be somebody we supposed to know!* I'm reading their minds. *Who is this nigger? Must be an important nigger, an important nigger Republican* AND WE DON'T KNOW HIM! *Jesus, let's don't fuck up. Somebody find out who he is!*

Nobody knew, except Mrs. Pat Boone. She saw me and came running over.

"Earl, what are you doing here?"

"Well hi, Shirley. How's Pat?"

"Wait, I'll get him!" And she went and gets Pat and we're shaking hands and hugging because I did a lot of work with him at Dot Records, and little Debbie's hugging me and Shirley's hugging me and Shirley goes and gets her daddy, the old country guy Red Foley, because she thought I knew him but I didn't. And the guests must have all breathed a great sigh of relief. *Now we can find out who this nigger is.* Everybody came swarming around Pat, who gave them the story.

Oh! He's an entertainment nigger! One of those kind, by God!

So now they all come up to me. "Oh, Mr. Palmer, are you having a nice time?" Mrs. Nixon, for one, very sweet lady.

"Yes, Mrs. President, I am, thank you very much." I *was* feeling pretty good—I'd just smoked some weed with Pete Fountain's band and Al Hirt.

I met them all, I'm telling you, everyone but Nixon. John Dean was the only one asked me anything about what I did.

"Who are you going to be playing with?"

"Well, I don't know yet. That's why Mr. Costa had me come along."

"You mean you'd be able to play with any of them?"

"Sure, that's what we do all the time, play with anybody we have to."

"Must be quite an experience." His wife walked up and he introduced us. Agnew was very busy; I must say the man was busy, the president not being there. Must have been writing his speech.

Like them or not, look who these people were! I'm not a celebrity-conscious motherfucker but you don't have to be told when you in the presence of power. I got introduced to Agnew by Ehrlichman or Haldeman, whichever. The bald, stern-faced one. Ehrlichman. Mean looking. Little jowls beginning.

I told Agnew, "Congratulations!" and said, "You remind me of somebody I've had occasion to have a couple of drinks with." He almost guessed who it was: Ed McMahon.

I was shocked when Sinatra exploded. They got their signals crossed and he introduced somebody, I can't remember who, but Joey Heatherton came on.

Wrong act. Sinatra hit the roof. I was in his dressing room with Costa and he storms in. "These cocksuckers don't know what the fuck they're doing!" I hadn't realized until then what a rough guy this was. "Wait till my man gets in there, he'll straighten this shit out." I'm wondering, "What does he mean, his man? Nixon's *in*." You know who he was talking about? Agnew. He didn't like Nixon worth a shit. That was his man, old Spiro.

Isn't it funny how nobody ever came up and asked me who I was? They all figured they supposed to know. The only other musicians who had this button were Costa and his brother Leo, who Costa brought along as contractor so Leo could make all that money contracting all them bands in one night. Contracting, man—that's a good-paying gig.

SEPTEMBER 25, 1973—*Midnight Special*, $300.00. She came up the hall at NBC when I was getting my shoes shined. I said, "Hello there." Nothing wrong with saying hello.

She turned and said hi. Slowed down.

I said, "How are you? My, you look awful good."

She said, "Thank you." I got down off the shoeshine stand and talked to her. She was pretty, and very shapely. Had an Afro, not too big. One feature I liked about her, she had a little space between her teeth. That do something to you, too? She said she was there to be on some kind of talk show.

I said, "What's your name?"

"Angela," she said. She never mentioned Davis.

I suggested we meet for lunch. She said, "Yeah, that would be nice." She didn't turn a cartwheel, but she responded. I wouldn't have imagined her to be receptive, and this is why I didn't grasp who she was till long after.

We met at the Carriage House, where Donte's is now. I told her what I did and how busy I was. She wanted to know, "Do you have any control over what you do, over your work situation?"

"Control? Yeah, I take the job or I don't."

"Well, you're rather prominent as a musician. You should be doing this and this and this," and suddenly she's talking all kind of politics.

I said, "Wait a minute—why?"

She said, "Because there's the exploiters and the exploited."

I said, "Honey, nobody's exploiting me, I'm just working." I got a little indignant right there. She don't know me from Adam and she's already made a decision as to I'm being exploited and I don't know what's what in my job. I didn't tell her she didn't know what she was doing in whatever she did. What made her think because I flirted with her and hit on her that I was automatically an idiot? This had turned into something that had nothing to do with two people meeting and flirting, it was a real confrontation.

She said, "Well, I can see there's no way of reaching you. You're just not prepared to hear what I have to say."

"You're damn right," I said, and got up and walked away.

Susan was forty-two when she died. She began to feel a lump in her breast, and they examined her and said, "We have to remove the breast." I wasn't too concerned, because they thought they caught it in time. But she started to suffer pains in her back. Come to find out, cancer had went into her liver.

And the doctors said if it had been in only one part of the liver, they could have cut that part out. But it was there and there and there, and they couldn't cut there and there and there.

Dr. Ted Haller was the one who told me. He was very sad. I'd had a clue right off the bat, he'd looked so sad. We knew Ted way back in '57. His brother Austin birthed both of our girls and Ted was our doctor, Dr. Ted Haller. Austin was a piano player; as a matter of fact, he'd worked his self through medical school that way.

When Ted told me, I almost dropped to my knees. What about they had doctors in Mexico had some kind of cure with apricots? What about that?

He said there was nothing to those things. "If there was I'd say so," he said, "though I'd be going against the rules of the AMA. You go ahead on and try it, but all it'll do is break you."

She was outside, in the examination room. When he called her in and told her, she and I both began to cry. She said, "Do I have any chance?"

"I'll never tell you you don't have any chances, Susan. Hopefully we'll find something that can slow it down."

You know, she took it so goddamn well. I always figured she wouldn't. We went and had some dinner and I was trying to be as normal as possible. That was my first thought, was keep things normal.

Susan didn't want to tell the children or her mother; she didn't want to break them up. The doctors agreed, for the simple reason that it would make things more traumatic for her. Because she was really fighting to live. If there was any way she could, she was going to live long enough to see her daughters grow up. They'd find some cure, something, so she could manage to see them grow up. Because she had such great hope for Shelly with that ice skating; Shelly was really getting good at that.

It was about eight months from getting the news until she died, winter to autumn 1972. I had to keep it from the girls and keep going. Drinking my ass off. After a while the girls knew. They knew she had cancer, they didn't know it was terminal. You don't burden them with that, man, they were hardly in junior high school.

The last few months Susan stayed in the hospital. She'd ask how they were. I'd say, "They doing fine." She'd say, "Well, how's your work going?" I'd say, "It's all right. I get so tired sometimes, I canceled some." She'd say, "I know." She'd smile. She was just fighting, doing everything they told her, always wanting to know what else she could do. She came home once, she just wanted to. She knew she couldn't stay.

Sometimes when I went to see her, I could tell she'd been crying. She never wanted to cry in front of me, but I could tell. I guess things would just get overbearing for her.

You could see her weakening, but she never gave up. I hope I face death with the courage she had. Because you hear a lot of talk about courage this, courage that, but I witnessed it, firsthand. She didn't resort to prayer, she never was a religious person. She didn't say, "I want to become a Christian." She would have considered that hypocritical.

She was really failing one day, and very weakly tried to joke. Said, "I sure wish I had a cigarette."

I said, "Girl, you don't want no cigarette, what you want is some hash." She said, "Well, maybe." We was both crying. That's the last conversation we had.

When she died, she had been unconscious for a day and a half. One of the nurses phoned me. "You might want to be here. Susan's very weak." So I did go there that evening, and I stayed, and early evening of the next day she passed. Her friend Lydia Land and I was there. We were sitting simply on the side of the bed, and watched that instrument fade to zero. I always expected there'd be something when you pass, some sign you're going, even if you're unconscious. There was nothing, other than that machine. And then you could see her stomach wasn't moving. I broke down crying. I kissed her hand. Lydia was crying really full. The nurse came in. Dr. Haller had just come in the hospital and they called him. He leaned over and kissed her forehead. She was just very pale, wasn't nothing distorted about her, just very pale, even her lips, there was no redness in her lips.

I went to Lydia and Harold's and we had a drink, and then I went home. Pamela started crying before I said anything. They didn't go to school anymore until after the funeral.

People spoke. Eleanor Slatkin, who'd given Susan flying lessons. Betty Agee, the girls' pediatrician. She and Susan used to go to the racetrack after

Susan took the girls for a checkup. Ernie Freeman spoke. He talked about how Susan had come to be like a sister, how he always knew where he could go and be comforted and sit down and get a little drink when he needed it. He said they all knew how I must feel because everyone knew how much the woman meant to me, what an anchor she was to me. Dr. Austin Haller spoke, said how he and his brother had become our friends, and that he would sorely miss her.

Lots of times afterwards, the girls and I went up to her grave site and sat and talked and thought about her. My grave site is there, next to hers and her mother's. We found a plot where if you stand right there you can see Baldwin Hills, because that's what Susan said she wanted. We went up there just last year, Shelly and Pamela and I, and we sat up there and remembered.

I can't think of anything I would want more, at this stage of my life, than to be with her. You couldn't have known a greater lady, man. She was my teacher. She made such sacrifices for me. I have so much to thank her for. And I wish she could see her daughters—how proud she'd be of those girls!

The first thing I'd noticed about that hippie era was the names the groups started taking on, the Grateful Dead, the Kitchen Sink. I didn't react much to hippies, I'd been getting high long before these kids were born. But Afros! I was pissed with that, and you know why? All of a sudden I had fifteen, sixteen beautiful hats in my closet I couldn't wear. The hat made a ring around your head; the top of your hair stood straight up, the sides stuck out! Take off your hat and your hair's a fright! I was pissed! I didn't wear an Afro but so long, but by that time hats were out. I was hoping they'd come back, but they never have. Afros killed them. But I'm still hoping. That's why I've got a closetful of them. Did I ever show you those shirts I have, big roll-collar shirts? Fifty years old. Wright's Tailor Shop on Rampart Street. It's what they call the cutaway roll. That was Eckstine's style. I told Billy before he died, "Man, I got some of these shirts." He said, "You think they'd fit me?" Maybe I'll start wearing them, start a new style.

Everything ends. I used to say, if I'd had a hell of a lot more ego when I saw it start to slip away, I'd have done one of two things: shot myself or already been a millionaire.

It didn't hit me right in the face. Maybe it should have. Ain't like I wasn't affected—I felt it in my pocket. Producers started letting groups record their own music, instead of session men doing it. We talked about this every day, talking about it and breaking it down, decimating it and trying to theorize it, what happened, what caused it—me, Tedesco, Carol Kaye, Bill Pittman, all these people who'd been working together, Red Callender, Buddy Collette. Damn near everyone saw his work start slowing down.

There was a whole new cadre of film composers and arrangers that wasn't Mancini and Schifrin. I look at film credits now and see people I don't even know; they all came up in the electronic era. I don't find any deficit in their underscoring, the music you put behind a scene. Where I find it is in their main titles. The theme songs are not memorable anymore. The older movie composers, they wrote main titles that became great standards.

And then it finally hit me straight on, where you say, "Oh! This is why it's happened and why it's going to get worse." If you remember, there was a movie called *Chariots of Fire* and one man, this Vangelis, did the whole score. Had electric drums, electric piano, had all this stuff. One man. And he got a Oscar. I said, "There you go. There's the end of it right there."

It wasn't just that work dropped off. There was younger guys now, the Johnny Guerins, Harvey Masons, Jim Keltners. I broke Paul Humphrey in, and you know when I knew he'd supplanted me? A Dixieland trombone player named Conrad Janis was always trying to hire me but I was too busy. One day I needed work and called him up. He'd hired Paul. I worked a job with Benny Carter where I couldn't make rehearsals, so I sent a guy in my place. Just so they had a drummer. Then I came in and cut the part straight through, sight unseen. Benny said it was the most impressive exhibit of sight-reading he'd seen in his life. But the guy that worked the rehearsals for me, Sherman Ferguson, has worked with Benny ever since.

I always knew one day it would happen to me. There's always somebody coming along that's real good. When I came out here, it happened to somebody else. *I* came along.

I sent out notices saying I was available. But the contractors I'd worked for, wasn't but a few of them still active and more and more they were calling younger guys. I got a message they needed a black drummer for a cop show, to work on-screen. I said, "Okay, when you want me?" It turned out they was thinking of my son Donald. He'd become a hell of a drummer—worked with Sly Stone, Willie Bobo. But I could never get him to read. I'd say, "Learn to read this music. I don't care how well you play, you've got to know how to read for me to recommend you."

He'd say, "Suppose I get with a group and get a hit record? I'll make a million dollars, won't need to learn to read."

"Go learn to read, if you're serious about this music. Sometime down the future, if you ain't a millionaire, you can teach."

"Are *you* going to teach?"

"If I have to, yes. I'm a graduate of music school." But he never learned. I sent him on gigs with Duane Eddy. We did a father-and-son drum bit on the Della Reese show that was a bitch. He was with Sly Stone when he got fucked up on acid, and by the time he got his head together, the doors wasn't open for him anymore.

Leaving Baldwin Hills wasn't sad, it was a good idea at the time. I married Yumiko in '76 and she moved in with me, Shelly, and Pamela. Everything was still the way Susan left it. Yumiko didn't want to hurt the girls' feelings by changing anything, so I sold the house. That backfired like a mother. The guy that bought it filed bankruptcy and I lost ninety thousand dollars. I never recovered from that.

I started touring a lot, any trip I could get. I made two tours with Maria Muldaur, one playing good jazz arrangements by Benny Carter and another with a rock group, Mike Finnegan, Amos Garrett, Michael Moore, and me. James Jamerson joined on bass for a while, not long, because he'd get drunk and hit on Maria and she let him go. He hit on every woman he saw; he seemed to have the impression it was all right to do that because he was James Jamerson. Who was James Jamerson to these people? They didn't know this man had created a sound, a whole way of playing bass. Jamerson and that drummer, Benny Benjamin—they made the Motown sound. Motown sabotaged them.

That rock tour with Maria was a lot of fun. Maria wrote down what everyone drank; we'd get to the hall and they'd have your drink for you. And the spreads! I'd never experienced this before. The one thing I hated was sound check. I hadn't never been around no sound check. Get you onstage at five-thirty in the afternoon. You had to go to work twice! Where I come from, the engineer already knew what to do, he didn't have to figure it out every day.

"It's routine now," they said.

"Oh! Routine! Sorry! I guess it's routine to build a fucking castle onstage too."

Shit yeah, I grumbled. But not too hard. I was making good money, the best I could at the time. Man, I'd like to go visit Maria up in Mill Valley. I taught her something Dinah Washington used to do. Say there was a chick you liked. You'd point her out to Dinah. She'd tell the chick to come in her dressing room. Dinah say, "Listen, my drummer likes you, so I'm going to tell you something. Don't tell my old man, but that's the best fuck you ever going to get." Next thing, the girl is knocking on your door.

Maria said, "Oh! I got to try that!" But we never got around to it.

Even if I couldn't compete with the young musicians, I wanted to have something to do with the only life I knew. Tommy Gumina, an accordion-player friend of mine, kept after me to run for union office. I was popular, I knew all the musicians. I put in for secretary-treasurer in 1983 and won. I didn't have the education to be president, I wasn't qualified. Besides, this way I was downstairs in the middle of the action, where the musicians came and got their checks and paid their dues and signed up to join and came to meetings. New people was always coming in and I let them know what the union was about.

The A. F. of M. [American Federation of Musicians] was at its strongest right after Petrillo, because of his tough ways of running the sumbitch. In those days, when you bought a musical instrument you joined the union. But this ain't a union country no more. I always talked to the young musicians, guys starting to make money but didn't want to join the union.

"Man, I know you earning a lot, but you not going to be busy like this always. You'll need money coming in someday. My pension is two thousand a month."

"Is that all?" they'd say. That's quite a bit!

One of the first things I did, I got on record companies' asses to pay what's called re-use fees. Lot of new movies were starting to use the old music, the Little Richard and Fats Domino. Practically using more old songs than new. Nobody policed it.

I was told, "This isn't a priority."

"I know it ain't," I said, "because the union don't make no money doing it. So you shouldn't be in this job. What are you being paid for but helping musicians? And you talking about this ain't your priority. What is?"

So I started doing it myself, and all the older musicians started getting checks: eight, nine hundred, sometimes a thousand dollars a year to guys like Justin Adams and Red Tyler. Lot of them had no idea they had any money coming. They saw a movie on TV and said to their buddies, "That's me!" They didn't realize they're supposed to get paid. They do now. I still do a lot of that watchdogging. Sitting home watching TV, I'll make lists of the songs I hear and send them to the union. A guy there checks into it. They're doing a better job of policing now.

Music is something you have fun on—you can't play it good *unless* you having fun. So the layman figures musicians shouldn't even get paid. Having fun, that's your pay. A woman called the union; she wanted a singer and five musicians for a wedding. She asked what it would cost.

I said, "Off the top of my head, roughly about two thousand dollars."

She say, "What? For music?"

Earl in the studio, 1981. (Rick Malkin)

I said, "Ma'am, I'll tell you what. Call the plumbers' union and ask for six plumbers to work from six to twelve o'clock on a Saturday night. Whatever they charge you, I'll work for half of that."

She called me back, said, "I get your point, Mr. Palmer."

I said, "Thank you, ma'am."

People pay to go to music school. Their instruments ain't free. Try going to the market and saying, "I play music, I make people happy, can I have that steak for less than this lady next to me?" Music your ass—you going to pay the $1.98 a pound.

I tried to help people who needed it. If a musician gets sick and can't work, he gets money from the union—not much, maybe forty dollars a week. But a lot of people didn't even know that. I let them know. There was always talk about kicking guys out if their dues was late. You're on the road, you forget about dues. I paid people's dues for them. Everyone always paid me back.

I wanted to be constructive, but it didn't work out that way. There was a faction of young guys, the prominent musicians in the studios now, that called themselves the Recording Musicians Association. I knew what they were doing and spoke against it bluntly and straight-out. I had been like them once. We had a group called the Musicians Guild. We were responsible for raising

Rock aristocracy, thirty years on, 1990. *Left to right:* Hal Blaine, bassist Lyle Ritz, Phil Spector, Jack Nitzsche, and Earl.

the pay scale, because when Sinatra insisted on certain guys for his sessions, the union said, "You can't use them. They've already done enough work." You can't put a limit on how much a person can work, this is America. So we formed the Musicians Guild, and its scale was higher than the union's, so the union had to go up, too. But we were all union men. This RMA is just for itself. They don't give a damn about regular guys in the union.

So I lost. If I'd been more two-faced and full of shit and everything you complain about in politicians, I'd have kept my job. My nature is to be angry a bit; the RMA's nature was to be very cool and calm and stick it in your ass. And the people I was representing assumed I'd win so overwhelmingly, most of them didn't bother to vote. Afterwards, they said, "Man, I voted for you." Then why I ain't in there?

I used to think I accomplished something. I don't know. If I said I did, they'd find a way to dispute it. I'd be better off if I hadn't went there. I'd have made a lot more if I'd kept on working.

I get scared nowadays, people dropping like flies. As a kid I can't remember reading any obituaries. The older you get, the more of them you read, believe me.

Earl in 1993.

One of my kids asked me, doesn't where I'm staying now feel like a come-down from Baldwin Hills? I never thought I'd have Baldwin Hills. I never thought I'd have this little house I'm in now! I always considered everything I got as found. When the stock market crashed, people killed themselves. They couldn't stand being poor. They were *born* poor, most of them! That's one reason I like New Orleans, because it brings me back to the reality of my beginnings.

I'm disappointed they didn't last longer, but I always knew the good years would end. A while ago Carol Kaye moved to Nashville. She used to call me

Earl preparing to play at a tribute to drummer Edward Blackwell, New Orleans Jazz and Heritage Festival, 1994.

up: "You ought to come down here, we can get a band together." Before you knew it she was in Arizona, then Colorado, always saying the same thing. "We could do well here. . . ." The days she's trying to re-create are gone. She was up around here for a year, now she's in Oceanside, down around San Diego. I hear she's thinking about moving again. "I hear there's a lot of work in Palm Springs. . . ."

I used to like to get high, I used to like spending money. I had the security of a beautiful wife, wonderful children, money in the bank. I'd sit back and say, "All is well with me. This is wonderful. From what I understand about religion, you can't smoke pot, can't get chicks, can't snort coke, can't drive your Cadillac, in Heaven. Why would I want to go? This is as close to Heaven as I'll get." And the times when life was at its lowest ebb, that was as close to Hell. I always came to the conclusion that Heaven and Hell was right here. If I didn't have happiness forever, I had it then, and what more could I want? What more? I didn't have a million dollars. I didn't need no million dollars, I had what I never had before, and I was happy. I want a cold glass of water.

NOTES

Unless otherwise noted, all interviews are by the author, who spoke with the following people, some a number of times, between 1991 and 1997: Vernel Bagneris, Dave Bartholomew, Harold Battiste, Warren Bell, Hal Blaine, Joseph Britto, Buddy Collette, Harold Dejan, Vernel Fournier, Paul Humphrey, Andrew "Puddinghead" Jones, Carol Kaye, Jim Keltner, Ellis Marsalis, Cosimo Matassa, Duke Oatis, Earl Palmer Jr., Bill Peterson, Walter Pichon Jr., Clark Terry, Red Tyler, and James van Eaton.

INTRODUCTION

xiv   *"If any single musician . . . surely Earl Palmer."*   Robert Palmer, *Rolling Stone*, April 19, 1990, 48.

xv   *"Bebop . . . too entrenched."*   Frank Driggs and Harris Lewine, *Black Beauty, White Heat: A Pictorial History of Classic Jazz, 1920–1950* (New York: William Morrow, 1982), 44.

xvii   *Alan Lomax writes . . .*   Alan Lomax, *Mister Jelly Roll*, 2d ed. (Berkeley and Los Angeles: University of California Press, 1973), ix.

1. THE TREMÉ JUMPED

1   *General comment about New Orleans music between the wars:*   Compared to the century's first decade and a half, when jazz exploded in New Orleans, the years of Earl Palmer's childhood and youth were a fallow period in the city's music. The city had become a musical backwater, its provincialism evident in

the local newspapers' anticipatory drumroll for Louis Armstrong's first appearance in town in four years, or in a *Louisiana Weekly* columnist's 1936 remark about a new nightclub that "tops everything . . . in this backward little town." Black New Orleanians enjoyed the same commercialized swing as the rest of the country; lost on most was the irony that the real thing had originated in their town. It was Jimmie Lunceford's smooth sounds that excited New Orleans jazz fans now, not a creative original like Big Eye Louis Nelson; unadvertised, Big Eye played in a Tremé dive.

"There is not much music to be heard these days in New Orleans," wrote jazz buff Ken Hulsizer in 1944 (in *Jazz Review*, ed. Max Jones and Albert McCarthy [London: Jazz Music Books, 1945], 5). But the flame still burned. Marching bands, Mardi Gras Indians, blues pianists like Tuts Washington, Burnell Santiago, and young Roy Byrd, the future Professor Longhair; local bandleaders like Fats Pichon, Papa Celestin, and Sidney Desvigne, who maintained high standards of professionalism—these embers glowed quietly but steadily, ultimately to spark the city's next explosion, in which Earl Palmer would play a big part: rhythm and blues.

2–3   *Leah Chase and Norman Smith, interviews.*   From Tremé Oral History Project (TOHP), 1993–94, courtesy of Amistad Research Center, Tulane University.

4   *In my neighborhood, the Tremé . . .*   Probing nineteenth-century New Orleans means entering a world unlike any that has ever existed in the United States, culturally as French and Caribbean as it was North American.

The story of the Tremé begins in the last decade of the eighteenth century, when a French-born hatter named Claude Tremé began developing a plot of land that lay directly behind what is now the French Quarter and was then the entire city. The Tremé was thus New Orleans's original suburb (faubourg). Its boundaries are somewhat nebulous. According to a 1980 architectural study, the Tremé extends from North Rampart to North Broad Streets and from Canal Street to St. Bernard Avenue (Roulhac Toledano and Mary Louise Christovich, *Faubourg Tremé and the Bayou Road*, vol. 6 of *New Orleans Architecture* [Gretna, La.: Pelican Publishing Co.], 141). Most people, however, consider it much smaller: the thirty-block area extending on one side from Rampart to North Claiborne, on the other from Orleans to Esplanade.

The bulk of the Tremé's early residents were *gens de couleur*: the New Orleanians of Franco-African descent who constituted a significant third stream in nineteenth-century New Orleans culture. Many of these so-called Creoles of color were solidly bourgeois, stamping the Tremé with its antebellum character: a bustling place alive with theaters, newspapers, salons, and the benevolent societies known as "social and pleasure" clubs. The last had a decisive and varied impact on the city's music. Not only did their halls give jazz one of its first venues, but as burial societies the clubs were important patrons of the brass bands whose rhythms underlie every genre of twentieth-century New Orleans music.

After the Civil War and the collapse of Reconstruction, the *gens de couleur* were stripped of their status and lumped with American blacks. Formerly a three-tiered society, New Orleans became as bipolar as the rest of America. Many Creoles fled the Tremé and New Orleans; most stayed behind, disenfranchised and impoverished, renting houses they had once owned.

Ironically, the Tremé's decline contributed directly to its musical importance. Musical training among well-to-do antebellum Creoles was a token of cultivation, an accoutrement of polite society. After the war it was suddenly a means of livelihood. A core of dance-band leaders and music masters formed: patriarchs of the Tremé's many musical families, the Picous, Barbarins, Dejans, Keppards, Santiagos, and Tios, jazz pioneers all.

By 1900, meanwhile, Jim Crow had taken hold of the Tremé; by 1920 the neighborhood was well along the path to slumhood. The worst blow fell in 1967 when a six-lane expressway was built over Claiborne Avenue and Claiborne's grassy neutral ground was paved over, its hundreds of sheltering oaks uprooted. "That strip of land, an essential element in the fabric of the community, became a strip of sterile dirt," reads a 1976 neighborhood group's report (Claiborne Avenue Design Team, "I-10 Multi-Use Study," 43). "At one stroke, a 13½-acre park was removed from the community." The conversion of Claiborne Avenue into a no-man's-land brought one tiny, unforeseen benefit: the drums of the marching bands and Mardi Gras Indians who still parade down Claiborne now have a spectacular, boomy resonance. Otherwise, the Tremé today is a blasted ruin.

Aside from its brass bands, concert halls, and heavy concentration of musicians, the neighborhood made one more crucial contribution to jazz. Among the legacies of French and Spanish rule was the city's relatively laissez-faire attitude toward slave activities. Nowhere else in North America were slaves allowed to preserve their ancestral, preslavery music and dance. An area was set aside for the slaves' Sunday gatherings: the Place Publique, later known as Congo Square, a swampy field in the uptown corner of the Tremé (the Municipal Auditorium stands there today). Here, early-nineteenth-century visitors "saw something . . . that had not been seen elsewhere in North America for nearly a century—native African music and dance still being performed" (Jerah Johnson, "Congo Square: La Place Publique," *Louisiana Cultural Vistas* [Winter 1997–98]: 63). One such traveler described his 1834 visit:

North of Rampart Street . . . is the celebrated Congo Square, [where] the lower order of colored people and negroes, bond and free, assemble in great numbers . . . to enjoy themselves in their own peculiar manner. . . . with banjos, tom-toms, violins, jawbones, triangles, and various other instruments from which harsh and dulcet sounds may be extracted; and a variety, indeed, of queer, grotesque, fantastic, strange, and merry dancers are to be seen. . . . [I]n all their movements, gyrations, and attitudenizing [*sic*] exhibitions, *the most perfect time is kept, making the beats with the feet, heads, or hands, or all, as correctly as a well-regulated metronome!* . . . To witness such a scene is a certain cure for ennui, blue-devils, mopes, horrors, and dyspepsia. . . . Every stranger should visit Congo Square when in its glory, once at least, and, my word for it, no one will ever regret or forget it. (Col. James R. Creecy, *Scenes in the South* [Washington, D.C.: Thomas McGill, 1860], 20–23; italics added.)

African music and dance survived in New Orleans into the 1880s, long enough for jazz's first generation to have absorbed some of it, and long enough to persist in the social memory of a New Orleanian born in 1924. Indeed, the foot-patting of the slave dancers not only presaged the tap dancing that Earl Palmer learned on the Tremé's unpaved streets, but the rhythms of Congo Square laid the groundwork for jazz itself. Jazz, said Sidney Bechet, one of its great pioneers, "was already born and making in the music they played at Congo Square" (Sidney Bechet, *Treat It Gentle* [New York: Hill & Wang, 1960], 8).

5   *As for the name of Walter Fats Pichon . . .*   The more Earl and I talked, the less clear became the circumstances of his birth. Walter "Fats" Pichon (1906–67) was a piano player whose name winds conspicuously through thirty years of New Orleans musical history. According to a number of older New Orleanians, one of his most significant contributions may have been to have fathered Earl Palmer.

Born and raised in the Tremé, Pichon spent the twenties and thirties shuttling between New Orleans and New York, recording with King Oliver, Luis Russell, and Fess Williams and arranging for Chick Webb. From the late thirties to 1942, he led an eleven-piece band on the Mississippi steamship *Capitol*, one of whose trumpeters was a teenaged Dave Bartholomew. "Being on that boat was my college degree," Bartholomew told me, "because Fats Pichon was on you hook, line, and sinker. There was nothing we didn't play."

Like many a New Orleans entertainer, Pichon had an advanced reputation as a roué. "My father was a rascal and I knew he was a rascal," says Walter Pichon Jr., who chauffeured Walter Sr. around town. "At 3:00 A.M. he'd say, 'Drop me off here and pick me up in a half-hour.' I knew he wasn't giving no piano lesson at 3:00 A.M."

In 1942 Fats became one of the first black entertainers to headline in the French Quarter, playing the Old Absinthe House on Bourbon Street for the next eighteen years. *Louisiana Weekly*'s "Scoop" Jones called him "New Orleans' highest-paid and most popular musician . . . the living example of the 'You Can Make Good in Your Home Town' philosophy" ("Potpourri," *Louisiana Weekly*, Dec. 14, 1946). He got his own weekly show on a local ABC affiliate in 1949, the city's first musician regularly featured on TV. Pichon's one major-label album, *Appearing Nightly at the Old Absinthe House* (Decca, 1956), sparkles with his virtuosic Earl Hines/Art Tatum–style piano.

Pichon moved to Chicago in 1962, where he died. His body came home for burial in St. Louis Cemetery II, a few blocks from where he'd lived in the early twenties, when he is said to have known Thelma Theophile very well indeed.

"When I met Walter Pichon, he was living with Earl's mama," says eighty-nine-year-old Harold Dejan, among the last of the old-time Crescent City jazzmen. "Then Earl came along. So I'd say, yeah, that's Earl's daddy." Walter Pichon Jr. agrees: "I believe deep within my heart that Earl is my brother." So does Dave Bartholomew: "We always did guess that Fats was actually Earl's father. We felt that way but we never voiced it. I've always felt that way."

Good Catholics, the Theophiles may have been unwilling to accept an illegitimate child. Is it possible that they sent Thelma to New York, where her sister Josephine was already living, to hide her pregnancy? An appropriate story could easily have been concocted; perhaps Josephine even knew a real Edward Palmer, conveniently dead at sea. There is no record of a marriage between an Edward Palmer and a Thelma Theophile in New York City or New York State during 1923 and 1924.

All of Earl's older relatives and in-laws are dead. Thelma's friend and fellow vaudevillian Mattie Jackson was living in Denver City, Texas, when I wrote her in 1996 (deaf, she was unable to talk on the telephone). She wrote back: "All I can remember is Sal [Thelma's nickname] saying Picon [*sic*] was Earls father and I always thought so." Mattie died a few months later, before I could visit her.

It may be that Earl Palmer, endowed with so many figurative fathers among New Orleans musicians, has a literal one. "The apple doesn't fall far from the tree," says Earl's old friend Cosimo Matassa, "and Fats was a great entertainer." Or as Walter Pichon Jr. says, "That bloodline tell."

9–10 *Vernel Fournier's daddy George . . .* and *Benny Powell grew up across the street.* Fournier and Powell became distinguished jazz musicians, Fournier as a drummer with Ahmad Jamal and others, Powell as a trombonist with Lionel Hampton's, Count Basie's, and Thad Jones and Mel Lewis's orchestras.

11 *Being born into a vaudeville family, I was a dancer by the time I was five.* Throughout the thirties Earl Palmer made frequent appearances in the *Louisiana Weekly:* "little Earl Palmer, 7-year-old song-and-dance boy" (Apr. 2, 1932); "at Roseland Dance Hall, the Theophile Sisters with 'Baby' Earl Palmer" (Dec. 7, 1935); "Earl Palmer, that cute little youngster" (Oct. 24, 1935). The Chicago *Defender*'s New Orleans correspondent told his readers on March 13, 1937, about "the Rhythm Club, a very beautiful spot where one can enjoy a floor show headed by Alvin Howey and Little Earl Palmer."

11 *Everybody around New Orleans knew my mama and my Aunt Nita.*   Cousin Joe, for instance. Pleasant Joseph (1907–92), better known as Cousin Joe, was a

well-traveled blues singer, cracker-barrel humorist, and Earl's onetime dancing partner. In his 1987 autobiography, Joseph says: "Thelma Fairfield [*sic*] and Anita Fairfield . . . were the top terpsichoreans — dancing teachers — in the city at that time. They were the chorus girls in every show that came to the Lyric Theatre or came to the Lincoln Theatre. They used to teach dancing to almost all the kids. Girls that were ambitious to be show girls and chorus dancers used to go to the Fairfield Sisters" (Pleasant "Cousin Joe" Joseph and Harriet J. Ottenheimer, *Cousin Joe: Blues from New Orleans* [Chicago: University of Chicago Press, 1987], 74).

But Cousin Joe reserves his highest praise for Thelma's boy: "Earl Palmer . . . was one of the greatest tap dancers in the *city*. . . . [His mother] used to make him white tails. White tux, tails, white satin shirt, white tie, and white shoes. And dance up a storm! He could outdance all of us. He was the cause that we could get in these big white nightclubs and do our number and pass our hat" (ibid., 50).

15   *When I was little, Louis Henry was about my biggest hero.*   Louis Henry was a figure around whom stories grew up like trees. "You'll never meet another character like that in your life!" says Walter Pichon Jr. "I'm going to tell you something about Louis Henry that Earl probably don't even know. Louis Henry's mama put him in a basket like in the Bible, and he floated down the river until another lady found him. Louis Henry! Had a personality out of this world, the way he laughed and the way he talked you couldn't help but remember him. And then that bowlegged walk with that big belly and that high behind and oh, man! Louis Henry married a nun, got her out of the sisterhood. Had a place here called the Cat and the Fiddle on Gravier Street. My father said to Louis Henry, 'How old are you?' and Louis Henry said, 'Two years older than God.' Oh, that's a terrible man! A big fat man, because you talk about eating! And had all the connections he wanted up in New York. If you wanted something up there, you went to see Louis Henry." (Earl gives a different picture of Louis Henry's eventual fortunes in New York, as we see in chapter 5.)

Cousin Joe remembers Louis Henry, too, as a cab driver and a first-rate "porch-climber": a second-story man. "He'd get Christ off the cross and then go back and get the cross!" (ibid., 50–51).

15   *They had another pimp by the name of Pete Robertson . . .*   Although Louis Henry may have piqued people's imaginations, his boon companion Pete Robertson figured more prominently in the city's social life. Robertson was a ubiquitous promoter and one of black New Orleans's most popular men. He moved to Harlem in 1938, opened Pete's Creole Restaurant, and became as much of a Harlem celebrity as he'd been in New Orleans.

16   *John McElroy was originally called Hats and Coats all by himself . . .*   On April 29, 1933, Earl Wright told his *Louisiana Weekly* readers that "J. D. McElroy

(Hats and Coats to you) wrote us from his home town, Chattanooga, Tenn. and declares that his mother has bought him a Lincoln car. That his wife's mother died recently (and he's fixed otherwise). That Green his dancing partner is with him and that his (Hats') next move will be to buy himself a show of his own and travel. . . . Well, you may live next door but you never know."

Thirty years later John D. McElroy, fifty-five, "one-time nationally famous entertainer who performed under the stage name 'Hats and Coats,'" was charged with the fatal stabbing of his friend Charles Warren Smith (*Louisiana Weekly*, Mar. 24, 1963). At the time of his arrest, McElroy was playing washtub bass on Bourbon Street; his dancing career, the newspaper said, had ended when his right leg was amputated years earlier. Convicted of second-degree murder, old Hats was sentenced to four years in prison (reflecting the casualness with which New Orleans courts regarded black-on-black crime as late as the sixties). After that, McElroy's trail vanishes. According to the March 24, 1963, article, he had served time "some years ago" for another murder.

20   *Blanche Thomas was the first chick I had anything to do with.*   Blanche Thomas grew up to become a beloved New Orleans entertainer, "one of New Orleans' rare singers of authentic blues" (Al Rose and Edmund Souchon, *New Orleans Jazz: A Family Album*, 3d ed. [Baton Rouge: Louisiana State University Press, 1984], 120). She had a regional hit, "You Ain't So Such a Much," in 1954. In the seventies she toured with the traditionalist Preservation Hall band; the last time Earl saw his old flame, she came to California in the mid-seventies with Preservation Hall. She always remained as earthy as she'd been when she deflowered Earl: "Blanche Thomas had just finished a throaty, insinuating rendition of 'You Got To See Your Mama Every Night (Or You Can't See Mama At All),'" the *New Orleans Times Picayune* reported on August 31, 1970, "and was propped against a white grand piano, laughing as waves of applause washed over her. 'I feel so good!' she called out, a hand on her hip as she took a step forward. 'You really got me today!'" Eight years older than Earl (not three or four as he recalled), Thomas died in 1977.

2. THE *DARKTOWN SCANDALS*

23   *"Admitting . . . going and getting nowhere."*   Mark Vance, "Color Show World," *Variety*, December 31, 1930, 23.

26   *I loved Miss Ida and she called me her baby.*   In 1961 Ida Cox gave jazz critic Whitney Balliett a few facts about her life:

I was born [in or around 1896] in Cedartown, Georgia. When I was fourteen, I ran away and joined a minstrel show, the Black and Tan [where she played Topsy in one of the innumerable minstrel versions of *Uncle Tom's Cabin* that toured America for decades]. I sang blues and ragtime songs, like "Put Your Arms Around Me, Honey," and an old, old one I learned from my brother, "Hard, Oh Lord." . . . Then I went with the Rabbit Foot Minstrels and the Florida Blossom Minstrels and into vaudeville. Jelly Roll Morton—he was a good-lookin' light-skinned boy—played for me at the Eight One Theatre, on Decatur Street, in Atlanta, and one of his tunes, "Jelly Roll Blues," was my first big success. I worked at the Plantation, in Chicago, with King Oliver and Louis Armstrong. Oliver was fat and plain, and almost as homely as I am. After that, I sang in every state in the Union. I had one of the most lovely colored shows on the road—a beautiful chorus line. I got to know everybody, and worked with the biggest portion of them. ("Yes Yes Yes Yes," *New Yorker*, Apr. 29, 1961, 30–31)

Cox was a member of the first generation of black popular musicians to record, extensively, in her case—she made dozens of records for Paramount between 1923 and 1929. She was among the greatest of the so-called classic blues singers: black women who gloried in their role as divas. As opposed to folk-based, self-taught bluesmen like Charley Patton and Blind Lemon Jefferson, classic singers (Cox, Bessie Smith, Ma Rainey, Ethel Waters) were self-conscious professionals trained in vaudeville and tent shows. Often accompanied by jazz bands, they tended to supplement their blues with Tin Pan Alley standards. Their appeal, at least in the twenties, was urban. Cox was on the down-home side of the classic blues spectrum: if her vocal timbre was less guttural and her diction less slurred than Bessie Smith's, she was earthier than Ethel Waters, and she sang almost nothing but basic twelve-bar blues.

On August 16, 1924, the *Defender* caught her in her prime: "Ida Cox . . . who would make you get an attack of 'looka-yander-listen-after' when you try to figure out which she hits hardest—her singing or her dressing—is simply mopping dry at all stands out through Oklahoma and Texas. We just had a letter from her in which she tells us about her chicken dinners and wanted to know if we liked chicken. Arf! Arf! Just wait! [A double entendre: "eating chicken" meant having sex.]"

Miss Ida was still going strong in 1930, when Kansas City theatergoers "literally stormed" the Lincoln Theater to see her then-current show, *Raisin' Cain* (Chicago *Defender*, Nov. 1, 1930). But by the mid-thirties her path led increasingly through whistle-stops; in 1936 and 1937 she played, among other towns, Greenfield, Massachusetts; Trenton, New Jersey; Sedalia, Missouri; Midland, Odessa, Ballinger, Brady, Georgetown, Belton, and Cleburne, Texas; Winnipeg, Manitoba; and Salt Lake City, Utah, where a *Variety* reviewer saw her on November 28, 1937. If *Variety*'s man considered the show a bit perfunctory —"There's no attempt whatsoever at production. Acts are run off in routine fashion."—he praised Miss Ida and a few others, including "kid orchestra leader [who] handles the baton with finesse": very likely Earl, one of whose specialties was miming Cab Calloway's celebrated conducting gyrations.

Already past her prime when John Hammond brought her to Carnegie Hall for his second "Spirituals to Swing" concert in 1939, Cox scored nonetheless: "Ida Cox," Hammond wrote, "appeared in heavy make-up and false eyelashes, not exactly what I thought a blues singer should look like, but she was a hit" (John Hammond, *On Record* [New York: Summit Books, 1977], 231).

Miss Ida toured until 1944, when a stroke forced her to retire. She died in Knoxville, Tennessee, in 1967.

26   *I traveled in vaudeville off and on for eleven years . . .*   Ida Cox wasn't Earl's first traveling-show boss. He turns out to have hit the road even earlier than he recalled. A December 13, 1930, *Defender* story, " 'Miss Broadway' Co. in Detroit; Lining 'Em Up," carries the byline of none other than Thelma Theophile. " 'Miss Broadway' company is carrying on here," she wrote. "Master Earl Palmer, 6-year-old tap specialist, closes the show." Two weeks later she wrote again, from Cleveland: "Earl Palmer, 5-year-old tap artist [his mother was either forgetting Earl's age or subtracting a year for effect], still holds his own as show stopper" (" 'Steppin High,' " Chicago *Defender*, Dec. 27, 1930). There he was, bringing down the house (if a proud mother can be believed): a hardworking, hard-traveling, six-year-old professional showman.

26–27 *I was with a show called the Georgia Minstrels for eight, nine months in 1936.* From the *Louisiana Weekly* of February 29 of that year, we learn that Earl, Thelma, and Nita joined the troupe when it passed through New Orleans: "The Georgia Minstrels attempted to clean the town of performers last week when they engaged the services of the three Theophiles, Nita, Thelma and 'Baby' Earl. Others who are making the tour are Juanita Gonzales, Lorraine Kauffman, Billy Freeman, comedian, and Alfred Williams, formerly a drummer with Piron's Orchestra."

27   *They had a famous comedian named Jazzlips Richardson . . .*   Jazzlips didn't stay with the Georgia Minstrels long that year: "He was touring the South with that crackshot unit," reported the *Pittsburgh Courier* ("Jazzlips Sails for London," Mar. 28, 1936), "when the good news reached him" that he'd been picked up for a $500-a-week, eighteen-week run in London. Richardson sailed on March 22. It seems he'd crossed the pond before: "Jazzlips has the distinction of giving a command performance before the late King George of Britain who openly expressed that he had enjoyed the performance immensely."

Jazzlips Richardson had Broadway credentials—in 1929 he appeared in the Broadway show *Hot Chocolates*, when the New York *Post* wrote that "an eel-like gentleman named Jazzlips" was the show's "surprise star" (June 21, 1929). The following year he was in *Blackbirds of 1930*, which starred Ethel Waters.

Dance historians Marshall and Jean Stearns consider Richardson "amateurish" (*Jazz Dance: The Story of American Vernacular Dance* [New York: Macmillan, 1968], 154). Not Earl: "Jazzlips was a class comedian."

28   *Single comedians like they have today, stand-ups, didn't come along until later.* In his history of Negro humor, *On the Real Side*, Mel Watkins makes an interesting point (and substantiates Earl's remark): "Stand-up comedy and its unmediated dialogue with audiences . . . did not become the principal form of stage humor until after the Depression. Most black comedy avoided direct interaction until the fifties. . . . A black performer who demanded a personal response would have transgressed a boundary by suggesting an equality intolerable to most non-blacks" (Mel Watkins, *On the Real Side* [New York: Simon & Schuster, 1994], 372).

31   *After I got my spot I did maybe six minutes.*   Where does "Baby" Earl fit into the evolution of tap?

Much of the history of tap dancing is the story of how performers gradually left the ground. In tap's first great era (1900–1920), dancers like King Rastus Brown, greatest of the old-time tappers, worked close to the ground, flat-footed, moving mostly from the hips down. Bill "Bojangles" Robinson, whose peak came in the teens and twenties, raised the center of gravity to the toes. By 1930 Robinson's straight, or rhythm, tapping, which relied on sound to make its impression, was fading; dancers began to augment their tapping with eye-catching, so-called flash, moves: flips, splits, knee drops, leaps, etc. As the great tap dancer Groundhog said, "If you take your feet more than one inch off the floor while you're doing rhythm tap, you're starting to do flash dancing" (quoted in Stearns and Stearns, *Jazz Dance*, 267).

Young Earl was especially taken with flash acts like the Four Step Brothers and Stump and Stumpy. "By my time flash was coming in, and you had to do some of what the great dancers were doing. The Step Brothers, the Berry Brothers, Stump and Stumpy, they all did a combination of flash steps and tap dance. And that's what I did, too. The flash steps—splits, spins, toe-stands—I did all of that."

44   *Tom Brooks—someone from St. Louis would know who I'm talking about.* Clark Terry hails from St. Louis and knows just whom Earl is talking about: "Tom Brooks. That was a mean motherfucker. And he had a patrolling buddy named Clarence Lee—a real black dude we used to call Buttermilk. Tom Brooks kept all the would-be delinquents in line. He was notorious. He demanded the proper decorum in public places. He'd sneak on the buses and streetcars and into crowds to see if anyone was doing anything that wasn't apropos and if you were, that was your ass. Buttermilk was even worse. This is the period when the style was Big Apple hats, you know, with the wide brims. Buttermilk kept a big pair of scissors. See a Big Apple hat, walk up, take it off your head, and cut the brim off."

3. NO KIND OF HERO

46 *"The policy of the War Department . . . national defense."* Ulysses Lee, *The Employment of Negro Troops* (Washington, D.C.: Center of Military History, 1963), 76.

46–47 *"The way we are sleeping and eating . . . fighting for Democracy."* Phillip McGuire, *Taps for a Jim Crow Army: Letters from Black Soldiers in World War II* (Santa Barbara, Calif.: ABC-Clio, 1983), 20.

47 *Writes historian Phillip McGuire.* Ibid., 59.

47 *"The inside story . . . steering wheel."* Randy Dixon, in *Pittsburgh Courier*, September 23, 1944.

47 *"All this build-up . . . a yardbird."* Lucy Milner, "Jim Crow in the Army," *New Republic*, March 13, 1944, 341.

47 *"Major Sheriden . . . chain gang."* McGuire, *Taps for a Jim Crow Army*, 99.

47 *"Now right at this moment . . . Negro soldier."* Ibid., 196.

47 *"There is a town . . . worse than hell itself."* Ibid., 192.

48 *"All of a sudden . . . God, it was awful."* Alex Albright, "Noon Parade and Midnight Ramble," in *Good Country People: An Irregular Journal of the Cultures of Eastern North Carolina* (Rocky Mount, N.C.: North Carolina Wesleyan College Press, 1995), 75.

48 *"If the invasion doesn't occur soon, trouble will."* Lee, *Employment of Negro Troops*, 627.

48 *"The thin-skinned and irritable Negro press . . . would stand."* *Time*, July 10, 1944, 65.

49 *"For the first time . . . first-class citizenship for the first time."* Neil A. Wynn, "The Impact of the Second World War on the American Negro," *Journal of Contemporary History* 6, no. 2 (1971): 51–52.

4. RUNNIN' WILD IN THIS BIG OLD TOWN

62 *"What's happening? . . . are 'treed.'"* Scoop Jones, "Potpourri," *Louisiana Weekly*, March 22, 1947.

62 *"Their story . . . decent wage."* *Louisiana Weekly*, December 27, 1947.

62–63 *"Ya shoulda seen . . . fine as dollar wine."* "Boogie Beat Jive," *Louisiana Weekly*, April 23, 1949.

68 *I hardly ever thought about the idea of father . . .* Earl sometimes struck me as oddly incurious about the question of his father's identity. It seems to have played a small role indeed in his life, more a piquant novelty, a topic of mild amusement, than anything else. As an only child with a strong mother—"my mama was father and mother to me both," he once told me—a warm extended family, and a family-like community, Earl may never have felt the lack of a

father, nor translated that felt lack into a need to probe the rumors, to establish with certainty who the missing father really was.

70　*I walked into a job with Harold Dejan at the Old Opera House.* "That's my genius," says old man Dejan. One of the old oaks who root Earl so deeply in New Orleans musical soil, "Duke" Dejan likes to take credit for starting Earl's drumming career, and some credit is due.

Born in 1909 in the Tremé, Harold Dejan studied with Lorenzo Tio Jr., one of the greats of early jazz. In the thirties Dejan led the pit band for the Palace Theater's vaudeville shows; his wife-to-be, Rose Angeline, danced with Thelma, Nita, and Earl. In the mid-forties Dejan worked a Bourbon Street strip joint called the Old Opera House with his trio, the Rhythm Boys. When the drummer left for the navy, Dejan decided to cultivate a new drummer from scratch. He told his wife, "I'm going to buy Earl a set of drums."

"Oh," said Rose, "he'll be so glad!"

"Earl had no drums of his own," Dejan says, "but I knew he could play the damn drums. I bought him a nice set." [Earl, as we've seen, disputes this last memory on more than one count.] "And Earl sit down at them drums and kill everybody. He was a natural. He was some drummer. If a mosquito fly past, hit the mosquito."

Sitting in his house in New Orleans East, the old man was hurt to learn that Earl (whom he still thought of as a boy despite Earl's seventy-plus years) had recently been in town without visiting. "I wanted him to come by and see the trophies I got. Tell Earl I'd like to see him next time. I want him to see I didn't go to school and eat lunch."

Dejan's nephew, saxophonist Warren Bell, insists that he remembers Earl's very first drumming job: an out-of-town gig in the summer of 1946 with several members of the Opera House band. "Earl was not really a drummer at that time," says Bell, "but he had so much natural ability it was almost like once he got the drums, he was transformed from a dancer to a drummer. But I know for a fact that that's the first time Earl actually tried to play a gig on drums. Neither one of us was really happening."

75　*The backbeat came about because the public wasn't buying jazz.* The basic pulse of rock and roll and rhythm and blues, the backbeat is a heavy emphasis on the second and fourth beats in every measure of a piece of music. (By way of contrast, listen to, say, bluegrass, where the emphasis is on one and three.) In forties jazz the backbeat was kept on the hi-hat to a crisp, light effect. To oversimplify, when drummers shifted the backbeat to the much louder snare drum, rock, with its pile-driving momentum (its monotony, say detractors), was born.

Forty years of laying into the backbeat gave Earl a carpenter's injury: a blood clot at the base of his thumb that needed to be surgically removed in the late eighties.

79   *New Orleans was a town that was known for drummers.*   From Baby Dodds at
one end of the century to Herlin Riley at the other, New Orleans has turned
out magnificent drummers with a heartbreaking prodigality—heartbreaking
because so many of them are so little known.

The cultural influence of West Africa, from which most New World slaves
came, was more deeply felt in nineteenth-century New Orleans than anywhere
else in the United States. Not only did the slave trade, outlawed in 1808, persist
sub rosa in New Orleans almost until the Civil War, but African music and
dance survived here almost a century longer than anywhere else in North
America. Congo Square's festivities ended just before the Civil War, but
African music persisted in pockets of the city almost until the twentieth century—in 1880, standing on Dumaine Street in the heart of the Tremé, Lafcadio
Hearn listened as "some old men and women chanted a song that appeared to
me to be purely African in its many vowelled syllabification" (quoted in Johnson, "Congo Square," 64; and in Frederic Ramsey Jr. and Charles Edward
Smith, *Jazzmen* [New York: Harcourt Brace Jovanovich, 1939], 8). As music
critic and historian Robert Palmer writes, such survivals ensured that "a very
strong African musical presence remains in the city even today, coloring its
folk and popular music" (*A Tale of Two Cities: Memphis Rock and New Orleans Roll*, I.S.A.M. Monographs, no. 12 [Brooklyn, N.Y.: Institute for Studies
in American Music, 1979], 6). To Palmer's "African" one ought to add "and
Afro-Caribbean"—a large percentage of the city's antebellum black population
came by way of the Caribbean, where the culture of African slaves had taken
on new, hybrid forms.

Rhythm is as central to West African music as harmony is to European music, a disposition that survives in the vernacular music of black New Orleans.
The streets themselves are a drumming school—thronging to parades, swelling
the second lines, New Orleanians grow up alive to percussion. No wonder so
many turn pro.

New Orleans drummers resist the usual generic labels—jazz, R&B, funk;
whatever their nominal orientation, a specific feel unites them, straddling genres. This is the famous second-line rhythm, "a dancing, marching, strutting
sort of step or beat," as drummer James Black described it (Val Wilmer, "James
Black and Freddie Kohlman," in Herlin Riley and Johnny Vidacovich, *New
Orleans Jazz and Second Line Drumming* [Miami: Warner Brothers Publications, 1995], 61). The hallmarks of the sound are a chattering snare drum and a
buoyant bass drum (the latter accenting the final beat of every second measure
to propel the music into the next two-bar phrase). In an especially useful insight, another member of the fraternity, Freddie Kohlman, explained how New
Orleans drummers developed their fancy bass-drum style: "All that footwork
comes from the New Orleans [parade] style of playing [the bass drum] with

their hands. That's why New Orleans drummers got it over all the different cats that are away from here" (ibid., 63).

In West African tradition, music is regenerative, not exhausting, a source, not an expense of energy. The same is true of New Orleans drumming. As Earl told interviewer Tad Jones in 1981: "You hear a relaxation in a New Orleans drummer that demonstrates his feeling of New Orleans. It's relaxed, it's good-times, it's a happy feeling. There's a happiness in it you don't feel from other drummers" (unpublished interview, William Ransom Hogan Jazz Archive, Tulane University). To borrow novelist William Gass's characterization of one of his heroes, New Orleans drumming is a wide and happy sound.

85   *Anxiously trying to shore up Jim Crow . . .*   See Tad Jones, "'Separate but Equal': The Laws of Segregation and Their Effect on New Orleans Black Musicians, 1950–1964," *Living Blues,* no. 77 (Dec. 1987), 24–25, 27.

89   *The first time I felt like a page was being turned was Little Richard.*   A minor myth deflated: Producer Bumps Blackwell is often said to have discovered Little Richard's true style during a lunch break at the fabled Dew Drop Inn when Richard pounded out "Tutti Frutti" on the Dew Drop's piano (see, for instance, Charles White, *The Life and Times of Little Richard* [New York: Harmony Books, 1984]). Everything about the story may well be true—except its locale. "We couldn't have went to lunch at no Dew Drop," says Earl. "We wouldn't have had time; the Dew Drop is miles away from J&M. We always went right next door to Buster's. Best red beans and rice in the city. If Bumps told people this happened at the Dew Drop, he's full of shit. Most likely it happened right there in the studio."

5. THE POWER AND THE GROOVE

101   *"That was a secret world."*   *Goldmine,* April 28, 1995, 124.

101   *"Los Angeles had more record companies . . . others wouldn't."*   Tom Reed, *The Black Music History of Los Angeles—Its Roots* (Los Angeles: Black Accent Press, 1994), 75.

101–2   *"In almost every region . . . Dave Bartholomew."*   *Goldmine,* October 26, 1984, 14.

103   *"It really was the studio musicians . . . to create a hit."*   Mark Cunningham, *Good Vibrations: A History of Record Production* (Chessington, England: Castle Communications, 1996), 75–76.

104   *The critic Leonard Feather called him "ubiquitous."*   Earl Palmer, personal memory.

105   *"I doubt . . . all types of challenges."*   Robert R. Faulkner, *Hollywood Studio Musicians: Their Work and Careers in the Recording Industry* (Chicago: Aldine-Atherton, 1971), 140.

105   *"[Session players were] expected to face . . . contingencies."*   Ibid., 38.

119   *. . . cartoon music, the hardest music I ever had to play.*   "Cartoons are particularly troublesome [for the studio musician] because of the quick shifts between fast and slow tempi, the former turning the player into a kind of musical speedometer—executing many notes within a short period of time" (ibid., 37).

122   *Rene came from New Orleans.*   Born circa 1905, Hall is among the few twentieth-century pop musicians who covered more stylistic ground than Earl. Banjoist with the great trumpeter Lee Collins's Astoria Ballroom Orchestra in 1929, Hall played with Sam Morgan's and Sidney Desvigne's bands in the thirties *and* played the blazing six-string bass intro to Ritchie Valens's "La Bamba" in 1958.

126   *"The power, groove and taste . . . at the time."*   Tony Scherman, "Earl Palmer the Rhythm Bomber, the Funk Machine from New Orleans," in *The Rock Musician,* ed. Tony Scherman (New York: St. Martin's, 1994), 232.

126   *Apt to run out to Vegas or down to Tijuana . . .*   Herb Alpert may owe the inspiration for his hugely successful Tijuana Brass to Earl and trumpeter Gerald Wilson. "Susan, me, Gerald Wilson, and Gerald's wife Josephine used to go down to Tijuana every weekend for the bullfights," says Earl. "I was doing a demo for Herbie Alpert one morning, hung over like mad. Someone said, 'Oh, down to Tijuana again?'

'Yeah,' I said, 'them bullfights.'

'Bullfights!' says Herbie. 'I never been to a bullfight, I'd like to go.' So he and his first wife Sandy went with the four of us. Herbie spent all day standing outside the bullring listening to the mariachi bands. Next thing you know, he wound up with the Tijuana Brass."

127   *"[Jazz] is no longer a dirty word in the film industry."*   Harvey Siders, "Keeping Score on Schifrin," *Down Beat,* March 6, 1969, 17.

127   *Item in* Addicted to Noise: A fuller account appeared in the following month's *Addicted to Noise* (Apr. 1996). In the article "Why Cracker Hates Their Generation," band members David Lowery and Johnny Hickman recalled the episode:

Lowery: [Video director] Sam Bayer, it's really his idea. He found old jazz musicians and guys that could actually really play the part and just really get fucking hectic. So we ended up with Earl Palmer who played with Little Richard and all of this stuff. Seventy-one years old. Totally dapper. Great guy. Really cool. [H]e comes out, sits at the drum set . . . and somebody goes, "Do you need to rehearse?" He goes, "Nah, I invented this shit."

Hickman: He played with Little Richard!

Lowery: He just played it, note for note, man. He checked out the fills. He goes, "The only thing I don't know is, cue me when that triplet fill happens at the end, man, OK?" Just played it note for note. Totally sweated. He's 71 years old, man. That was awesome. . . . "I invented this shit." It was beautiful.

136   *Motown had two sisters called the Lewis Sisters.*   Other Los Angeles session stars, including Carol Kaye and Hal Blaine, make the same claim: that they played on many early Motown hits, deceived into thinking they were cutting mere demos. Kaye is the most vocal: that's her, she says, and not Motown's legendary staff bassist James Jamerson on the Four Tops' "Bernadette," the Supremes' "Stop! In the Name of Love," Stevie Wonder's "I Was Made to Love Her," Martha and the Vandellas' "Dancing in the Street," and many more. According to Kaye, Earl plays drums on "Bernadette," Mary Wells's "My Guy," Marvin Gaye and Tammi Terrell's "If I Could Build My Whole World around You," the Temptations' "Get Ready," and others. Earl himself doesn't remember any titles, which isn't surprising; he rarely paid attention to song titles.

Solid evidence here is hard to come by—contracts for demo recordings rarely list song titles (besides, many of the sessions were purportedly off the books). Over the years a number of Motown figures—singer/songwriter/former VP Smokey Robinson, songwriter Brian Holland, and (of course) Jamerson—have denied Kaye's claims. No response of any sort is likely to come from Motown founder Berry Gordy, with his reputation for avoiding controversy.

A 1989 statement from Lester Sill, then in charge of Motown's publishing arm, reads: "Carol Kaye has played bass on several Motown hits that were cut between the years 1963 to 1969." Yet this reveals nothing that wasn't already known. Whatever they did on the sly, Motown held plenty of legitimate, on-the-books, mid-sixties sessions in Los Angeles. Earl played on several, for Marvin Gaye, the Supremes, and Brenda Holloway. Only one was a hit, and not a big one: Holloway's "You've Made Me So Very Happy." (There's also a four-day Temptations session in Earl's 1966 log, but I haven't been able to find out which songs were cut.)

The mystery is not likely to be cleared up (barring some sort of computer analysis of the musicians' characteristic sounds, which probably wouldn't be conclusive anyway). What remains is a tantalizing possibility: did the California musicians, aside from the hundreds of hits they created for the Beach Boys, Phil Spector, Jan and Dean, etc., also play a role in the rise of Motown?

137 *Teddy once tried to hire me to join Basie.*   Hal Blaine has a Basie story, too: "I was working with Tommy Sands, and Basie asked me if I thought I could play with his band. I said, 'Are you kidding? I know every arrangement backwards.' Basie offered me the chair for a hundred a week. I was already making three-fifty. I said, 'Bill, I just love this band and I'd love to play with you but I'm making big money with this guy. Basie said, 'I'll tell you what. I'll let you be road manager and I'll give you a hundred and a quarter.' "

146 *I married Yumiko in '76.*   Earl's third wife was Yumiko Makino, a Tokyoite he met on one of his Japanese tours with Percy Faith. Penny, Earl's seventh child, was born in 1978. Yumiko and Earl separated in 1980 and were divorced several years later. Earl hasn't remarried. He has eighteen grandchildren and three great-grandchildren.

APPENDIX

SELECTED SINGLES, ALBUMS, AND FILM AND TELEVISION SOUNDTRACKS FEATURING EARL PALMER

This list is not intended to be complete but rather to give readers an idea of the tremendous range of Earl Palmer's recorded work. The list was compiled from a number of sources, including recording-session contracts on file at the American Federation of Musicians (Los Angeles and New Orleans branches), Earl Palmer's session logs, interviews with other musicians, liner-note credits, and several discographies and film and television reference books, including Bruyninckx's *60 Years of Recorded Jazz, 1917–1977*, Lord's *The Jazz Discography*, and *Halliwell's Film and Video Guide*. Much of the research for this list was done by Russell Wapensky.

SINGLES

The date given is the date of release, as best determined. The listing includes (in brackets) chart position if single reached top 10 on *Billboard* pop or R&B charts. Chart information is from Joel Whitburn's books *Top R&B Singles, 1942–1995*; *Top Pop Singles, 1955–1990*; *Top Pop Albums, 1955–1992*; and *Top Country Singles, 1944–1993* (Menomenee Falls, Wis.: Record Research).

1947

Dave Bartholomew   "Dave's Boogie Woogie" / "Bum Mae" (DeLuxe)
                                  "Stardust" / "She's Got Great Big Eyes" (DeLuxe)

1949

Dave Bartholomew   "Carnival Day" (DeLuxe)
                       "Country Boy" (DeLuxe)
Fats Domino   "The Fat Man" [#2 R&B] / "Detroit City Blues"
                           (Imperial)

1950

Dave Bartholomew   "Good Jax Boogie" (Imperial)
                       "That's How You Got Killed Before" (Imperial)
Fats Domino   "Every Night About This Time" (Imperial) [#5 R&B]
Jewel King   "3 × 7 = 21" (Imperial) [#4 R&B]
Tommy Ridgley   "Looped" / "Junie Mae" (Imperial)
Joe Turner   "Jumpin' Tonight (Midnight Rockin')" (Imperial)

1951

Fats Domino   "Rockin' Chair" (Imperial) [#9 R&B]

1952

Dave Bartholomew   "Little Girl Sing Ding-a-ling" (Imperial)
                       "Who Drank My Beer While I Was in the Rear?"
                           (Imperial)
Fats Domino   "Mardi Gras in New Orleans" (Imperial)
Smiley Lewis   "The Bells Are Ringing" (Imperial) [#10 R&B]
Lloyd Price   "Lawdy Miss Clawdy" (Specialty) [#1 R&B]
Shirley and Lee   "I'm Gone" (Aladdin) [#2 R&B]

1953

Fats Domino   "Little School Girl" (Imperial)
                       "Rose Mary" (Imperial) [#10 R&B]
                       "Swanee River Hop" (Imperial)
Smiley Lewis   "Big Mamou" / "Play Girl" (Imperial)

1954

Dave Bartholomew   "Jump Children" / "Cat Music" (Imperial)
                       "When the Saints Go Marching In" (Imperial)

James Booker	"Thinkin' 'bout My Baby" / "Doin' the Ham Bone" (Imperial)
Ernie K-Doe	"No Money" (Savoy)
Earl King	"I'm Your Best Bet, Baby" / "A Mother's Love" (Specialty)
Professor Longhair	"In the Night" (Atlantic)
Spiders	"I Didn't Want to Do It" [#3 R&B] / "You're the One" [#8 R&B] (Imperial)
	"I'm Slippin' In" (Imperial) [#6 R&B]
Earl Williams	"I Can't Go On" / "Let's Make Love Tonight" (Savoy)

1955

Fats Domino	"Bo Weevil" (Imperial) [#5 R&B]
	"I'm in Love Again" (Imperial) [#3 pop, #1 R&B]
	"My Blue Heaven" (Imperial) [#5 R&B]
	"Poor Me" (Imperial) [#1 R&B]
Smiley Lewis	"I Hear You Knocking" (Imperial) [#2 R&B]
	"One Night" (Imperial)
Little Richard	"Directly from My Heart" (Specialty)
	"Kansas City" (Specialty)
	"Tutti Frutti" (Specialty) [#2 R&B]
Bob Luman	"Red Hot" (Imperial)
Roy Montrell	"Ooh Wow!" / "Every Time I Hear That Mellow Saxophone" (Specialty)
Shirley and Lee	"Feel So Good" (Aladdin) [#2 R&B]

1956

Lee Allen	"Shimmy" / "Rockin' at Cosimo's" (Aladdin)
Charles Brown	"I'll Always Be in Love with You" (Aladdin)
	"Merry Christmas Baby" (Aladdin)
Roy Brown	"Saturday Night (That's My Night)" (Imperial)
Fats Domino	"When My Dreamboat Comes Home" (Imperial) [#2 R&B]
Merle Kilgore	"Teenager's Holiday" / "Please Please Please" (Imperial)
Earl King	"Mother Told Me Not to Go" / "Is Everything Alright?" (Ace)
Little Richard	"The Girl Can't Help It" (Specialty) [#7 R&B]
	"Long Tall Sally" [#1 R&B] / "Slippin' and Slidin'" [#2 R&B] (Specialty)

	"Rip It Up" [#1 R&B] / "Ready Teddy" [#8 R&B] (Specialty)
Amos Milburn	"Chicken Shack Boogie" (Aladdin)
Art Neville	"Ooh-Whee Baby" (Specialty)
Shirley and Lee	"Let the Good Times Roll" (Aladdin) [#1 R&B]
Spiders	"That's My Desire" (Imperial)

1957

Roy Brown	"Let the Four Winds Blow" (Imperial) [#5 R&B]
	"Party Doll" (Imperial)
Sam Cooke	"Forever" (Specialty)
	"You Send Me" (Keen) [#1 pop, #1 R&B]
Sugarboy Crawford	"She's Got a Wobble When She Walks" (Imperial)
Fats Domino	"I'm Walkin'" (Imperial) [#4 pop, #1 R&B]
Don and Dewey	"I'm Leavin' It All Up to You" (Specialty)
Thurston Harris	"Little Bitty Pretty One" (Aladdin) [#6 pop, #2 R&B]
Hollywood Flames	"Buzz Buzz" (Ebb) [#5 R&B]
Little Richard	"Baby Face" (Specialty)
	"Jenny Jenny" [#10 pop, #2 R&B] / "Miss Ann" [#6 R&B] (Specialty)
	"Lucille" (Specialty) [#1 R&B]
Marvin and Johnny	"Pretty Eyes" (Specialty)
Percy Mayfield	"Please Believe Me" (Specialty)
Ricky Nelson	"Be-Bop Baby" (Imperial) [#3 pop]
	"Boppin' the Blues" (Imperial)
	"I'm Walkin'" (Verve) [#4 pop]
Earl Palmer's Party Rockers	"Johnny's House Party," pts. 1 and 2 (Aladdin)
Tommy Sands	"Sing Boy Sing" (Capitol)
Slim Whitman	"Unchain My Heart" (Imperial)
Larry Williams	"Bony Maronie" [#4 R&B] / "Slow Down" (Specialty)
	"Short Fat Fannie" (Specialty) [#5 pop, #1 R&B]

1958

Burnette Brothers	"Warm Love" / "My Honey" (Imperial)
Eugene Church	"Pretty Girls Everywhere" (Class) [#6 R&B]
Eddie Cochran	"Jeannie Jeannie Jeannie" (Liberty)
	"Nervous Breakdown" (Liberty)
	"Summertime Blues" (Liberty) [#8 pop]

Bobby Day	"The Bluebird, the Buzzard, and the Oriole" (Class)
	"Rockin' Robin" [#2 pop, #1 R&B] / "Over and Over" (Class)
Doris Day	"Everybody Loves a Lover" (Columbia) [#6 pop]
Fats Domino	"I Hear You Knocking" (Imperial)
	"Margie" (Imperial)
Don and Dewey	"Koko Joe" (Specialty)
Jan and Arnie	"Jennie Lee" (Arwin) [#8 pop, #4 R&B]
Johnny Otis Show	"Willie and the Hand Jive" (Capitol) [#9 pop, #3 R&B]
Little Richard	"Good Golly Miss Molly" (Specialty) [#10 pop, #4 R&B]
Earl Palmer	"Drum Village," pts. 1 and 2 (Capitol)
Art and Dotty Todd	"Chanson d'amour (Song of Love)" (Era) [#6 pop]
Ritchie Valens	"Come On, Let's Go" (Del-Fi)
	"Donna" (Del-Fi) [#2 pop]
	"La Bamba" (Del-Fi)
Larry Williams	"Heebie Jeebies" (Specialty)
Sheb Wooley	"The Purple People Eater" (MGM) [#1 pop]

1959

Dorsey Burnette	"There Was a Tall Oak Tree" (Era)
Edd Byrnes	"Kookie, Kookie (Lend Me Your Comb)" (Warner Bros.) [#4 pop]
	"Like I Love You" / "Kookie's Mad" (Warner Bros.)
Eddie Cochran	"Teenage Heaven" (Liberty)
	"Weekend" (Liberty)
Don and Dewey	"Farmer John" (Specialty)
	"Pink Champagne" (Specialty)
Ernie Fields	"In the Mood" (Rendezvous) [#4 pop, #7 R&B]
Jan and Dean	"Baby Talk" (Dore) [#10 pop]
Don Ralke	"Bourbon Street Beat" (Warner Bros.)
Chan Romero	"Hippy Hippy Shake" (Del-Fi)
Spectors Three	"I Really Do" (Trey)
April Stevens	"Teach Me Tiger" (Imperial)
Connie Stevens	"Sixteen Reasons" (Warner Bros.) [#3 pop]
Teddy Bears	"Oh, Why" (Imperial)
Ritchie Valens	"Stay beside Me" (Del-Fi)
Larry Williams	"She Said Yeah" / "Bad Boy (Junior Behave Yourself)" (Specialty)

1960

Bobby Bare	"Book of Love" (Fraternity)
Walter Brennan	"Dutchman's Gold" (Dot)
Dorsey Burnette	"Hey Little One" (Era)
Dante and the Evergreens	"Alley Oop" (Madison)
Bobby Vee	"Devil or Angel" (Liberty) [#6 pop]
	"Rubber Ball" (Liberty) [#6 pop]
Dinah Washington	"Love Walked In" (Mercury)

1961

Paul Anka	"Dance On Little Girl" (ABC-Paramount) [#10 pop]
B. Bumble and the Stingers	"Bumble Boogie" (Rendezvous)
	"Caravan" (Rendezvous)
	"Nutrocker" (Rendezvous)
Glen Campbell	"Turn Around, Look at Me" (Crest)
Castelles	"Sacred" (Era)
Sam Cooke	"Cupid" (RCA)
	"Twistin' the Night Away" (RCA) [#9 pop, #1 R&B]
Bobby Darin	"You Must Have Been a Beautiful Baby" (Atco) [#5 pop]
Jackie DeShannon	"Heaven Is Being with You" (Liberty)
Fleetwoods	"(He's the) Great Impostor" (Dolton)
	"Tragedy" (Dolton) [#10 pop]
Lettermen	"When I Fall in Love" (Capitol) [#7 pop]
Limeliters	"A Dollar Down" (RCA)
Gene McDaniels	"Chip Chip" (Liberty) [#10 pop]
	"A Hundred Pounds of Clay" (Liberty) [#3 pop]
	"Tower of Strength" (Liberty) [#5 pop, #5 R&B]
Lou Rawls	"Above My Head" (Capitol)
Simms Twins	"Soothe Me" (SAR) [#4 R&B]
Bobby Vee	"Run to Him" (Liberty) [#2 pop]
	"Take Good Care of My Baby" (Liberty) [#1 pop]
Dinah Washington	"Our Love Is Here to Stay" (Mercury)
	"September in the Rain" (Mercury) [#5 R&B]
Jimmy Witherspoon	"Warm Your Heart" (Reprise)
Timi Yuro	"Hurt" (Liberty) [#4 pop]

1962

Herb Alpert and the Tijuana Brass	"The Lonely Bull" (A&M) [#6 pop]

Walter Brennan	"Mama Sang a Song" (Liberty)
Anita Bryant	"Till There Was You" (Carlton)
Vikki Carr	"He's a Rebel" (Liberty)
Ray Charles	"I Can't Stop Lovin' You" (ABC-Paramount) [#1 pop, #1 R&B]
	"You Don't Know Me" (ABC-Paramount) [#2 pop, #5 R&B]
Nat King Cole	"Ramblin' Rose" (Capitol) [#2 pop, #7 R&B]
Johnny Crawford	"Cindy's Birthday" (Del-Fi) [#8 pop]
Bobby Darin	"You're the Reason I'm Living" (Capitol) [#3 pop, #9 R&B]
Duane Eddy	"The Ballad of Paladin" (RCA)
	"Deep in the Heart of Texas" (RCA)
Everly Brothers	"Don't Ask Me to Be Friends" (Warner Bros.)
Ketty Lester	"Love Letters" (Era) [#5 pop]
Willie Nelson	"Half a Man" (Liberty) [#25 country]
Clifford Scott	"The Kangaroo" / "Skee-dattle to Seattle" (King)
	"Walk That Twist" / "Half Fast Twist" (King)
Frank Sinatra	"Ev'rybody's Twistin' " (Reprise)
Bobby Vee	"The Night Has a Thousand Eyes" (Liberty) [#3 pop, #8 R&B]

1963

Roy Clark	"Through the Eyes of a Fool" (Capitol)
Bobby Darin	"Treat My Baby Good" (Capitol)
Everly Brothers	"It's Been Nice" (Warner Bros.)
Jan and Dean	"Drag City" (Liberty) [#10 pop]
	"Surf City" (Liberty) [#1 pop, #3 R&B]
Waylon Jennings	"Rave On" (A&M)
Willie Nelson	"Opportunity to Cry" (Liberty)
Nino Tempo and April Stevens	"Deep Purple" (Atco) [#1 pop, #4 R&B]
Andy Williams	"Can't Get Used to Losing You" (Columbia) [#2 pop, #7 R&B]

1964

| Beefeaters [later the Byrds] | "Please Let Me Love You" / "It Won't Be Wrong" (Elektra) |
| Roy Clark | "When the Wind Blows in Chicago" (Capitol) |

Sam Cooke	"Shake" [#7 pop, #2 R&B] / "A Change Is Gonna Come" [#9 R&B] (RCA)
Vic Damone	"On the Street Where You Live" (Columbia) [#4 pop]
Jan and Dean	"Dead Man's Curve" (Liberty) [#8 pop]
	"The Little Old Lady from Pasadena" (Liberty) [#3 pop]
	"New Girl in School" (Liberty)
Little Richard	"Bama Lama Bama Lou" (Specialty)
Righteous Brothers	"You've Lost That Lovin' Feelin'" (Philles) [#1 pop, #3 R&B]
Ronettes	"Born to Be Together" (Philles)
	"You Baby" (Philles)
Glenn Yarbrough	"Baby the Rain Must Fall" (RCA)

1965

Beach Boys	"Please Let Me Wonder" (Capitol)
Stan Kenton	"Theme from *Peyton Place*" (Capitol)
Righteous Brothers	"Just Once in My Life" (Philles) [#9 pop]
	"Unchained Melody" (Philles) [#4 pop, #6 R&B]
Sonny and Cher	"What Now My Love" (Atco)
Supremes	"A Lovers' Concerto" (Motown)

1966

Ray Charles	"Let's Go Get Stoned" (ABC) [#1 R&B]
Jackie DeShannon	"I Can Make It with You" (Imperial)
Tim Hardin	"It'll Never Happen Again" (Verve)
	"Misty Roses" (Verve)
Neal Hefti	"Batman Theme" (RCA)
Brenda Holloway	"Where Were You?" (Tamla)
Marketts	"Batman Theme" (Warner Bros.)
P. J. Proby	"Niki Hoeky" (Liberty)
Righteous Brothers	"Soul and Inspiration" (Verve) [#1 pop]
Ike and Tina Turner	"A Love Like Yours" (Philles)
	"River Deep—Mountain High" (Philles)

1967

Bobbie Gentry	"Okolona River Bottom Band" (Capitol)
Brenda Holloway	"You've Made Me So Very Happy" (Tamla)

Monkees	"Tapioca Tundra" (Colgems)
Lou Rawls	"Dead End Street" (Capitol) [#3 R&B]
Paul Revere and the Raiders	"Legend of Paul Revere" (Columbia)
Lalo Schifrin	"Mission Impossible Theme" (Dot)

1968

Ray Charles	"Eleanor Rigby" (ABC)
Fats Domino	"Lady Madonna" (Reprise)
Little Richard	"Baby Don't You Tear My Clothes" /
	"Stingy Jenny" (Brunswick)
Monkees	"It's Nice to Be with You" (Colgems)
Lou Rawls	"Down Here on the Ground" (Capitol)
Marty Robbins	"Padre" (Columbia) [#5 country]

1969

Sonny Charles and	
the Checkmates, Ltd.	"Proud Mary" (A&M)
James Brown	"World (Part 1)" (King) [#8 R&B]
Jimmy Durante	"He Ain't Heavy He's My Brother" (Warner Bros.)
Screamin' Jay Hawkins	"Constipation Blues" (Mercury)

1970

| José Feliciano | "Marley Purt Drive" (RCA) |

NOTE: Earl Palmer's 1970–74 logbooks contain a number of sessions with high-profile artists that no doubt resulted in more hit singles. Unfortunately, it has not been possible to determine which songs were recorded at these sessions. The artists include the Beach Boys, Ella Fitzgerald, the Jackson Five, Gladys Knight and the Pips, Peggy Lee, Diana Ross, Frank Sinatra, Barbra Streisand, the Temptations, and Dionne Warwick.

ALBUMS

Albums on which Earl Palmer plays one or more tracks are listed here by year of release. The listing includes (in brackets) the position of the album on the *Billboard* chart if it reached the top 40. Chart information is from Joel Whitburn's *The Billboard Book of Top 40 Albums* (New York: Billboard Publications, 1987).

1955

Jack Martin   *New Orleans Suite* (Patio)

1956

Fats Domino   *Fats Domino Rock and Rollin'* (Imperial) [#18]
                               Rock and Rollin' with Fats Domino (Imperial) [#17]

1957

Buddy Collette   *Buddy's Best* (Dootone)
Fats Domino   *This Is Fats Domino!* (Imperial) [#19]
Little Richard   *Here's Little Richard* (Specialty) [#13]
Ricky Nelson   *Ricky* (Imperial) [#1]

1958

Ernie Andrews   *Travelin' Light* (GNP)
Earl Bostic   *Bostic Rocks Hits of the Swing Age* (King)
Sam Cooke   *Sam Cooke* (Keen) [#16]
Alton Purnell   *Alton Purnell Quartet* (Warner Bros.)
Strollers   *Swingin' Flute in Hi-Fi* (Score)

1959

Ritchie Valens   *Ritchie Valens* (Del-Fi) [#23]

1960

Julie London   *Julie . . . at Home* (Liberty)
King Pleasure   *Golden Days* (Hi Fi)
T-Bone Walker   *T-Bone Blues* (Atlantic)

1961

Barbara Dane   *On My Way* (Capitol)
Tommy Garrett
  (50 Guitars of)   *50 Guitars Go South of the Border* (Liberty) [#36]
Earl Palmer   *Drumsville* (Liberty)
Bobby Vee   *Bobby Vee* (Liberty) [#18]

Dinah Washington   *September in the Rain* (Mercury)
Jimmy Witherspoon   *Spoon* (Reprise)

1962

Herb Alpert and the
   Tijuana Brass   *The Lonely Bull* (A&M) [#24]
Ray Charles   *Modern Sounds in Country and Western*
                     (ABC-Paramount) [#1]
Sam Cooke   *Twistin' the Night Away* (RCA)
Bobby Darin   *Bobby Darin Sings Ray Charles* (Atco)
                                Twist with Bobby Darin (Atco)
Willie Nelson   *. . . And Then I Wrote* (Liberty)
Earl Palmer   *Percolator Twist* (Liberty)
Frank Sinatra   *Sinatra and Swingin' Brass* (Reprise) [#18]
Sarah Vaughan   *The Explosive Side of Sarah Vaughan* (Roulette)
Speedy West   *Guitar Spectacular* (Capitol)
Andy Williams   *"Danny Boy" and Other Songs I Love to Sing*
                     (Columbia) [#19]
Jimmy Witherspoon   *Hey Mrs. Jones* (Reprise)

1963

Howard Roberts   *Color Him Funky* (Capitol)
Mel Tormé   *Sunday in New York and Other Songs about New York*
                     (Atlantic)

1964

Harry "Sweets" Edison   *Sweets for the Sweet Taste of Love* (Vee-Jay)
Marvin Gaye   *Hello Broadway* (Motown)
Jan and Dean   *Surf City and Other Swingin' Cities* (Liberty)
Howard Roberts   *H. R. Is a Dirty Guitar Player* (Capitol)
Ronettes   *Presenting the Fabulous Ronettes Featuring Veronica*
                     (Philles)

1965

Beach Boys   *The Beach Boys Today!* (Capitol) [#4]
Sam Cooke   *Shake* (RCA)

Dizzy Gillespie	*Dizzy Gillespie with Gil Fuller & the Monterey Jazz Orchestra* (Pacific Jazz)
Righteous Brothers	*Just Once in My Life* (Philles) [#9]
	You've Lost That Lovin' Feelin' (Philles) [#4]
Glenn Yarbrough	*Baby the Rain Must Fall* (RCA) [#35]

1966

Tim Hardin	*Tim Hardin 1* (Verve)
Lightnin' Hopkins	*Lightnin' Strikes* (Verve)
Lou Rawls	*Lou Rawls Live!* (Capitol) [#4]
Righteous Brothers	*Soul and Inspiration* (Verve) [#7]
Sonny and Cher	*The Wondrous World of Sonny and Cher* (Atco) [#34]
Supremes	*I Hear a Symphony* (Motown) [#8]

1967

Gene Clark	*Gene Clark with the Gosdin Brothers* (Columbia)
Phil Ochs	*Pleasures of the Harbor* (A&M)
Van Dyke Parks	*Song Cycle* (Warner Bros.)

1968

Count Basie and Jackie Wilson	*Manufacturers of Soul* (Brunswick)
Roy Brown	*Hard Times* (Bluesway)
Ray Charles	*A Portrait of Ray* (ABC-TRC)
Everly Brothers	*Roots* (Warner Bros.)
Monkees	*The Birds, the Bees, and the Monkees* (Colgems) [#39]
Michael Nesmith	*Michael Nesmith Produces/The Wichita Train Whistle Sings* (Dot)

1969

Byrds	*Preflyte* (Together)
Checkmates, Ltd.	*Love Is All We Have to Give* (A&M)
Taj Mahal	*The Natch'l Blues* (Columbia)
Ike and Tina Turner	*River Deep—Mountain High* (A&M)
Eric von Schmidt	*Catch It* (Smash)
Eddie "Cleanhead" Vinson	*The Original Cleanhead* (Blues Time)
Neil Young	*Neil Young* (Reprise)

1970

Johnny Almond   *Hollywood Blues* (Deram)
James Brown   *It's a New Day So Let a Man Come In* (King)
Milt Jackson   *Memphis Jackson* (Impulse)
Barbra Streisand   *Stoney End* (Columbia) [#10]

1972

Randy Newman   *Sail Away* (Reprise)
Dory Previn   *Mary C. Brown* (United Artists)
Professor Longhair   *New Orleans Piano* (Atlantic) [Earl Palmer's tracks
                            recorded 1953]
Sarah Vaughan   *A Time in My Life* (Mainstream)

1973

Bonnie Raitt   *Takin' My Time* (Warner Bros.)

1974

Tim Buckley   *Look at the Fool* (DiscReet)
Maria Muldaur   *Waitress in the Donut Shop* (Reprise) [#23]

1975

Splinter   *Harder to Live* (Dark Horse)

1976

Maria Muldaur   *Sweet Harmony* (Warner Bros.)

1978

Joe Sample   *Swing Street Cafe* (MCA)
Tom Waits   *Blue Valentine* (Asylum)

1979

Little Feat   *Down on the Farm* (Warner Bros.) [#29]
Teena Marie   *Wild and Peaceful* (Motown)

1981
Johnny Otis   *The New Johnny Otis Show* (Alligator)

1982
Elvis Costello   *King of America* (Columbia) [#39]
Lalo Schifrin   *Ins and Outs* (Palo Alto)

1988
Willie Dixon   *Hidden Charms* (Capitol)

1993
Lowell George   *Lowell George* (WEA/Atlantic/Rhino) [recorded late
                                  sixties]

1994
Dr. John, Earl Parlmer,
   Allen Toussaint, etc.   *Crescent City Gold* (High Street)

1999
B. B. King   *Let the Good Times Roll* (MCA)

MOTION PICTURES

Films to whose soundtracks Earl Palmer contributed are listed here. Names in parentheses are soundtrack composer and/or music director (md).

1961
Judgment at Nuremberg (Ernest Gold) ·

1963
Hud (Elmer Bernstein)
It's a Mad Mad Mad Mad World (Ernest Gold)

1964
Baby the Rain Must Fall (Elmer Bernstein)

Ride the Wild Surf (Stu Phillips)
Robin and the Seven Hoods (Nelson Riddle)

1965

Boeing-Boeing (Neal Hefti)
Harlow (Neal Hefti)
How to Stuff a Wild Bikini (Les Baxter)
A *Patch of Blue* (Jerry Goldsmith)

1966

Grand Prix (Maurice Jarre)
Murderer's Row (Lalo Schifrin)
Three Bites of the Apple (Eddy Manson)
Walk, Don't Run (Quincy Jones)

1967

Banning (Quincy Jones)
Barefoot in the Park (Neal Hefti)
Cool Hand Luke (Lalo Schifrin)
Guess Who's Coming to Dinner (md: Frank de Vol)
Hotel (Johnny Keating)
In Cold Blood (Quincy Jones)
In the Heat of the Night (Quincy Jones)
Riot on Sunset Strip (Fred Karger)
Tony Rome (Billy May)
Valley of the Dolls (André Previn; md: John Williams)

1968

Bullitt (Lalo Schifrin)
Candy (Dave Grusin)
Coogan's Bluff (Lalo Schifrin)
A *Dandy in Aspic* (Quincy Jones)
Faces (Jack Ackerman)
Finian's Rainbow (Burton Lane/E. Y. Harburg; md: Ray Heindorf)
The Heart Is a Lonely Hunter (Dave Grusin)
The Impossible Years (Don Costa)

Madigan (Don Costa)
Rosemary's Baby (Krzysztof Komeda)
Up Tight (Booker T. Jones)
With Six You Get Egg Roll (Robert Mersey)

1969

Cactus Flower (Quincy Jones)
The Killing of Sister George (Gerald Fried)
The Sterile Cuckoo (Fred Karlin)
Sweet Charity (Cy Coleman/Dorothy Fields; md: Joseph Gershenson)

1970

Alex in Wonderland (Tom O'Horgan)
Kelly's Heroes (Lalo Schifrin)
The Liberation of Lord Byron Jones (Elmer Bernstein)
On a Clear Day You Can See Forever (Alan Jay Lerner/Burton Lane)

1971

Bless the Beasts and Children (Perry Botkin Jr./Barry de Vorzon)
Buck and the Preacher (Benny Carter)
Harold and Maude (Cat Stevens)
Plaza Suite (Maurice Jarre)
Zachariah (Jimmy Haskell)

1972

Lady Sings the Blues (Michel Legrand; md: Gil Askey)
The New Centurions (Quincy Jones)
What's Up, Doc? (Artie Butler)

1973

The Laughing Policeman (Charles Fox)
Lost Horizon (Burt Bacharach)
Macon County Line (Stu Phillips)
Walking Tall (Walter Scharf)

1974

Cinderella Liberty (John Williams)
For Pete's Sake (Artie Butler)
Freebie and the Bean (Dominic Frontière)
Harry and Tonto (Bill Conti)
The Longest Yard (Frank de Vol)

1975

Matt Helm (Jerry Fielding/Oliver Nelson)

1977

The Deep (John Barry)
Greased Lightning (Fred Karlin)
The Island of Dr. Moreau (Laurence Rosenthal)
New York, New York (Ralph Burns)

1978

An Unmarried Woman (Bill Conti)

1979

Breaking Away (Patrick Williams; md: Lionel Newman)
The Rose (Paul A. Rothchild)

1982

The Best Little Whorehouse in Texas (Patrick Williams)
Cannery Row (Jack Nitzsche)
Honkytonk Man (Steve Dorff)

1984

Gremlins (Jerry Goldsmith)

1985

Armed and Dangerous (Bill Meyers)

1986

The Money Pit (Michel Colombier)
Top Gun (Harold Faltermeyer)

1987

The Big Town (Michael Melvoin)
Predator (Alan Silvestri)
Tin Men (David Steele)

1988

Cocktail (Pete Robinson)

1989

The Fabulous Baker Boys (Dave Grusin)

1990

The Hot Spot (Jack Nitzsche)

TELEVISION

Television shows in which Earl Palmer played on theme song and/or incidental music are listed here. The years are those of show's prime-time run. Names in parentheses are composers or music directors.

M Squad, 1957–60 (Count Basie/Benny Carter/Stanley Wilson)
77 Sunset Strip, 1958–64 (Jerry Livingston/Mack David/Jerry Fielding et al.)
Bourbon Street Beat, 1959–60 (Jerry Livingston/Mack David/Paul Sawtell)
Hawaiian Eye, 1959–63 (Jerry Livingston/Mack David/Paul Sawtell)
Peyton Place, 1964–69 (Lionel Newman/Franz Waxman et al.)
I Dream of Jeannie, 1965–70 (Hugo Montenegro/Ed Forsyth et al.)
Green Acres, 1965–71 (Vic Mizzy/Dave Kahn)
Ironside, 1967–75 (Quincy Jones)
The Outsider, 1968–69 (Pete Rugolo)
It Takes a Thief, 1968–70 (Benny Golson/Ralph Ferraro/Dave Grusin)
The Leslie Uggams Show, 1969 (Ernie Freeman)

The Brady Bunch, 1969–74 (Frank de Vol)
Della, 1970–71 (H. B. Barnum)
The Partridge Family, 1970–74 (Hugo Montenegro/Shorty Rogers/George
    Duning/Benny Golson)
The Odd Couple, 1970–75 and 1982–83 (Neal Hefti/Kenyon Hopkins/Leith Stevens)
The Pearl Bailey Show, 1971 (Louis Bellson)
M.A.S.H., 1972–83 (Johnny Mandel et al.)
The Midnight Special, 1973–81

INDEX

Page numbers in bold indicate photographs

LaVergne, TN USA
07 July 2010
188630LV00003B/72/A